The Best
Stage Scenes
of 1996

Other books by Jocelyn A. Beard

100 Men's Stage Monologues from the 1980s

100 Women's Stage Monologues from the 1980s

The Best Men's/Women's Stage Monologues of 1990

The Best Men's/Women's Stage Monologues of 1991

The Best Men's/Women's Stage Monologues of 1992

The Best Men's/Women's Stage Monologues of 1993

The Best Men's/Women's Stage Monologues of 1994

The Best Men's/Women's Stage Monologues of 1995

The Best Stage Scenes for Men from the 1980s

The Best Stage Scenes for Women from the 1980s

The Best Stage Scenes of 1992

The Best Stage Scenes of 1993

The Best Stage Scenes of 1994

The Best Stage Scenes of 1995

Monologues from Classic Plays 468 B.C. to 1960 A.D.

Scenes from Classic Plays 468 B.C. to 1970 A.D.

100 Great Monologues from the Renaissance Theatre

100 Great Monologues from the Neo-Classical Theatre

100 Great Monologues from the 19th C. Romantic & Realistic Theatres

The Best
Stage Scenes
of 1996

edited by Jocelyn A. Beard

SCENE STUDY SERIES

A SMITH AND KRAUS BOOK

Published by Smith and Kraus, Inc.
One Main Street, Lyme, NH 03768

Copyright © 1997 by Smith and Kraus, Inc.
All rights reserved
Manufactured in the United States of America

First Edition: September 1997
10 9 8 7 6 5 4 3 2 1

The Scene Study Series 1067-3253

Contents

MEN'S AND WOMEN'S SCENES

WOMEN'S SCENES

MEN'S SCENES

MEN'S AND WOMEN'S SCENES

AFTERLIFE
Jack Gilhooley

serio-comedic, 1 Man, 1 Woman
Mother Kathleen (30s) a Catholic priest, and Mickey (30s) a criminal seeking absolution…and a bit more.

Scene: a church confessional, AD 2025

> *In the not-too-distant future, women have finally broken down the sexist barriers in Rome and won the right to enter the Catholic clergy. Here, Mother Kathleen is paid a confessional visit by the man with whom she once was in love.*

○ ○ ○

Confession

> *(Kathleen sits in a twenty-first century confessional. She's in the darkened center section and faces out towards the audience. She wears a Roman collar. She is reading a missal while buffing her nails. In a moment, Mickey Reilly enters. He looks around suspiciously then enters one of the two side compartments of the confessional and sits in a comfortable padded armchair. The compartment is closer to a small, cozy room with a sliding panel between the penitent and the priest. It is equipped with temperature control and a dimmer switch for the light. He immediately dims the overhead light for anonymity though Kathleen hasn't even acknowledged him. For her, business as usual. She'll set the missal down but she'll continue on her nails. For the purposes of staging, the doors to each of the three units should be cut off slightly above the handles. Or of course, the doors can be mimed on opening and closing. Or the (imaginary) doors can slide open and shut with a simple handheld, remote control device issued upon entry to the church. The latter option would be the most theatrical. Kathleen slides the panel open between*

her and Mickey. She's set to hear his confession with no great enthusiasm.)

MICKEY: Bless me Father, for I have sinned. It has been a—

KATHLEEN: Mother! "Bless me, *Mother,* for I have sinned."

MICKEY: Yeah, yeah…forgot. I have trouble with that.

KATHLEEN: Get used to it.

MICKEY: Bless me, *Mother,* for I have sinned. It has been fourteen years since my last confession.

KATHLEEN: Fourteen years??? What have you been doing since…what, two thousand and six???

MICKEY: Give or take a year.

KATHLEEN: It's nice to have an infrequent miscreant. All I get lately are career sinners.

MICKEY: Actually, it's been fourteen years since a *true* confession. Honest. Unedited. My soul laid bare.

KATHLEEN: What happened fourteen years ago to provoke your *bogus* confessions?

MICKEY: Puberty.

KATHLEEN: Mickey???

MICKEY: Yeah.

KATHLEEN: God…

MICKEY: *(Nervous amusement.)* Hey, if I was God, I wouldn't need con—

KATHLEEN: *(Unamused.)* Don't say it. How'd you get past the metal detector?

MICKEY: I don't pack a heater in church.

KATHLEEN: I hope this is *not* about that gangland rub-out. Because if it is, it's my worst nightmare come true.

MICKEY: Look, you chose to be a priest, you gotta take the baggage that comes with it.

KATHLEEN: Baggage I can deal with. It's the garbage…Can't you confess to someone else? We're too close, you and I.

MICKEY: Does that mean you'd squeal?

KATHLEEN: Priests can't "squeal." I'm bound to silence. I've had this fear of hearing two confessors. My mother and you.

2 men's and women's scenes

MICKEY: Your mother? No wonder. You'd spend the weekend in there. Send out for meals.

KATHLEEN: With her it's all *petty* sins. Venial, not mortal. She'll embellish, though. For instance, she doesn't just park over- time. She *"defrauds* the government." Pumping up minor sins gives her a sense of accomplishment. Without the con- sequences.

MICKEY: Not me, I'm in and out of here in a minute. Max. One sin is all.

KATHLEEN: *One* sin in fourteen years? C'mon, Mick.

MICKEY: One sin...a few times. One big-time sin.

KATHLEEN: Why don't you shop around for another confessor?

MICKEY: "Shop around"? We're talking about my eternal soul, not a Toyota.

KATHLEEN: Go to Father Murphy at St. Gregory's? Confession should be a man-to-man thing.

MICKEY: What about for women?

KATHLEEN: Same thing. Woman-to-woman. It's less awkward. More intimate. Like guys in the locker room. Or women in the powder room.

MICKEY: Men talk about home runs and tennis in the locker room. And women. Unless it's Super Bowl time. I never feel guilty confessing to men.

KATHLEEN: Well, *I'll* make you feel guilty.

MICKEY: Women traditionally make me feel guilty. I need to change my life. And *you've* always been out to change the world.

KATHLEEN: How am I ,going to change your rotten life?

MICKEY: We go way back. St. Rita's. You exert a powerful influence on me.

KATHLEEN: Because I've become a priest?

MICKEY: Because I still love you.

(She slams the panel shut, rises and paces.)

KATHLEEN: *(Quietly prayerful.)* Oh, Mother Mary, why do you test me? You know thy love for thee. *(Beat...prayerfully...)* Hail

Mary, full of grace, The Lord is with Thee. Blessed art thou amongst women and blessed is the fruit of Thy womb,—
(He taps lightly on the panel. After a moment, she slides open the panel vehemently.)

KATHLEEN: Is that an overture?"..."fruit of Thy womb..." Knock, knock! Aggression time.

MICKEY: I never even *heard* you It's soundproofed. And in the old days *you* were the aggressor.

KATHLEEN: *(Rising, indignantly.)* Owwwww. You...I had the strength—and the good sense—to stop at the crucial moment.

MICKEY: Make that the "climactic moment."

KATHLEEN: I was only human.

MICKEY: If you were only human, we'd have been lovers.

KATHLEEN: Well, we were...uh, sort of.

MICKEY: It was unconsummated. Emily Dickinson-type love. We were in *love*. That's all. At least *I* was.

KATHLEEN: That's *all???* That was no small commitment, Mick.

MICKEY: How did *you* feel?

KATHLEEN: *(Pondering.)* Hmmm...infatuated. And unprepared to hear your confession, *now*.

MICKEY: Certainly you're unprepared. The Church gave you a crash course before the Supreme Court declared gender discrimination.

KATHLEEN: Thankfully, church and state are in harmony.

MICKEY: Look, forget that I've always loved you. Just hear my confession.

KATHLEEN: I'm too subjective...torn between the sin and the son.

MICKEY: Sin and sun??? What are you babbling about? Las Vegas???

KATHLEEN: You're my child now. All my subjects look to me as Mother Kathleen. Just as traditional priests have been fathers to their flock.

MICKEY: I think that's like...a *metaphor*, Kathleen. I mean, I'm two months older than you, "Mom." I know that the church gets off on miracles but—

4 men's and women's scenes

KATHLEEN: I can't make an exception of you just because of our past.

MICKEY: The last thing you said was how tough it would be. To leave me for… (Indicating the area.) …this.

KATHLEEN: This???

MICKEY: Religion. Maybe that's cause *you* still love *me,* too. Chew on that!

(He's up and out [utilizing the remote]. She's after him [using her own remote].)

KATHLEEN: Look…we had a thing back in high school!!! It wasn't meant to be a…lifetime commitment!!!

MICKEY: *(Sheepishly returning.)* We vowed that it was! Marriage, even. Then this new guy moved into Vatican City and started pontificating—no pun intended—that women could be priests. And you began to change.

KATHLEEN: I thought I had a higher calling.

MICKEY: Than me?

KATHLEEN: I should hope so. Mickey, you're a professional assassin.

MICKEY: I wasn't then. If we had stayed together, I wouldn't be now.

KATHLEEN: Don't lay your guilt trip on me. I'm not responsible for your f—…your screwed-up life.

MICKEY: *(Bolting to attention.)* Kathleen!!! You nearly said the F-word. In church!

KATHLEEN: It's not a curse. It's a swear word. Venial sin, not mortal. A curse is taking The Lord Thy God's name in vain.

MICKEY: Still. We're in church.

KATHLEEN: It's not part of my Sunday sermon. Only you and God heard it. And She forgives me.

MICKEY: I don't.

KATHLEEN: You don't count. I lost my temper. Priests are mortal. You're so bogged down in tradition, Mick…

MICKEY: Me? What's more tradition-bound than the church?

KATHLEEN: Not me. I'm a radical churchwoman. Like Pope Joan…

MICKEY: Who?

KATHLEEN: There was a female pope named Joan.

MICKEY: G'wan. All those lavender robes…swishy capes. Pope Joan was a drag queen.

KATHLEEN: What would your dear old mother say if she heard you say that?

MICKEY: Dear old Mom never heard me swear in church.

KATHLEEN: What if she heard that you shoot people?

MICKEY: She wouldn't believe it. You know mothers.

(A heavy door slams, off. Both scamper back to their respective compartments. Kathleen continues…)

KATHLEEN: Y'know, maybe you should be seeing a psychiatrist.

MICKEY: A psychiatrist could go to the cops. Anyway, you're a psychiatrist to working people.

KATHLEEN: *(Truly enlightened.)* Gee, I never saw myself that way. Look,…*you've* got to forget about our past life. You're married. I'm a priest. At peace with my calling. Subservient to God. Something you should reflect on.

MICKEY: I've reflected. And I've determined that God's the ultimate hit man. He gave me carte blanche to kill all those innocent people in the China War.

KATHLEEN: Combat. Not the same thing.

MICKEY: Right. That was mass murder. For which I was decorated…and awarded the Medal of Honor. And praised from the pulpit of this very church.

KATHLEEN: Not by me. And even if priests could marry, they couldn't marry already-married people That's Mormon priests.

MICKEY: I left her. I'm getting an annulment.

KATHLEEN: (Pause…quietly.) What? Do you think it will be granted?
[Bridget saunters on. She is flashily dressed and beautiful.]

MICKEY: From Noreen? I'll get an annulment and a free ticket to heaven. I've already served in hell.

KATHLEEN: *(Cynically.)* If you don't get the annulment you could just shoot her.

MICKEY: I don't shoot people just cause I want to. I have standards.

KATHLEEN: Right. You've got to be paid! I never knew why you married Noreen. A nut case from the get-go.

6 men's and women's scenes

MICKEY: I married her on the rebound. From you. She was wild but I thought I could tame her.

[Bridget tries her remote on Mickey's confessional. Nothing. She bangs on the door. Mickey responds by shouting from within.]

MICKEY: Buzz Off!

KATHLEEN: (Offended.) Beg pardon? I'm here to reconcile you with your soul, Mick.

MICKEY: (To Kathleen.) Not you!

[Bridget: (To the door.) You need this space more than me, you cretin.]

[She withdraws and meanders to the other cubicle. She enters. She's awe-stricken, never having seen one of these new facilities. She tinkers with the dimmer control. Light up…light down. She leaves it low and slouches. She's in no way prepared for a religious experience. She indicates the heat, wipes her brow then adjusts the thermostat. The A-C kicks in. She re-seats herself.]

KATHLEEN: When I heard that you were marrying Noreen, I felt guilty. And depressed. She didn't shower after gym class. And she was a druggie. A drunk too, in time. It rums in that family.

MICKEY: That's grounds for an annulment. Look at what the drinking did to our daughter.

KATHLEEN: (Sincerely.) You didn't deserve that.

MICKEY: To say nothing of Mary Catherine. I didn't know that Noreen was drinking during pregnancy. And now— (On the verge of tears.) I'll pay anything if it will help the baby. I owe a fortune in medical bills but—

KATHLEEN: Still, assassinating is not a viable career-choice.

MICKEY: My day job doesn't have group insurance. Killing's not something I aspired to, believe me. But it's big money, fast. Unfortunately, it's tough to resign from.

KATHLEEN: (Pause.) I can't give you absolution.

MICKEY: What d'you mean??? I go to confession. I spill my guts. I'm clean. It's a rule.

men's and women's scenes 7

KATHLEEN: Wrong. You must have remorse.

MICKEY: I have remorse. I had nothing against this guy Martelli, last night. Personally, I liked him for the few seconds I knew him. But they tell me he was the worst sort of scumbag. That's a requirement with me. I've got to know that each hit I score makes the world a little safer. Like they told us in the air force. So, while I'm providing a social service,. I nonetheless have a sense of remorse.

KATHLEEN: It's the wrong kind of remorse.

MICKEY: How many kinds are there?

KATHLEEN: There's remorse…and then there's…repentance.

MICKEY: Explain, please.

KATHLEEN: You have no *real* remorse for the victim.

MICKEY: I have repentance! Joey Martelli was a hit man, himself. Citizens approve of what I'm doing. Especially the Christian militia. By the way, I try to let the hit make a quick Act of Contrition. So, Martelli's in heaven now. Thanks to me. It's win-win for my victims.

KATHLEEN: A real Angel of Mercy. What if the guy's not a Catholic?

MICKEY: Sorry to say, most gangland rub-outs are. Work to be done there, Mother Kathleen. But RCs don't have a monopoly on contrition. It's not an exclusive club despite what Sister Leo said in the fifth grade.

[Bridget reads a fashion magazine.]

KATHLEEN: Sister Leo nearly made me a pre-teen atheist.

MICKEY: I once whacked a Muslim. I told him to bow towards Mecca. He said he'd have to make a *pilgrimage.* Sorry, Abdul. Bang! So I have remorse for Joey like he had for *his* victims.

KATHLEEN: You only have remorse for yourself.

MICKEY: So be it! Remorse is established. Seal the deal so I can go to communion tomorrow.

KATHLEEN: Self-pity is not remorse.

MICKEY: I pity Martelli's wife and kids. Though they may not miss his abuse. Now, do I pass your remorse litmus test?

KATHLEEN: They never prepared me for this in the seminary.

8 men's and women's scenes

MICKEY: Naturally. The Church doesn't deal with everyday problems.

KATHLEEN: Like yours, huh? Will you do your penance when I assign it?

MICKEY: Certainly, how else could I go to communion?

KATHLEEN: The penance is…Man, there aren't enough hours in the day.

MICKEY: Try me. I speed pray. Something I picked up in combat.

KATHLEEN: You promise not to sin again?

MICKEY: You don't really want that. You'd be out of business.

KATHLEEN: Promise not to *kill* again.

MICKEY: Look Kathleen, I never *want* to kill again. Ever. But, if the kid needs another operation—

KATHLEEN: Jesus!

MICKEY: Aside from my one, ongoing sin, I've led a pretty exemplary life. Make allowances. And *you* just took The Lord's name in vain in church!

KATHLEEN: I said "Jesus" as in a prayer.

[Bridget lights up a cigarette.]

MICKEY: A mortal sin is not a prayer.

KATHLEEN: *(Defensively.)* It was an invocation.

MICKEY: A one-word prayer? Give me one-word prayers as penance. I'll reel off a thousand.

KATHLEEN: I was about to say, "Jesus, hear my prayers." But you cut me off.

MICKEY: You used to swear a blue streak back in high school. And you'd confess on Saturday, receive communion on Sunday. Then all week long you'd outdo a platoon of Marines. Until Saturday.

KATHLEEN: *Are you implying that blasphemy is equal to what you've been*—

MICKEY: *(Nervously cautioning.)* Shhhhh. You're bound to secrecy.

KATHLEEN: It's soundproofed, remember? There are degrees of sin. And you've been committing the whopper of them all.

MICKEY: I don't remember anyone handicapping the Ten

Commandments. Not like golf. Or horse racing. They're all equal in God's eyes. There's no sinner's "top ten."

KATHLEEN: Sister Aquinas did. Remember?

MICKEY: Seventh grade. Yeah, she ranked 'em.

KATHLEEN: And killing was the worst. The big time taboo. She moved that commandment from fifth place to first. She said that killing was not so prevalent when Exodus was written.

MICKEY: She never read The Bible, then. And "Thou Shalt Not Covet Thy Neighbor's Wife." She canceled that right out. Called it a victimless sin. Venial, if that.

KATHLEEN: When we got older we determined why.

MICKEY: She coveted a *few* neighbor's wives.

KATHLEEN: And daughters. She was weird, man. Not many nuns taught us but they were usually more fun than the lay teachers.

MICKEY: We were their whole lives. Poor women.

KATHLEEN: Aquinas would come to the girls' locker after gym class. She'd want to dry us off after we'd shower.

MICKEY: *That's* why Noreen didn't shower.

KATHLEEN: Sister said she did it because she loved us. And Noreen said, "Go love the boys."

MICKEY: That's why Noreen was always getting detention. She had a big trap. Still does.

KATHLEEN: Noreen was her favorite. No wonder. She was the prettiest.

MICKEY: I thought *you* were prettiest.

[Bridget extracts a paper cup from her bag. She removes the lid and drinks the entire contents then rolls her eyes in satisfaction.]

KATHLEEN: *(Slightly unnerved.)* I wasn't even prettiest in my family. Bridget is. Sister Mary Aquinas said that all the girls would meet her in heaven. That put a whole new twist on eternity and it's rewards.

MICKEY: And she said all the boys would go to hell.

KATHLEEN: She was right about you, Mickey.

10 men's and women's scenes

MICKEY: Not now. I'm in the state of grace. Give me penance and I'll skedaddle.

KATHLEEN: You'll kill again.

MICKEY: If Mary Catherine needs another operation, and I can ice a drug dealer…before he kills a schoolkid—

KATHLEEN: Come to me. I'll try to help.

MICKEY: My daughter needs the help. Fetal alcohol syndrome. You a surgeon, too?

KATHLEEN: Come to me for counseling. Anything else to confess?

MICKEY: Nothing. Except that I cheated.

KATHLEEN: On Noreen? That's not sin, it's self-preservation. *(Concerned.)* If I thought you cheated on me back in school—
[Bridget: (Looking at her watch, to herself.) Who's she in there with, Torquemade? (She punches out the bottom of the paper cup and applies the cylinder flush against the wall trying to hear. After a few futile moments, she'll resettle.)]

MICKEY: I was faithful. I idealized you. I thought we were destined for each other. Then came the revolution. If it was still the old church, you and me would be married now. And I wouldn't have a gun full of notches. No, I cheated on the IRS. Primarily because my veteran's benefits don't kick in for the kid.

KATHLEEN: How did you ever get into this…line of work?

MICKEY: I was recruited. They went against type. Nobody expects Mick Reilly, an ex-altar boy who studies accounting at night…repairs laser telepathy modules during the day… nobody figures me for a hired killer. But the mob heard about the baby…about how I needed dough. And they knew I'd flown all those bombing missions in Asia. Killed thousands.

KATHLEEN: I can see that. You don't fit the profile. I mean, it's a sort of Italian profession.

MICKEY: Not any more. Lately, some motivated immigrants. Peruvians…Nigerians…Mongolians…On second thought, if I get an assignment, I'll take you up on your counseling offer. We'll go out and talk.

KATHLEEN: No more back-seat-of-the-car-tryna-get-your-hands-up-my-dress—

MICKEY: Kathleen! Man, I can't believe this conversation. If anyone had told me when I was an altar boy that I'd be talking sex in church to a priest with tits—

KATHLEEN: Will you promise not to kill again?

MICKEY: I already have…for now.

KATHLEEN: That's conditional. Look me in the eye.

MICKEY: I can't.

KATHLEEN: You can't look me in the eye?

MICKEY: I can't see through this screen.

KATHLEEN: We should talk head on, face-to-face. Obscurity shouldn't be an option. The confessor and the confessee should be eye-to-eye. Mandatory. We'd have a lot fewer sinners that way.

MICKEY: You'd have a lot fewer confessors, too. But I do miss your eyes. I love your eyes. Why not come over into my compartment? *(He rises in anticipation of her cross to his side.)* There's no one around.
(Kathleen thinks about the option. She hits her remote, steps into the aisle. Mickey hits his and steps smiling into the aisle to welcome her to his compartment. Just as Kathleen is about to enter Mickey's area, [Bridget hits her remote in order to check them. The sound is heard although Bridget merely peeks out at them.] Kathleen panics and runs back into her compartment. [Bridget withdraws.] Mick dejectedly re-enters his area.)

MICKEY: What happened???

KATHLEEN: We're being watched. There's someone here. It was a warning from The Holy Ghost. No good could have come from you and I in a tiny space

MICKEY: The Holy Ghost's in the other compartment? *(Sarcastically.)* Maybe he'll give me an instant annulment.
(Kathleen closes his panel and opens Bridget's.)

KATHLEEN: You might want to take a powder for awhile. This guy's a serious sinner.

12 men's and women's scenes

[Bridget: What's he done?]

KATHLEEN: Nothing doing, toots. I'm new at this but I don't disclose. *(Kathleen absolutely slams the panel shut.)*

[Bridget: Jeez. Kate is still Kate, priest or no priest.]

KATHLEEN: *(Reopening Mickey's panel.)* The quality of sinner is hitting rock bottom.

MICKEY: Can I come back after you're through this evening?

KATHLEEN: Well...come to the cathedral tomorrow. For the Gospel Song-a-long Ecumenical Mass. With AME Tabernacle Church. Always fun. A full house. Then we'll go to my mother's.

MICKEY: To your mother's? From the sublime to the ridiculous.

KATHLEEN: She's very sick. About to expire. My sisters have come in. She'd just like to know...well, that we're not alone in the world. That we'll have one another...and our...friends. My phone number is—

MICKEY: I know it, I've got it memorized.

KATHLEEN: Impressive. You had trouble with numbers in school.

MICKEY: Those numbers didn't motivate me. You live alone?

KATHLEEN: I live with another priest but she's usually at her boyfriend's.

MICKEY: We could have that.

KATHLEEN: For all I know they just pray together.

MICKEY: Get real.

KATHLEEN: It's none of my business.

MICKEY: It's your business if they're sinning.

KATHLEEN: Bye, Mick.

MICKEY: *(Starting off.)* I just want to tell you that...well, I was really twisted when you left me for the church.

KATHLEEN: I had to choose between you and God.

MICKEY: For that decision you didn't a Tibetan mountaintop. But I had no option. I'd fallen for you. Abandoning me wasn't very Christian. You could have loved God and me at the same ti—

KATHLEEN: *(Interrupting.)* Hold on, Mickey Riley. The leopard never changes his spots. You're sneaking off without paying your dues. It's penance time. *(She administers the sign of the cross* and recites as he kneels.)* "In The Name of The Mother, The Daughter and The Holy Spirit."

MICKEY: Why not "Sprit*ess*"?

KATHLEEN: Shut up!

MICKEY: If this rewrite isn't kosher, I'm up the creek.

KATHLEEN: I absolve you of your sins in The Name of—

MICKEY: "Sin"! Singular. One sin.

KATHLEEN: Frequently committed. Ergo, "sins." Say three rosaries a day.

MICKEY: *Three rosaries a day?* I've got a full-time job. Until when?

KATHLEEN: Indefinitely. Keep busy. You won't have time to kill.

MICKEY: Three rosaries a day is too severe. I'm appealing to a higher authority.

KATHLEEN: There's none higher than mine. *(She slams his panel. He's off. She sits staring ahead and reflecting for a long moment. A smile. She blesses herself and quietly…)* St. Jude? Are you listening? I have this *seemingly* lost cause and I need your help.

CUTE BOYS IN THEIR UNDER-PANTS MAKE IT BIG (IN SHOW BUSINESS)

Robert Coles

serio-comedic, 1 Man, 1 Woman

Orson (40s) and Giselle (40s) performers; a theatrical couple.

Scene: the dressing room of an old theatre in Ft. Meyers, FL

As Orson and Giselle prepare for yet another performance, they bicker about their costumes and their lives.

○　○　○

GISELLE: What are you doing over there?

ORSON: Nothing. *(He hides what he's been working on.)* What are *you* doing?

GISELLE: I'm fixing your fez.

ORSON: My fez? What fez?

GISELLE: The fez you wear.

ORSON: I wear a fez?

GISELLE: In the show.

ORSON: I wear a fez in the show?

GISELLE: *Yes,* you wear a fez.

ORSON: When do I wear a fez?

GISELLE: In the Casbah scene.

ORSON: I wear that Moroccan hat.

GISELLE: It's a fez.

ORSON: A fez?

GISELLE: *Yes.* See? *(She holds up the fez.)*

ORSON: That's a fez?

GISELLE: Yes. Of course. What did you think a fez was?

ORSON: I don't know.

GISELLE: You don't know what you thought a fez was?

ORSON: No.

GISELLE: You must have thought something.

ORSON: I don't know what I thought.

GISELLE: When I said, "I'm fixing your fez," you said, "What fez?" Like you thought you knew what a fez was. I mean, obviously, you were picturing something.

ORSON: Not necessarily.

GISELLE: Oh, come on. You thought you knew what it was. Otherwise, you would have said, "What the hell is a fez?" But you didn't. You said, "What fez?" Like it was a familiar thing. Like you knew what it was.

ORSON: That doesn't mean I *visualized* it.

GISELLE: You just don't want to admit you were wrong. You don't want to admit you pictured what a fez looked like and it was something else that you were thinking of, not a real fez.

ORSON: That's not true.

GISELLE: Oh, come on. Admit it. I don't see what the big deal is. Admit you thought a fez was something else.

ORSON: I *didn't* think it was something else.

GISELLE: You are such a liar. I don't see what the big deal is.

ORSON: Because the plain truth is that I *didn't* think a fez was something else. I simply didn't know *exactly* what a fez looked like. I didn't *picture* it. All right? Does that satisfy you? I admit that I *didn't* know that what a fez looked like. All right?

GISELLE: All right. *(Pause.) This* is a fez.

(Orson continues with his previous business, still hiding it. She continues futzing with the fez.)

ORSON: What's wrong with it?

GISELLE: It's coming apart inside. Didn't you notice?

ORSON: No.

GISELLE: See? *(She holds inside of fez before his face.)*

ORSON: Oh. It probably should be glued.

GISELLE: Yeah, I guess so. *(She puts it upside down on table and futzes inside it.)*

ORSON: Don't do that—you'll shmoosh the tassel.

16 men's and women's scenes

GISELLE: Do *you* want to fix it?

ORSON: It probably just needs some glue.

GISELLE: I guess so. What sort of glue does one use on a fez?

ORSON: There's a hardware store next to the deli.

GISELLE: What deli?

ORSON: The deli next to the— *(He stops himself.)* The deli next door.

GISELLE: There's a hardware store?

ORSON: Next to the deli.

GISELLE: What sort of glue should I ask for?

ORSON: I don't know—Elmer's?

GISELLE: *Elmer's* glue? On a *fez?*

ORSON: I don't think there's such a thing as "fez glue."

GISELLE: Don't you think Elmer's is sort of...*extreme?* I mean, I would think we don't need anything quite so...*industrial.*

ORSON: "Industrial"?

GISELLE: Well, don't they glue tables together with Elmer's? Things like that. I've seen people *build sets* with Elmer's glue. I would think we'd want a...*gentler* sort of glue. I mean, I want to make sure it *holds, but...*I don't want it to seep through and discolor the top of the fez. I mean, we'd be doing that Moroccan love scene and you'd have this big old ugly glue stain on your fez. You know, our *hats* are *important* in this show. We don't have whole costumes, so we rely on the hats to indicate the various locales.

ORSON: Presenting "DeTouche & Rogers in 'Meal Ticket', a pleasant evening of hats across the globe at two in the afternoon."

GISELLE: *The hats work!!* They give an immediate feeling of *place* and *time,* an *atmosphere,* without distracting from our performance. It's our characterizations, our performances, that are important. That's what people focus on, but they also want a little color, a little variety. That's why we go across the globe. To see all our different relationships, the different love relationships you find in all these exotic places. The hats work perfectly to suggest the locale, to give the atmosphere, without getting in the way. A whole costume would be too much. Besides, we'd never stop changing the entire show. Either there'd be these big holes of emptiness while we changed costume, or else *you* would change and I would have this patter to fill the time, and then *I* would change, and *you* would have to talk to the audience. It would be a *nightmare.* The *hats* are *perfect.* It takes two seconds. Put the hats on and voila! We're in Tangiers, I'm an innocent Moroccan maiden and you're a powerful vizier attempting to seduce me. The *hats* are *important,* so I'm not gonna mess up this fez. I'm going to that hardware store. You want anything?

ORSON: Could you pick me up three nine-foot lengths of one-by-three, a screw gun, and a bucket of joint compound?

GISELLE: *(Acknowledging his sarcasm.)* I mean, from the deli.

ORSON: What deli?

(Fed up with his jokes, she stomps out.)

ORSON: I thought she'd never leave.

DANCE WITH ME

Stephen Temperly

serio-comedic, 2 Men, 2 Women

Sally (30s) a woman encountering her old flame, Jack (30s) the old flame, Daisy (20s) an ex-pat Brit seeking literary adventure in the USA and Talbot (30s) Sally's current beau.

Scene: New York City

> *Sally and Talbot are cheating on each other with Jack and Daisy respectively. When they all wind up in the same restaurant for lunch, mayhem ensues.*

> *(Despairing, Sally and Talbot turn from their respective partners and come face to face with each other; it takes a moment or two for them to comprehend the situation.)*

SALLY: *(Wonderingly.)* Talbot?

TALBOT: Sally?

SALLY: I thought you were…

TALBOT: You said you were…

SALLY: Talbot?

TALBOT: Sally?

SALLY: Who's that with…?

TALBOT: What are you doing?

SALLY: Talbot?

TALBOT: Sally?

JACK: *(Impatiently.)* Sally!

DAISY: Talbot!

SALLY: *(Turning to Jack.)* It's Talbot.

TALBOT: *(Turning to Daisy.)* It's Sally.

JACK: Where?

DAISY: Where?

SALLY: There.

TALBOT: There.

    (They peer at one another.)

JACK: *(Disbelieving).* Him?—That's him?

SALLY: Sh!

DAISY: She doesn't look drunk.

JACK: This is worse than I thought.

TALBOT: *(Indignant.)* She's with a man!

SALLY: *(Looking in her pocketbook.)* Have I got any Advil?

DAISY: Maybe she's sick of you, too.

TALBOT: Very funny.

    (Waiter crosses with Daisy's new drink.)

TALBOT: What the fuck's going on?

WAITER: *(To Jack.)* How is everything?

JACK: Couldn't be better.

WAITER: *(To Talbot.)* Seen anyone famous?

TALBOT: I think we might need a minute more.

WAITER: Okay. No rush. Take your time.

DAISY: Thanks.

WAITER: We get them all here. Nathan Lane, Mandy Patinkin…

    (He sets the drink down and goes. Silence.)

JACK: We have to do something.

SALLY: No!

JACK: We can't just sit here.

TALBOT: He was holding her hand.

DAISY: *(Poking his arm.)* Well. Go on.

TALBOT: What?

DAISY: Do something. Now's your chance.

TALBOT: Let *her* come to *me.*

SALLY: *(Faint.)* I can't deal with this.

JACK: Then I'll deal with it for you.

    (He stands: Sally can't speak; she doesn't like what's happening but can't seem to stop it.)

DAISY: He stood up.

TALBOT: (Furious.) He better not come near me.

    (Jack crosses to Talbot. Sally crawls under the table to hide.)

DAISY: He's coming this way.

20 men's and women's scenes

TALBOT: He better not start anything with me.

JACK: *(Simply.)* Hi.

TALBOT: *(Brightly.)* Hi!

(Jack, his eye on Daisy, looms over Talbot.)

TALBOT: Wait a minute, wait a minute, you're…

JACK: Jack.

TALBOT: *(Relieved.)* That explains it. He was the one before me.

JACK: Talbot. Man to man. She never wanted it to be this way.

DAISY: What way?

TALBOT: I'll deal with this. What way?

JACK: She wanted to able to let you down gently. It's so like her. *(To Daisy.)* She's a wonderful person. *(To Talbot.)* I guess you must mean something to her somewhere, somehow. *(To Daisy: big smile.)* Hi.

DAISY: Hello.

JACK: Who are you?

DAISY: Me?

JACK: Yes.

DAISY: Who am I?

JACK: Yes.

DAISY: I'm Talbot's little friend.

TALBOT: *(A rebuke.)* Daisy.

JACK: *(Pleased.)* Daisy!

DAISY: Just an old-fashioned girl.

JACK: The pick of the bunch.

(Daisy notes this in her book.)

DAISY: "Pick of the bunch…" Tell me…

JACK: Mmm?

DAISY: Are you this charming all the time or just on special occasions?

JACK: This is kind of spooky. Don't you think? All four of us arriving at the same place, at the same time…Quite a coincidence.

DAISY: I'll say.

JACK: Seems almost too good to be true. Like a movie or something. Maybe it was meant to be? Maybe we've been thrown together for a reason? The question is...what reason?

TALBOT: *(Confused.)* What movie?

JACK: Talbot. Sally wants to leave you. It's nothing personal. Don't feel inadequate: she needs someone strong. So she's coming to live with me.

(Talbot tries to work this out: Jack and Daisy observe his efforts.)

DAISY: He's gone a funny color.

JACK: *(Helpfully.)* Try to keep breathing.

TALBOT: *(To Jack: finally and with difficulty.)* Live with...you?

JACK: Let it out, don't bottle it up.

TALBOT: She lived with you. You drove her nuts.

DAISY: *(As if to a child).* Temper.

TALBOT: This is crazy! I don't believe this. It makes no sense.

JACK: Let's all say hi to Sally.

DAISY: Now?

JACK: Or shall I get Sally to say hi to you?

DAISY: Never mind. Come on, Talbot.

JACK: We'll all say hi to Sally.

DAISY: Brilliant.

(They stand. Talbot is dazed; Jack leads the way, bringing the remains of Daisy's drink.)

JACK: Sally? Sally. Talbot's come to say hi.

TALBOT: *(Grim.)* Hi, Sally.

JACK: Sally? Talbot says hi.

SALLY: *(From under the table.)* Hi, Talbot.

JACK: *(Enthusiastically.)* This is Daisy.

DAISY: Hello.

JACK: Daisy's here with Talbot. She's a...well, she's a...

DAISY: Friend.

JACK: She's a friend. Sally say hi.

SALLY: Hi, Daisy.

DAISY: Hi, Sally.

JACK: There! We all said hi.

DAISY: I'm going to throw up.

22 men's and women's scenes

SALLY: *(Coming out from under the table.)* You, too?

JACK: *(Taking charge.)* Now why don't we all sit down? Sally sit here and Daisy here and I'll sit...No. *(To Sally.)* I'll sit here and you sit...Talbot, bring Sally a chair, will you?

(They sit. An awkward pause. Talbot turns to Sally.)

TALBOT: So. You're leaving me.

SALLY: *(Aghast.)* What?

DAISY: That's broken the ice.

TALBOT: That's what *he* said.

(Sally turns to Jack.)

JACK: I merely told him the truth as I saw it.

DAISY: *(To Jack.)* You work fast.

TALBOT: If you wanted out why didn't you say?

SALLY: I didn't know.

JACK: Sal's a great one for denial.

TALBOT: *(To Jack.)* "Sal?"

JACK: *(Putting his hand on Sally's.)* Sal.

TALBOT: *(To Sally.)* "Sal?"

DAISY: *(To Talbot: "shut up.")* Sal.

SALLY: Look, all that's happened...Jack called me.

TALBOT: I feel so betrayed.

SALLY: But it was just...talk!

JACK: Talk?

SALLY: You know what I mean.

JACK: But Sally, I thought we'd broken through.

SALLY: We did.

JACK: I thought we were in a different place.

SALLY: We are.

JACK: Then how can you say it's just...talk?

SALLY: What I mean is.

JACK: Yes. Tell me. So I can understand.

SALLY: Everything's happening so fast.

JACK: I thought you wanted this. I thought you were happy.

SALLY: I am.

JACK: I'm getting double-signals here.

men's and women's scenes 23

DAISY: *(Practical.)* So you'll be moving, then? When would that be?

SALLY: But my apartment!

DAISY: *(To Sally.)* *Your* apartment?

TALBOT: *Our* apartment.

SALLY: It's in my name.

DAISY: *(To Talbot.)* You said you had the lease.

SALLY: I've got the lease.

DAISY: No, he said they assigned it to him the last time you were arrested.

SALLY: Arrested? When was I arrested?

TALBOT: I don't know if I actually said "arrested…"

DAISY: You had a psychotic episode at "Sunset Boulevard." They put you in detox.

SALLY: Talbot!

JACK: *(Dubious.)* "Sunset Boulevard?"

DAISY: He's got the CD.

TALBOT: So?

SALLY: *(Indignantly.)* I've never even seen "Sunset Boulevard."

DAISY: You haven't missed much.

TALBOT: I quite liked it.

JACK: You did?

TALBOT: Okay, it's got it's problems…

SALLY: How do you know he's got the CD?

  (Both women turn on Talbot.)

SALLY: *(To Talbot.)* In *my* apartment!

TALBOT: *Our* apartment!

SALLY: Not any more.

JACK: Talbot can sublet.

DAISY: That could work.

SALLY: Talbot can burn in hell!

JACK: Sally, let it go.

DAISY: Today's the thirteenth. How much time will you need?

SALLY: I can't just walk out.

JACK: Why not?

SALLY: Well…all my things!

24 men's and women's scenes

DAISY: We'll take it furnished.

JACK: Just bring a few clothes.

DAISY: I'll get a night's sleep!

TALBOT: This is quite a commitment.

DAISY: I thought you'd be happy.

TALBOT: I am happy.

DAISY: You don't *look* happy.

JACK: I'm *very* happy.

TALBOT: *(Irritated.)* I'm happy, *too.*

SALLY: *(Too loud.)* Look, can we just *drop it!*
    (Talbot, shocked by her vehemence, starts to cry again.)

DAISY: *(Disgusted.)* Oh my God!

JACK: What is he doing?

SALLY: Talbot, stop that.

TALBOT: You scared me.

SALLY: I'm sorry.

TALBOT: You shouldn't snap at people that way.

SALLY: I'm *sorry.*

TALBOT: All I ask is some consideration.

SALLY: Alright. I didn't mean it. I'm sorry.

TALBOT: That's not much to ask.

SALLY: Okay, I'm sorry, okay?

DAISY: *(To Talbot.)* If you don't stop this right now I'll stick my fork in your ear. Got it?
    (Talbot is still.)

DAISY: *(To Sally.)* You've got to be firm with him. Show him who's boss.

SALLY: *(Placing Daisy.)* Don and Betty! You look after the twins! I knew I'd seen you. We came to dinner. Talbot, how could you! They're our best friends.

DAISY: That marriage is not long for this world. Not since Betty found Don in bed with the Super.

TALBOT: The Super, my God!

DAISY: She wants to go to Montana and join a sect.

TALBOT: My God! What's he like?

SALLY: Talbot, we shouldn't be listening to this.

DAISY: It's the kiddies I feel sorry for. *(Pointing at Talbot.)* They'll probably grow up just like him. Thing. It.

JACK: You're here as a nanny? You look far too young.

DAISY: I'll say this for you, you're predictable.

DOUBLE OR NOTHING

Michael Ajakwe, Jr.

serio-comedic, 2 Men, 1 Woman

Frank (28) a blue-collar brother from the 'hood, Sherry (26) the woman he'd like to date and Chance (8) Sherry's over-protective son.

Scene: here and now

> *When unsuspecting Frank arrives at Sherry's apartment to pick her up for their first date, he's put through the wringer by the precocious Chance.*

○ ○ ○

(Sherry's living room. Night. Chance, 8, is sitting on the sofa playing a handheld video game. Knocking at the front door. Chance is too engrossed in his video game to care. More knocking.)

SHERRY: *(Offstage.)* Chance, would you get that for me?

CHANCE: (Calling back.) Who is it?

SHERRY: *(Offstage.)* My date.

(Chance stops playing the game and looks up, stone-faced. Then, with the subtlest of ease, a devilish grin soon covers his face.)

CHANCE: Don't worry, Mama, I'll take care of it.

(Chance puts down the video game and crosses to the door. He opens it, sees Frank standing there—flowers in one hand, a box of candy in the other, and a billfold clip full of money in his mouth. Chance reaches up, takes the money clip and slams the door in Frank's face. He starts back to the sofa, counting the money. More knocking.)

SHERRY: *(Offstage.)* Have you let that man in yet, Chance? Don't make me come out there and embarrass you.

(Chance reluctantly crosses back to the door again. Frank is still standing there. He looks pissed).

CHANCE: Just playin', man. *(Giving him back the money.)* Come on in. *(Frank enters.)*

FRANK: Who are you?

CHANCE: Who are you?

FRANK: *(Taken aback.)* Johnson. *Mister* Frank Johnson.

CHANCE: Have a seat, Frank.

(Frank shoots him a look. Chance starts back for the sofa.)

FRANK: Hang on. You didn't tell me your name.

CHANCE: Just call me "The Man of the House." *(Chance starts down and resumes playing his video game.)*

SHERRY: *(Offstage. Calling out.)* Hi, Frank.

FRANK: *(Calling back.)* How ya doin'?

SHERRY: *(Offstage.)* Oh, fine. Did you meet Chance?

FRANK: No. I...No; I met "The Man."

SHERRY: *(Offstage.)* Huh?

FRANK: I said, I like him. He's a character.

SHERRY: *(Offstage.)* Isn't he? I'll be ready in a few minutes, okay?

FRANK: Take your time.

(Frank sits next to Chance. He puts the box of candy on the living room table and leans back, holding the flowers. He takes in the place. Chance opens the box of candy and takes one. Frank grabs his hand.)

FRANK: Those are for your mother.

CHANCE: My mother doesn't eat candy.

FRANK: But she said—

CHANCE: —"bring some candy." *(Off his look.)* She always says that. And I always wind up eating it all up 'cause she don't wanna get fat.

(Frank looks at Chance for a long beat before finally releasing his hand. Chance eats a piece of chocolate. He looks at Frank and laughs, shaking his head.)

CHANCE: Sucker.

(Frank grabs Chance by the collar.)

CHANCE: Touch me and I'll tell my Mama.

28 men's and women's scenes

(Frank looks at Chance for a long beat, a glare in his eyes like hot coals, then finally releases him.)

FRANK: *(Whispering.)* Little punk.

CHANCE: *(Cupping his ear.)* Huh? I can't hear you. Speak up.

(Frank starts for him again, ready to wring his neck.)

CHANCE: Mama…!

(Frank covers his mouth, reducing Chance's pleas to mumbles.)

FRANK: *(Whispering.)* All right! All right! *(Off his defiant stare.)* I'm…I'm sorry.

(Chance finally calms down. Frank slowly removes his hand from Chance's mouth. Chance smiles, sardonically.)

FRANK: You're a devil.

CHANCE: Don't you forget it. *(Pointing.)* Have my Mama home by midnight or else.

FRANK: Or else, what? My car's gonna turn into a pumpkin? *(Laughs at his own joke.)*

CHANCE: No, I'm gonna call nine-one-one and say you kidnapped her.

FRANK: What?!

CHANCE: You heard me, sucker.

(Sherry enters from her bedroom. She looks like a million bucks. She gives Frank a big hug. As he spins her around, Frank shoots Chance a sly victorious grin. Chance sits back on the sofa, arms folded, staring at Frank the whole while. He's not a happy camper. Sherry looks at her watch and leads Frank towards the door.)

SHERRY: Let's go. I don't want to be late for the movie.

FRANK: What movie?

SHERRY: The movie you're taking me to *after* dinner.

(Sherry exits. Frank follows her, turning back to Chance with a teasing tongue, before Frank exits. Chance stands, pointing.)

CHANCE: Remember what I said, punk! Midnight or you're a fugitive! *(Black out.)*

FAMILY OF HORRORS

William Gadea

serio-comedic, 1 Man, 2 Women
Herman (30–40) a man who has murdered his wife, Vanessa
(20–30) his mistress and Katharine (30–40) his wife's vengeful
spirit.

Scene: here and now

> *As punishment for killing Katharine, Herman and Vanessa are*
> *forbidden to touch one another; a situation that suits*
> *Katharine just fine.*

○ ○ ○

(A night full of rain. Ominous music plays. Herman is dressed
in sweats. He sits on the sofa watching television. Katharine
enters carrying a bag of groceries and a dripping umbrella.
She announces herself to Herman and the audience.)

KATHARINE: I'm home! *(Thunder claps.)* Oh! It is awful out. Be glad
you can stay home all nice and warm, Herman. *(Katharine*
takes the groceries to the kitchen.) Heavens. What a day.
Anything good on television?

HERMAN: Usual crap.

KATHARINE: Well, don't forget, honey. There's always those re-runs
on Nick at Night. *(Katharine collapses on the sofa.)* Oh! I am
exhausted! Do you want me to cook for you now? Or if you
like I can make us a big bowl of popcorn and we can watch
TV. We'll eat later. Only not too much later or we won't sleep
well.

HERMAN: Whatever.

KATHARINE: Maybe I should heat up some of that nice french bread
pizza you like. But then you wouldn't have them when I'm
not home to cook a proper meal for you. I don't know. What
do you think, dear?

30 men's and women's scenes

HERMAN: I don't care.

KATHARINE: You have to have a preference.

HERMAN: Christ, I said I don't care! *(Brusquely, Herman turns off the TV with his remote. He throws the remote on the sofa and walks away.)* Jesus.

KATHARINE: *(Walking on eggshells.)* Oh. Okay. Is there something you want to talk about, honey?

HERMAN: No. There's not.

KATHARINE: Honey…I've been doing some reading. I think we need to work on our communication. What do you think? Can you sit with me here? Please? *(Reluctantly, Herman joins Katharine on the couch.)* Thank you. Now, do you want to tell me why you're in such a grumpy mood?

HERMAN: You know why.

KATHARINE: No, I don't. I've done all I can. Haven't I?

HERMAN: Well, then I'm not in a grumpy mood. You know what it is, Katharine.

KATHARINE: It seems to me I've done everything to make you happy.

HERMAN: What good am I doing you here? You know what I want. It's simple. Tear up the agreement. Please.

KATHARINE: I can't do that, Herman.

HERMAN: Why not?

KATHARINE: Because I love you.

HERMAN: Haven't you heard the expression: if you love somebody, set them free?

KATHARINE: Why, that's ridiculous. To love someone is to need them. To not be able to give them up. *(Herman groans in despair.)* How about you, Herman? Do you ever ask yourself whether you're trying as hard as you should? You could start by asking me how my day was. *(Herman doesn't reply. Katharine is perky and oblivious.)* It was a nice day…although very busy. What with having to shuttle between here and Vanessa's. It's not easy taking care of both of you, you know. The buses were actually on time today, but the lines at the supermarket! Goodness.

HERMAN: Vanessa. How is she?

KATHARINE: Now Herman.

HERMAN: I'm just asking. You're the one that wanted communication!

KATHARINE: You know that's not an appropriate question.

HERMAN: You brought it up. Who mentioned Vanessa? You did. Oh, Katharine. I'm just asking. We're talking. What harm can it do?

KATHARINE: All right, Herman. If it'll make you happy. Ask away.

HERMAN: Good.

KATHARINE: I'll answer because I love you.

HERMAN: Whatever. How's she doing?

KATHARINE: Vanessa is fine.

HERMAN: What was she wearing today?

KATHARINE: Some hideous housedress. Nothing special.

HERMAN: Did she…ummm, does she ever ask about me?

KATHARINE: I'm sorry, Herman. This isn't healthy.

HERMAN: Well?

KATHARINE: No, I can't answer any more questions. It's for your own good.

HERMAN: For my own good? You sadistic bitch. I can't take this nice-nice shit anymore. Why don't you torture me with a sneer on your face! Growling through your teeth! Why do you have to do it smiley-face sweetie-pie like you're doing me some favor? *(The door swings open. It is Vanessa. She is wearing a trench-coat wet from the rain.)* Vanessa!

KATHARINE: Vanessa! How did you get here!

VANESSA: I followed you when you left, Katharine. I had to see him.

HERMAN: Vanessa! *(Vanessa and Herman run to embrace each other. Katharine intercedes to prevent a clinch.)*

KATHARINE: No! No! This is not supposed to happen. Go home now. Leave! Go, go, go!

VANESSA: No, I'm not leaving.

KATHARINE: You have to.

VANESSA: Why?

KATHARINE: Because he's my husband!

VANESSA: Who cares. You can't use him. You're dead.

32 men's and women's scenes

(A portentous music cue accompanies this revelation. Katharine turns to stare big-eyed at the audience; the characters freeze as the cue plays out.)

KATHARINE: *(Turning back to address Vanessa.)* All the more reason you shouldn't mess with me.

HERMAN: Don't listen to her, Vanessa. Stay with me!

VANESSA: That's what I intend to do.

KATHARINE: Nooooooooooo!

HERMAN: I can't think of anything but you…when I wake up in the morning…when I go to bed at night.

VANESSA: Oh, darling! Me too. I was outside—I wanted to wait until Katharine left again but I couldn't! I had to see you.

HERMAN: Is she terrible to you?

VANESSA: She curses at me for hours on end…

KATHARINE: I do not, you scheming little tramp!

VANESSA: Like that.

HERMAN: Poor darling! How do you manage? How do I manage?

KATHARINE: This is against the agreement! You both signed the agreement! Need I remind you? *(Katharine pulls a scroll of paper from under her skirt. She unfurls it and reads…)* We, the undersigned, will be allowed to forego an eternal perdition in hell. In return, we agree not to touch another creature—living or dead—ever! Should we default from these terms, we will be condemned to the fiery reaches of… *(A thunder clap and another music cue drenched in horror. The set lights dim and brighten rhythmically.)* …hell! Immediately and forever! *(Katharine shows the document to the audience.)* Signed in blood, Herman and Vanessa!
(The music stops. The lights stop flashing. It is suddenly quiet.)

HERMAN: It doesn't say anything about not visiting each other.

KATHARINE: Don't try looking for loopholes.

VANESSA: Besides, hell couldn't be any worse than this!

KATHARINE: You don't know what hell is, you little slut.

VANESSA: Aren't I right, Herman? We can't throw our lives away like this. This *isn't* life!

HERMAN: Don't worry about that now. We've got each other now.

VANESSA: Yes, Herman, yes! Say you'll touch me.

KATHARINE: Watch it, Herman.

HERMAN: Darling…just seeing you is feast enough.

VANESSA: Mmmm!

HERMAN: Drink to me only with thine eyes!

VANESSA: Oh! Poetry!

HERMAN: Hearing your voice is like…a really great dessert, a chocolate mousse or something.

VANESSA: I love you, I love you, I love you!

HERMAN: Come sit with me!

VANESSA: Yes!

KATHARINE: Not in my house! Not on my sofa!

(Vanessa takes off her trench coat and joins Herman on the sofa.)

HERMAN: Let me take you in!

VANESSA: Yes!

HERMAN: Darling…imagine that I'm kissing you.

VANESSA: *(Closing her eyes.)* Oh! I can feel your tongue…

HERMAN: Mmmm…let me slip it in your ear like you like it.

KATHARINE: No!

VANESSA: *(Giggling.)* Oh, darling! Don't stop! Oh! It doesn't taste like ear wax, does it?

HERMAN: No. It tastes like…an orange souffle! I'm running my hands up and down your body!

VANESSA: I'm doing the same to you!

KATHARINE: Disgusting!

HERMAN: Wait! Let me look at you! Oh!

VANESSA: *(Cupping her breasts.)* You like what you see?

HERMAN: Yes!

(Katharine blocks Herman's vision with her hands.)

KATHARINE: Stop it! Stop it! Stop it!

HERMAN: *(In disgust.)* Christ, Katharine! Haven't you done enough to torment me? Can't I have this little crumb?

KATHARINE: *(Her bravado breaking into weepiness.)* You should have thought of that…before you killed me! *(Another music cue, this one melancholic.)* Oh, honey. I don't want to sound unforgiving. After you fooled around with that hussy. After you asked for a divorce. Even after you stuck a knife in my chest when I wouldn't give it to you, I've still been willing to forgive. All I ask is that you try to make up for it, that's all.

HERMAN: Never! Never! I'll never treat you with the slightest bit of affection, you rotten bitch! If you're hoping that some day I'll stop hating the sight of you, you're hoping for too much. *(Katharine purses her lips. She turns to Vanessa.)*

KATHARINE: Out of my house, you little whore.

VANESSA: I'm not going anywhere!

HERMAN: That's right.

KATHARINE: Isn't it enough that you've stolen a good woman's husband? That you've plotted murder with him? Do you also have to wear those tight little dresses, and swing your hips back and forth, so men undress you with their eyes!

VANESSA: So what if they do?

KATHARINE: They grab their crotches and think what they'd do with you naked…

VANESSA: You're just jealous because you can't keep a man happy!

KATHARINE: At least I'm not a slut. Slut! Slut!

VANESSA: Bitch! Bitch!

KATHARINE: Leave!

VANESSA: No!

KATHARINE: *(Starting to weep.)* Oh, no! No, no, no, no! *(Katharine crumbles into a heap on the floor. She asks the audience…)* What did I do wrong? All I did was love a man with all my heart. All I wanted was to make a beautiful home with him!

HERMAN: Oh, Christ.

KATHARINE: If it was just me you killed I wouldn't mind. If it was just my dream I wouldn't mind. But we could have had babies! *(Katharine's weeping gains volume. Pointing to Herman.)* You killed the babies!

HERMAN: Bullshit I did. They're right here… *(Herman grabs his crotch.)* All dressed up with no place to go! Who's fault is that, Katharine? Huh?

men's and women's scenes 35

VANESSA: Look at her. She's desperate. Maybe she's just been bluffing.

KATHARINE: Don't kid yourself, trollop.

VANESSA: Why should we believe you can send us to hell?

KATHARINE: Try me out. You're more than welcome. Just don't take my hubby with you.

VANESSA: Herman: act on an impulse. Wrap your arms around me. Now!

KATHARINE: Don't try it, Herman. I've warned you about this.

HERMAN: I so much want to.

KATHARINE: The howls of the damned, packed together like sardines. The smell of rotting flesh! The smell of burning flesh! Torture! Torment!

VANESSA: She's lying!

HERMAN: I don't know. The thunderclaps? She's been very persuasive.

VANESSA: It's a stormy night. She got lucky.

HERMAN: Yeah, but the music, the lights. I don't know.

VANESSA: She's lying, I tell you.

KATHARINE: You don't believe me? All right. All right. *(Katharine goes to the phone and dials.)* Hello? The Prince of Darkness, please. Katharine Mould.

HERMAN: Katharine, what are you doing? We didn't do anything.

KATHARINE: Yes, I'll hold. Well, then. Ask her to leave.

HERMAN: We're not breaking the agreement or anything.

VANESSA: She's bluffing, but even if she wasn't. Even if she was telling the truth. So what?

HERMAN: What do you mean, so what?

VANESSA: Wouldn't it be worth it?

HERMAN: A touch, you mean?

VANESSA: Yes.

HERMAN: Depends. If I touched you and then right away we got beamed to hell, then no.

KATHARINE: Of course it wouldn't.

VANESSA: Shut up. She's on hold. It sounds like they're backed up.

Maybe there's paperwork involved. Maybe it would take a long time. What if it took them a month?

HERMAN: Oh! A month.

VANESSA: Would it be worth it? Huh? 'Cause I think it would.

HERMAN: Mmmm.

VANESSA: If it was just a day…a day we could spend together. Even then it would be worth it. Don't you think? I'd draw you a hot bath. Drop in a few teaspoonfuls of exotic mideastern love oils! Let some red rose petals float on top! Then I'd get in with you, soak up the water like I was a sponge, and scrub every inch of you clean!

HERMAN: Oh, God. You're killing me here.

VANESSA: If it was just one minute! One minute of that. Wouldn't it be worth it?

HERMAN: Oh, Vanessa.

VANESSA: Well?

HERMAN: I don't know. Eternity can really stretch out.

VANESSA: What's that supposed to mean?

HERMAN: It means we don't know the score.

VANESSA: Touch me, Herman. I'm begging you. I'll never ask anything more. If you love me…please! Touch me. Touch me. *(Herman doesn't reply. Vanessa stretches her hand towards Herman's face. He shrinks back. Vanessa advances toward him. Herman retreats to avoid her. Finally, she's backed him up to the wall. She stretches her hand to his face…he recoils. Vanessa withdraws her hand.)* So that's what it's worth to you. Nothing.

HERMAN: No. Everything. Just not forever in flames.

VANESSA: You shrink from me. Like I was a leper.

HERMAN: I love you.

VANESSA: It's not love! It's not love unless you'll do anything!

HERMAN: Anything but! Everything…but this one thing.

VANESSA: You're a coward, Herman. You shrink from me. Coward.

HERMAN: This isn't all there is, Vanessa. We can talk. Look into each other's eyes. We can have each other.

VANESSA: Look into the eyes of a coward? Why? Have someone who's so scared of dying they won't live? Why?
(*Vanessa leaves. Katharine hangs up. Herman stands immobilized, staring after Vanessa.*)

KATHARINE: Well. I suppose that's the end of that. Now it *is* time for dinner. Would you like some pork chops, Herman? Pork chops with apple sauce? What do you think? Do you want to see some TV? Here I'll put it on for you. (*Herman ambles slowly to sofa.*) I know you're feeling a little blue, honey. I understand. But I wish you'd stop being so silly. This dizzy-headedness you feel…it's not love! Love isn't shaken by little inconveniences…like not being able to touch. No! It faces down all things: infidelity, contempt, cruelty…even the murderer's knife. That… (*From behind Herman, Katharine puts her arms around his shoulders to brace them, but her hands stop an inch shy from contact. She bends to kiss the top of his head and again stops an inch shy.*) …that is true love! (*Blackout.*)

FRAGMENTS

John Jay Garrett

dramatic, 1 Man, 1 Woman

Jack (18) a young recruit preparing to leave for Vietnam and Rachel (18) the woman he loves.

Scene: an airport, 1967

Here, as the two young lovers bid a final farewell, Rachel is unable to tell Jack that she is pregnant.

(Rachel turns to Jack who is at the other end of the stage. He seems hesitant.)

VOICE (P.A.): Pam Archer, your party is waiting for you at the TWA ticket counter.

JACK: Hi.

RACHEL: Hi. Did you say good-bye to your parents?

JACK: Yeah, they dropped me off. My mom didn't wanna come in, she just…yeah.

RACHEL: You fly out of Oakland, right?

JACK: In three days. We're flying to Chicago first, then to Oakland, then, well, you know, Vietnam.

RACHEL: Why are you way over there?

JACK: I don't think I can do this Rachel.

RACHEL: What do you mean exactly?

JACK: I know…I know that if I hold you, that if I kiss you, I'll be admitting things I'm not ready to deal with. It's gonna be best if I just leave. If I just leave then I can come back and it's like this whole thing never happened. It's like…I don't know Rachel, I 'm just so afraid.

RACHEL: You don't think I'm afraid? Do you know what it feels like to have to stand here and watch you leave?

JACK: Rachel, if I come over there, if I smell you next to me, if I touch your face, I'm never going to leave. I'll just run. I'll run like I really want to and not even the hand of God will be able to push me into Vietnam.

RACHEL: Would that be so bad?

JACK: Yes, it would. It would be for me. Look I'm not saying this war is right, or that we have any place being over there, or that it makes any kind of difference whatsoever, I just know that I have to go.

VOICE (P.A.): TWA flight one-one-three to Chicago now boarding gate twenty.

RACHEL: Why, I don't understand why?

(Jack walks closer to her.)

JACK: I don't know why. I really don't. "Because?" That's my best answer. Mr. Canty would fail me if I gave it to him on a test. But things are more confusing out here, you know?

RACHEL: No, I don't. I'm selfish and I'm greedy and I don't understand why you're going away for a year, why you might get killed, and why you "have" to do all this. I don't understand any of it.

JACK: Maybe it's not supposed to make sense. Maybe that's the part about being a grown-up they forgot to tell us. *(Beat.)* Do you remember when we drove to Toronto?

RACHEL: *(Smiles.)* Yeah.

(As he talks, Jack slowly gets closer to Rachel and the sounds of the airport fade.)

JACK: It was the middle of the night, you said you couldn't stay awake any more. You asked me to pull over so we could sleep, but I told you to put your head in my lap, that I'd be fine to keep driving.

RACHEL: I remember, I remember all of it.

JACK: Yeah, but what you didn't know was that I was falling asleep too. I could barely keep my eyes open when you asked me to pull over. But I don't know, I just didn't want to stop right then. You put a pillow down on my lap, I remember it was one of the old ones from the couch on our front porch. All the tassel things on it's sides were missing because I'd pulled them off as a kid. You laid down and I kept driving and I started running my hand in your hair. And as soon as I did, I was really awake. I could see the road like it was daylight. The clanging sound my dad's Chevy makes was like a circus in my ears. I felt your chest rising and falling as you took in each breath, and I can distinctly remember thinking, "This is the best moment of my life." Isn't that strange? I mean, it was such a stupid thing, I'm just driving, but I thought that, I said it even. "This is the best moment of my life." Everything made sense in that moment, Rachel. There were no questions. *(He rubs her arms and places his forehead against hers.)* Good-bye. *(Jack picks up his duffel and starts away.)*

RACHEL: Jack, I need to tell you something…

JACK: No. No Rachel, this needs to be quick. I'm sorry, I just…I know, I love you too. *(He kisses her on the cheek but winds up standing there for a moment, kissing her, before he can finally pull away.)* Bye.

(Jack exits and Rachel is left standing alone as the sounds of the airport resume full blast. People start walking past and around her, all in a hurry. Rachel just stands there for several moments, watching Jack who must be far down the corridor by now.)

VOICE (P.A.): Last call flight one-one-three to Chicago. Last call flight one-one-three.

RACHEL: Good-bye.

THE LADY WITH THE TOY DOG

Sari Bodi

Adapted From a Short Story by Anton Chekov

dramatic, 1 Man, 1 Woman

Dimitri (30–40) a pleasant womanizer, and Anna (20s) a married woman flirting with emotional disaster.

Scene: a resort in Yalta, turn of the century

Dimitri has been pursuing Anna for several days. Here his seduction is finally a success.

(Anna and Dimitri at the pier. Anna holds a bouquet of flowers.)

DIMITRI: Here, Anna. Another iced tea.

ANNA: Thank you. And thank you for the last one. And the one before that.

DIMITRI: And I will continue through the rest of the day if this heat keeps up.

ANNA: The sun should go down soon. The steamer is still having difficulty turning into the jetty. Does such a crowd always turn up to see the passengers disembark?

DIMITRI: Of course. It is one of the highlights of Yalta. You'll notice another peculiarity of Yalta. Here, the elderly ladies always dress like young women. They try to disguise old age with ribbons. And there are far more generals than one is accustomed to seeing in Petersburg or Moscow.

ANNA: The generals seem to take themselves very seriously. They must polish their buttons every morning.

DIMITRI: Would you respect me more if I wore such buttons?

ANNA: I am not one who is impressed with men in uniform. I can never tell them apart.

DIMITRI: Why do you play with your necklace like that? Is it precious to you?

ANNA: No, it is just a cross, given to me by my husband before I left Petersburg. It is supposed to protect me here in Yalta.

DIMITRI: And has it protected you?

ANNA: Yes, so far. No horrible fate has befallen me.

DIMITRI: May I see the cross?

ANNA: Yes. *(Anna hands Dimitri the cross.)*

DIMITRI: It's been a long time since I have been to church. I used to sing in the church choir when I was a boy. Now, all I remember is the way the incense always made me cough. *(Looking at the cross.)* It is such a tiny little thing and yet it holds such power for some people.

ANNA: Oh, here come the passengers. *(Anna looks through her lorgnette at the steamer.)* It's so exciting. Where are they coming from? Who do they know? Oh, look at the children. And more dogs. Though none so white as mine.

DIMITRI: Are you looking for someone?

ANNA: What? No. I don't think so. Why did you ask? Oh, I'm sorry, I'm babbling. It's just too thrilling. I've never seen so many fashionable people. What could they all be thinking about? *(She grabs Dimitri's arms.)* Oh, let's get closer to the steamer. I want to see everything.

DIMITRI: Anna, when you pulled my arm, I dropped the cross.

ANNA: What? Oh no. Where is it? I can't lose it.

DIMITRI: Calm down, Anna. We'll find it. You're getting flushed.

ANNA: Oh no. I can't see it. I can't see it anywhere. It's buried in the grass. I have to find it. My husband won't understand. He says I always lose things. He says he should never give me anything because I don't appreciate it. It's the first thing he'll look for when he sees me.

DIMITRI: Anna, I'm sorry. I don't see it anywhere.

ANNA: No. It's lost. Never mind.

DIMITRI: I will buy you another.

ANNA: It was made by a particular friend of my husband's in Petersburg. He would know the difference. Don't worry. He will yell and sulk, but he will get over it in about ten years time.

DIMITRI: I am sorry.

ANNA: Good-bye little cross. I feel as if a weight has been lifted off of me.

(Anna and Dimitri sit down on a bench. Anna smells the flowers and doesn't look at Dimitri.)

DIMITRI: The weather has got pleasanter now that the sun has started to go down. Where shall we go now? Shall we take a carriage? *(Anna doesn't answer. Dimitri gazes at her, and suddenly embraces her, and kisses her lips. He then looks around.)* Let's go to your... *(Anna and Dimitri get up quickly and walk away.)*

LAGOON

Frank Cossa

dramatic, 1 Man, 1 Woman
Heather (20s) a young woman discovering herself in Venice, and
Stampalia (60) a Venetian with a keen eye for potential.

Scene: Venice

> *Heather and her boorish husband, Doug, encounter the enig-*
> *matic Stampalia while honeymooning in Venice. Stampalia*
> *has been watching Heather react to the mesmerizing light of*
> *his beloved Venice and has decided to offer her an opportu-*
> *nity to stay. His plan unfolds when he offers Doug two hun-*
> *dred and fifty thousand dollars to spend the night with*
> *Heather. Here, she angrily confronts the older man.*

(The Cafe. Stampalia sits alone, reading a newspaper.
Heather enters and watches him for a moment.)

HEATHER: Signor Stampalia.

STAMPALIA: *(Putting down his paper.)* Ah…Under the circumstances
I think you should call me by my given name. Adriano.

HEATHER: Under the circumstances I should call you all kinds of
names, but for now Signor Stampalia will do.

STAMPALIA: You are angry with me. I am sorry.

HEATHER: Are you surprised?

STAMPALIA: No. But I am sorry.

HEATHER: I have one question for you.

STAMPALIA: Of course you have.

HEATHER: Don't you patronize me, I used to play soccer.

STAMPALIA: In that case I will not patronize you, if you promise not
to kick me.

HEATHER: What I want to know is…

STAMPALIA: Yes?

HEATHER: If this is what it was all about…

STAMPALIA: If what was…?

HEATHER: Everything. The last two weeks. The whole performance…

STAMPALIA: Yes?

HEATHER: Was all because…you wanted me. Why did you offer the money to *Doug? (Pause.)* It was *me* you wanted, right?

STAMPALIA: *(A small laugh.)* Oh yes. You may rest assured.

HEATHER: Well?

STAMPALIA: I do not discuss money with women. With women I discuss art, poetry, love, the light on San Giorgio… *(Gesturing.)* …not money.

HEATHER: That's not good enough. I want the truth.

STAMPALIA: Oh, the *truth.* You would have refused.

HEATHER: Doug refused. *(Pause.)* Didn't he? *(Pause.)*

STAMPALIA: Yes, of course. I did not expect him to shake my hand and say 'It's a deal.' Although…you are here.

HEATHER: What *did* you expect?

STAMPALIA: I wanted to make a crisis. You have had a crisis?

HEATHER: Yes.

STAMPALIA: It is a crisis that would have come in two years or five years. I brought it sooner. I think you learned something about your husband today. That he loves too much the money. Already his heart is poisoned. He is not a bad man. He is not even unusual. He is typical.

HEATHER: I don't really see…

STAMPALIA: And you are not. *(Pause.)*

HEATHER: Did I miss the answer to my question or haven't you gotten to it yet?

STAMPALIA: I am…in the middle.

HEATHER: I'm waiting.

STAMPALIA: Won't you sit down? *(She does.)* Want a Campari?

HEATHER: No, I think I should be clear headed for this.

STAMPALIA: When I first spoke to you in front of San Zaccaria, you remember?

HEATHER: Yes.

46 men's and women's scenes

STAMPALIA: I was…following you already some hours.

HEATHER: You were…?

STAMPALIA: I was watching you as you went from Church to Palazzo to gallery, to Church. Always with the guide book and the map. I was watching.

HEATHER: Watching what?

STAMPALIA: Every movement, every gesture. At first I thought, 'Ah, the young women of America, so eager, so ignorant, so perfect!'

HEATHER: Thanks.

STAMPALIA: Then I began to see something more. Something in the eyes as you looked at the paintings, the statues, the churches. It was something like fear and something like…ecstasy. You were frightened by what you were feeling, no?

HEATHER: Yes.

STAMPALIA: You wanted to escape. To rest, to eat, to go to the lavatory, anything to get away. *E vero?*

HEATHER: Si.

STAMPALIA: And your innocent husband with the camera, dragged you to see more. Not knowing what was happening. How could he?

HEATHER: What was happening?

STAMPALIA: You were being seduced.

HEATHER: It was the light. I felt like it was going right through my head.

STAMPALIA: You were blinded so that you could *see.*

HEATHER: *(Slightly dazed.)* I was…blinded… *(Trying to snap out of it.)* Are we getting close to the part about the money?

STAMPALIA: I decided to speak to you. I had to…know you. I did not know why. I had no idea how to approach you, but I could see what would appeal to your husband. An expensive restaurant so he would feel better than the other American tourists. The hotel, the villa, as long as I could amuse him with such things I could keep you here. I could hope to… reach you. You resisted, as I knew you would. I succeeded once only.

men's and women's scenes 47

HEATHER: That day in front of the Bellini altarpiece.

STAMPALIA: You were so frightened…the beauty, the mystery…

HEATHER: I thought I would faint…it was the heat…the wine we had at lunch!

STAMPALIA: *(Rising, over her.)* No! It was cool and dark in the church. You were alert, *alive.* You were living through your *eyes.* You were frightened by your own emotions. *E vero?*

HEATHER: *(Defeated.) Si. E vero. (Pause.)*

STAMPALIA: The time was over. I was about to lose you. I made this bizarre offer of money, to create a disaster.

HEATHER: And what do you think you've accomplished?

STAMPALIA: I don't know. I have perhaps lost your friendship forever. It was a great risk, but I was desperate. *(Pause.)* I know that you have seen the light of Venice. You can never return to …'outside Chicago.' To live in the darkness. Oh, you can get on an airplane and go there. You can sit all day with the computer, and drive up and down the street in the car. And fill your house with lamps and televisions and the…the compact disc. And keep your appointments at the dentist, and pay your bills on time. And most of the time believe you are living your life. *(Pause.)* But once every day you will look up from your terminal computer, or your checkbook or your VCR because something…a sound, a color, a scent, will remind you. And you will know that this is terribly wrong. That something is always…missing.

HEATHER: The light.

STAMPALIA: The light. *(Pause.)* I knew from the beginning that you were one of those persons…blessed or cursed, I know not which…who must remain in Venice.

HEATHER: I can't stay here! I have a job, a marriage.

STAMPALIA: You cannot return to the darkness.

HEATHER: *(Greatly disturbed.)* This place is crazy. It makes *me* crazy! *(Pause, thoughtfully.)* I'll die if I stay here.

STAMPALIA: Perhaps. But you will not *live* if you go away.

HEATHER: I'll…I'll come back to Venice.

STAMPALIA: Certainly, in two years or five years you come back with

48 men's and women's scenes

the husband, the children, the cameras. For what? The…the nostalgia? To see if Stampalia still sits at the cafe or is he dead? Or San Marco has crumbled into the sea? No! To return this way is a desecration! Stay…'outside Chicago,' or go to the Disney World, or the Great Wall of China and hit the golf ball like your President. But Venice will be lost to you! You will never find her again.

HEATHER: I feel like I'm caught in some kind of spell.

STAMPALIA: Yes! Yes! Look at it. Venice after the thunder storm. And San Marco, the wet stones, as if they are made of silk! The sky that was painted by Tiepolo! The water, silver, splashing at your feet, the breeze, from the sea with the sweetness of the east. The light…

HEATHER: That's what I mean! Nothing is real here, nothing is solid. It's all light and water, reflections of reflections. Everything…shimmers. How can you live in a place like this?

STAMPALIA: How can you live in any other place? Now you have truly seen, truly felt La Serenissima?

HEATHER: I can't just…I have to think.

STAMPALIA: This is not a time to think! It is a time to *know*. You have the truth before your eyes, you have it in your soul. What is to think? To go…'outside Chicago'? To drown in your possessions. Stay in Venice. Possess nothing. *Be* possessed!

LEMONADE

Michael T. Folie

serio-comedic, 1 Man, 1 Woman

Jim, a vitamin salesman in love (30s) and Betsy, his best friend's lover (30s).

Scene: here and now

> *Betsy has been having an affair with Carl, an old friend of Jim's. Jim has fallen in love with Carl's wife, Jane. Here, Jim reveals a plan which he hopes will split up Carl and Jane to his and Betsy's benefit.*

> *(Jim's apartment. Jim and Betsy in bed or on a couch, disheveled and half-dressed. Betsy lights a cigarette.)*

JIM: I guess I should finish making dinner.

BETSY: Forget it.

JIM: Beg pardon?

BETSY: I'm not hungry. I couldn't eat that macrobiotic crap anyway.

JIM: Oh. *(Pause.)* I guess you know that's really bad for you.

BETSY: Does it bother you?

JIM: Sort of.

BETSY: Too bad.

JIM: Let me get you an ashtray.

BETSY: Oh, the hell with it. *(She puts the cigarette out in a wine glass.)*

JIM: You seem upset.

BETSY: Whatever gave you that idea?

JIM: Would you like something to calm you down?

BETSY: What've you got?

JIM: B-12.

BETSY: I'll take another glass of wine.

JIM: You know, I don't usually do this.

50 men's and women's scenes

BETSY: It showed.

JIM: I mean on the first date. I'm not this easy usually.

BETSY: You think I am?

JIM: I don't know. Are you?

BETSY: Of course not. You could have AIDS for all I know.

JIM: So could you.

BETSY: Well I don't!

JIM: Well I don't either.

BETSY: I'm sorry.

JIM: You're just upset about Carl.

BETSY: What do you mean?

JIM: I heard you and Carl on the baby monitor. *(Pause.)*

BETSY: Did Jane?

JIM: No. I stopped her from coming into the room.

BETSY: Thanks.

JIM: You're welcome.

BETSY: Thanks for nothing.

JIM: I didn't know what to do.

BETSY: So why did you…do what we just did? If you knew about me and Carl? You must have known I was just using you to get back at him.

JIM: I thought it might make you feel better.

BETSY: It didn't.

JIM: And I didn't want to hand you another rejection on top of last night.

BETSY: Thank you. That was actually sweet of you.

JIM: I don't mind being used once in a while. For a good cause.

BETSY: I don't know how I ever fell for that line of bullshit Carl was feeding me. He's never going to leave Jane.

JIM: Are you sure you're not getting hungry? I could order out for something.

BETSY: But why have an affair with me if he's happy with Jane?

JIM: Because he can.

BETSY: What?

JIM: If he can have you and Jane, why not? That's how men think. Women think that if you're happy with somebody and in love, then you shouldn't want anybody else. But men want all the sex they can get, from all the women they can convince to give it to them. And they want a comfortable home life with a faithful wife and children, too. They want it all.

BETSY: Is that what you want?

JIM: Well, most guys realize they can't have both. So they settle for one or the other. But guys like Carl think they can break the rules. They think the reason they're successful in business is because they break the rules. So they just go ahead and try to get away with everything they can.

BETSY: That's disgusting.

JIM: Women seem to find it attractive.

BETSY: I should leave.

JIM: Why?

BETSY: I'm not such great company tonight.

JIM: You've been great so far.

BETSY: Why on Earth would you want me to stay?

JIM: We could talk.

BETSY: You don't want to hear my problems.

JIM: Look, if you leave now, I'm going to sit here and turn on the television and have another boring, lonely evening feeling sorry for myself. And you'll probably go home and do the same thing. Right? So why don't you just hang out here with me for a while and we'll talk to each other. You tell me your problems and I'll tell you mine. I'll get some Chinese food delivered. What the hell, I'll even eat some. *(Pause.)*

BETSY: Can I have some more wine?

JIM: Sure.

BETSY: Okay.

JIM: How long has it been going on with Carl?

BETSY: Two years.

JIM: Long time.

BETSY: Too long.

JIM: Do you love him?

BETSY: Yes.

JIM: What are you going to do now?

52 men's and women's scenes

BETSY: I don't know. Tell me your problems.

JIM: I'm in love with Jane.

BETSY: What?

JIM: I'm in love with Jane. I'm in love with Carl's wife.

BETSY: You just met her last night.

JIM: I fell in love with her the moment I saw her. That's how it happens sometimes, I guess.

BETSY: I wouldn't know. It's never happened to me. Do you think she might love you, too?

JIM: Not yet. But she will.

BETSY: What makes you so sure?

JIM: Because I'm going to make her fall in love with me. Then I'm going to convince her to leave Carl and marry me.

BETSY: Woo! That won't be easy. She's a married woman with a kid.

JIM: I'll find some way. I know I will. I just know it somehow. The minute I met her my insides began to vibrate differently. I became different. Does that make sense?

BETSY: Yes.

JIM: It's like, all my life I've been just galumphing along without direction, waiting to find this right thing to vibrate to. And now that I've found it, nothing's going to keep me from it. Nothing.

BETSY: That's…beautiful.

JIM: I'm thinking in fact, that if you and I pretended to fall in love and started seeing each other, then we could arrange to see them as a couple. I could see Jane and you could see Carl.

BETSY: Are you serious?

JIM: Look, what are your options? You can dump Carl and try to forget about him, which I don't think you're ready to do. You can expose the affair to Jane, which would be poison. Carl would never come near you again. Or you can go on being his mistress, kidding yourself that he's going to leave his wife and making yourself miserable until you get old and Carl dumps you anyway.

BETSY: Don't try to sugarcoat it, Jim, give it to me straight why don't you.

JIM: But my way you'd be taking some action. You'd be helping me to break up his marriage. And what's Carl going to do if I take Jane away from him? His ego will be destroyed. He'll need emergency ego first aid like crazy. And where's he going to go for it?

BETSY: Me?

JIM: Absolutely.

BETSY: I didn't figure you for the devious type.

JIM: I've never wanted something this badly before. I'm willing to do anything to have Jane.

BETSY: It makes you much more attractive.

JIM: Thank you.

BETSY: I think I'm going to enjoy this. *(She kisses him.)*

JIM: Do you think we should…

BETSY: Yes. I think we should. I think we'll be much more convincing as a couple if we do. *(They kiss.)*

JIM: I'm a lot better the second time.

BETSY: I'm counting on it.

   (End of scene.)

MR. MELANCHOLY

Matt Cameron

serio-comedic, 1 Man, 1 Woman
Ollie (30s) a lighthouse keeper living as a hermit and Dolores (20–30) a circus clown who has washed up in a trunk on his shore.

Scene: a desolate lighthouse

> *When Dolores arrives on Ollie's desolate beach, his self-imposed isolation is violated in a way he never would have imagined. Helplessly drawn to the vivacious Dolores, Ollie feels his sense of self both stimulated and threatened. Here, in an extremely awkward moment, these two extremely awkward people attempt an extremely awkward seduction of one another.*

○ ○ ○

DOLORES: Are there bones?
    (Ollie stops.)
OLLIE: I don't think so.
DOLORES: I don't like bones in my fish. *(Circus music creeps in. Dolores prods at the fish with a fork which disappears down into the fish along with her arm.)* Oh… *(When she pulls it out, she is holding a very large dogbone. She looks to Ollie.)*
OLLIE: Slice of lemon? Tartare sauce?
DOLORES: There's death in that fish.
OLLIE: Death comes to us all.
DOLORES: That's true. A meteor could wipe us all out at any moment.
OLLIE: *(Looks up fearfully.)* Really?
DOLORES: Possibly.
OLLIE: I hate the sky.
DOLORES: You hate the sky?

OLLIE: Never know what's going to fall on you. Someone's throwing things at us.

DOLORES: Oh yes, there are all kinds of disasters and doom hurtling towards us.

OLLIE: There are?

DOLORES: Meteors! They shave by all the time, just missing us.

OLLIE: By how much?

DOLORES: One hundred fifty thousand miles.

OLLIE: Phew.

DOLORES: When you think of how big space is...

OLLIE: I often do. I'd like to go into space.

DOLORES: And do what?

OLLIE: Just sit there.

DOLORES: I'd like to go to the horizon.

OLLIE: How would you know you've made it?

DOLORES: There'd be a sign: "You are now leaving the horizon...missing you already," then I'd just go back a bit.

OLLIE: I don't think you can go there. It's unreachable, it's indefinable, it's like—

DOLORES: Stealing a beach?

OLLIE: The horizon doesn't actually exist, it can't be located, it's an unknown—

DOLORES: We're all heads, that's the problem. Take a look at any ship sailing by, full of disembodied passengers. *(She bobs her head.)* All these heads bobbing about in the porthole, looking out, trying to spot their body.
(Ollie is staring at Dolores.)

OLLIE: Would you like to dance?

DOLORES: As long as you don't tread on my feet.
(He looks at her clown shoes.)

OLLIE: You're making it hard... *(She looks at him. They stare at each other.)* What's your face look like?

DOLORES: *(Indicates.)* This.

OLLIE: Under that one?

DOLORES: I don't know.

OLLIE: You could take it off...

56 men's and women's scenes

DOLORES: Um… *(Ollie holds out a cloth to wipe her makeup. Dolores grabs the cloth and backs away.)* Do you want to kiss me?

(The circus music disappears. They both look away, stunned.)

DOLORES: *(Pointing.)* Meet me at that spot there if you want to.

OLLIE: *(Pointing.)* That spot there?

DOLORES: *(Pointing.)* There. That spot.

(They tentatively move towards the spot, taking a non-committal, circuitous route.)

OLLIE: Are you going to that spot?

DOLORES: I'll meet you there if I am.

(They arrive and stop, facing each other, looking down.)

OLLIE: This is the spot.

DOLORES: This is the spot.

(They awkwardly but tenderly kiss. The clown shoes get in the way and they fall in a tangled mess on the floor.)

OLLIE: That went well.

DOLORES: Swept me off my feet.

OLLIE: I haven't done this in a long time.

DOLORES: It's these shoes… *(He helps her up and she stands right in close.)* I could take them off.

OLLIE: *(Muttering.)* Dead cat, dead cat, dead cat, dead cat…

DOLORES: "Dead cat," what is that?

OLLIE: It's an anti-arousal phrase that I use. Dead cat, dead cat, dead cat…

DOLORES: What about "old nun, old nun, old nun"?

OLLIE: Doesn't work.

DOLORES: Old nun, old nun, old—

OLLIE: In fact, can you stop saying that?

DOLORES: Old nun, old nun, old nun—

OLLIE: Please, I'm in the middle of a drought.

DOLORES: I think I'll take a bath. *(She steps away.)*

OLLIE: Now?

DOLORES: Before bed.

OLLIE: *(Smiles.)* Right.

(Dolores leaves. Ollie takes out a condom packet from his

wallet and lays it out on the pillow of his suitcase bed. He
casually reclines. Dolores screams and enters.)

DOLORES: There's a spider in the bath.

OLLIE: Hope it hasn't used up all your hot water.

DOLORES: I'm serious!

OLLIE: *(Scared.)* You're serious? It's back?!

DOLORES: You can't be scared, I'm scared.

OLLIE: That's good. Fear is good.

DOLORES: It is?

OLLIE: Crucial! Brings people together.

DOLORES: But you're a hermit. *(Pause.)*

OLLIE: Is it big?!

DOLORES: There's legs everywhere!

OLLIE: I'm putting the lighthouse on the market—

DOLORES: You'd think with all those limbs it could manage a door
handle and leave—

OLLIE: Don't panic, this is what it wants us to do—

DOLORES: You said fear is good—

OLLIE: I never go anywhere without it—

DOLORES: Let's make it an offer. Cash, unmarked bills—

OLLIE: We're playing right into its hands—

DOLORES: Legs—

OLLIE: What'll we do?

DOLORES: Face it.

(She hands him a clown shoe. Ollie holds it up, poised.)

OLLIE: Listen to that.

DOLORES: It's quiet.

OLLIE: Too quiet. I hate creatures that don't make a noise. At least
if there's a leopard in your living room it makes a growling
sound so you know it's there.

DOLORES: Then all you need is a really big jar to coax it into.

OLLIE: Is it really big and hairy?

DOLORES: It looks like there's a yak in your bath.

(Ollie shudders as he exits, clown shoe poised. Dolores pre-
tends to follow but doesn't.)

OLLIE: *(Off.)* What if the spider leaps at me?

58 men's and women's scenes

DOLORES: *(Calls.)* It's just a fear, Ollie. Face it.

(Ollie screams and runs in with his hand clasped across his face. Dolores grabs the shoe from him.)

OLLIE: I'm facing it! Hit me, *(She hits him.)* hit me, *(She hits him.)* hit me! *(Dolores smacks Ollie's face again with the clown shoe.)* Stop hitting me. *(Ollie flips the unseen spider off.)* There it is!

DOLORES: Where?

OLLIE: There! *(Dolores slams her clown shoe on top of it.)* Don't take your shoe off it.

DOLORES: Why, what are you going to do?

OLLIE: Nothing.

DOLORES: When can I take my shoe off?

OLLIE: Never.

DOLORES: I didn't actually see it…

OLLIE: Oh, believe me, it's there.

(They step back from the shoe. Dolores' eye catches the condom packet on the bed.)

DOLORES: What's that on your bed?

OLLIE: Not another one. *(Realizing.)* The bed! Oh, it's er—

DOLORES: Is that a condom?

(Ollie dashes to grab it.)

OLLIE: It's an, ah, after dinner mint.

DOLORES: Let me see.

(Ollie rips the packet open and puts the condom in his mouth.)

OLLIE: Mmm, that's good.

DOLORES: Do you want to have sex with me on that *(Points to bed.)* spot there? *(Ollie nods and gulps.)* But we needed that after dinner mint.

NAKED MOLE RATS IN THE WORLD OF DARKNESS

Michael T. Folie

serio-comedic, 1 Man, 1 Woman

Mary Becker, an officer with the DEA (30s) and Frank Pulone, a suspected felon (30s).

Scene: here and now

When Mary attempts to arrest Frank, she is flabbergasted to discover that he is the same Frank Pulone who stood her up for the senior prom and broke her heart.

○ ○ ○

(A city alley at night. We hear the sound of a police siren rise and fade. Frank Pulone, a well-dressed man in his 30s, runs on stage, sees no way out and starts to go the way he entered. Mary Becker, a Drug Enforcement Agency officer, wearing a windbreaker with the letters "DEA" on the back, runs at him, gun drawn. She takes a police pose with gun trained on Frank, blocking his escape.)

MARY: Freeze! Lemme see your hands! Now, now, now! Hands in the air! Do it!

FRANK: Alright, alright, calm down.

MARY: On your knees. Keep those hands up!

FRANK: Alright! Don't wet your pants. *(He begins to pull handkerchief out of breast pocket. She pulls hammer back on gun, screaming at him.)*

MARY: What do you think you're doing!? Get those hands up!

FRANK: I'm just getting my handkerchief. See? I'll do it slow. *(He removes handkerchief and places it on ground, kneels on handkerchief.)* Jeez, lady, don't get so excited.

MARY: On your face. Keep those hands where I can see 'em.

FRANK: Aw come on! This suit costs more than you earn in a month.

60 men's and women's scenes

MARY: I count to three. One. Two.

FRANK: Can't I just lean up against the wall? You sound like you watch enough cops shows with all that "freeze!" bullshit.

MARY: Three. *(She knocks him to the ground. Puts gun against his head.)* You do what you're told. *(She cuffs his hands behind him, frisks him.)*

FRANK: Fuck you, bitch. *(She whacks him hard with the gun in his ribs.)* Owwww!

MARY: You got something else to say?

FRANK: Yeah. Fuck you, bitch. *(She whacks him again, hard.)*

MARY: Excuse me? *(Pause.)*

FRANK: May I get up now? Please? *(She pulls him up to a standing position.)*

MARY: Come on, let's go.

FRANK: Wait a second, I know you from someplace.

MARY: You're under arrest. You have the right to remain silent.

FRANK: Mary. Mary Becker?

MARY: Anything you say…How'd you know that?

FRANK: Mary Becker. Hoboken High. Class of 1980.

MARY: Yeah.

FRANK: Mary, don't you recognize me? Frank? Frankie Pulone.

MARY: Frankie Pulone.

FRANK: Jesus Christ! Mary Becker.

MARY: Frankie Pulone.

FRANK: How the hell are you?

MARY: Not bad, not bad. How're you?

FRANK: Doin' okay, y'know? *(Suddenly she whacks him again.)*

MARY: You creep! You stood me up for the senior prom!

FRANK: I can explain that, Mary.

MARY: I spent a fortune on that dress. *(She hits him.)*

FRANK: Ow! Mary, Mary. Come on! I didn't do it on purpose. Something came up.

MARY: And you couldn't call?

FRANK: No, I couldn't call! I hadda go away. On business! It was unavoidable, doll. I always felt bad about it. Really. *(Pause.)* So I guess you're married by now, huh?

men's and women's scenes 61

MARY: I wish. How about you?

FRANK: Married? Well, yeah. I'm married. But, you know, it ain't serious.

MARY: Frankie fucking Pulone.

FRANK: Mary goddamn Becker. *(Pause.)* So you wanna get together sometime?

MARY: When? In about 10 to 15 years?

FRANK: Lemme go, Mary.

MARY: I can't do that, Frankie.

FRANK: Sure you can. For old time's sake. Nobody saw. Take off the cuffs and lemme go. Then you and me can get together later on.

MARY: What?

FRANK: You and me, we were meant for each other. Remember that night on the bluff, Mary? I swore I'd love you forever. I meant it.

MARY: You love me?!

FRANK: Yeah!

MARY: All of a sudden you love me!? After standing me up at the prom all those years ago?!

FRANK: Yeah!

MARY: You gotta a lot of goddamn nerve! Do you know how long I sat beside that phone? Crying my eyes out?

FRANK: Jeeze, Mary, I said I was sorry. What're we talking about here, a stupid dance?

MARY: Do you know how humiliating that was? Do you know how much I've been messed up with men ever since, unable to trust, unable to love? Do you know what you did to me?!

FRANK: And I'll make it up to you, honey. I will. Just let me go. Give me another chance, please, baby!

MARY: Another chance? Sure. I'll give you a chance. I'll give you a sporting chance. Here. *(She turns him around and takes off the cuffs.)*

FRANK: You won't regret this, Mary.

MARY: I know. *(She pulls her gun.)* Now go on. Get!

FRANK: Uh, what's with the gun, Sweetie?

62 men's and women's scenes

MARY: I gotta make this look good, don't I? Go on. Run. I'll fire a couple of shots into the air.

FRANK: Uh, you sure that's necessary?

MARY: Absolutely.

FRANK: You're going to shoot? Into the air?

MARY: Bang, bang.

FRANK: You do know how to work that thing, don't you?

MARY: I'm an instructor at the academy, Frankie. I can shoot the balls off a perp at two hundred feet. What are you waiting for? Scoot.

FRANK: Mary, about the senior prom…

MARY: *(She points gun at him.)* Move, scumbag! *(Pause. He looks at her. Looks at gun. He looks off in the direction he might run. Looks back at her.)* What're we doing, Frankie? What's the matter? Don't you trust me? I trusted you. I never trusted anybody ever again, but I trusted you. *(Long pause.)*

FRANK: Aw, fuck me, man. *(He turns around and puts his arms behind his back to be cuffed again. She puts the cuffs on him.)*

MARY: Let's go, punk.

FRANK: Mary, tell me the truth. Would you've shot me for standing you up for the goddamn senior prom? *(Pause.)*

MARY: *(She smiles.)* You have the right to remain silent. *(As she leads him off.)* Anything you say can and will be used against you in a court of law. You have the right to an attorney. If you cannot afford an attorney, one will be provided by the court. *(Blackout.)*

SAD LAUGHTER

Charles Deemer

dramatic, 2 Men, 1 Woman
Moliere (50s) the playwright and actor, Madeleine (40s) an actress and former lover and La Grange (40s) a member of the company.

Scene: seventeenth century France

Here, the volatile genius is confronted by his former lover about the possibility that he has unwittingly married his own daughter.

○ ○ ○

MOLIERE: What's the matter with you? Charles is as much a part of the family as we are.

MADELEINE: Don't say that.

MOLIERE: He's been with the company almost as long as you have. Longer, counting the time you were gone.

MADELEINE: That's what we have to talk about, Jean. *(A beat: she is having a hard time starting, getting to the real subject.)*

MOLIERE: Let me guess. You don't like "Don Juan."

MADELEINE: Those whom "Tartuffe" upset, "Don Juan" will upset twice over.

MOLIERE: Don Juan is a hypocrite.

MADELEINE: So is Tartuffe but few recognize the fact. I think you want trouble. You want scandal. And that troubles me very much.

MOLIERE: I merely satirize the vices I see—

MADELEINE: I know the explanation, Jean. You recite it like a litany. But I didn't come here to talk about "Don Juan."

MOLIERE: Then what is it? What's bothering you?

MADELEINE: My soul is bothering me.

(Moliere laughs. When he sees that Madeleine is sincerely upset, he stops. He is confused.)

64 men's and women's scenes

MOLIERE: Sorry. I didn't mean to interrupt.

MADELEINE: When I returned to the troupe in the provinces, bringing Armande with me, I came under false pretenses.

MOLIERE: I don't recall any pretenses at all. Theater's in your blood and you wanted to return. We welcomed you with open arms.

MADELEINE: I shouldn't have brought Armande.

(Moliere thinks he understands what is going on.)

MOLIERE: So that's it! For all the women I put on stage, I'll never understand where female jealousy comes from. I'm surprised at you. The love we shared, Madeleine, the love I still feel for you—it's a spiritual love, not physical. Don't be jealous of Armande because she's having my child.

MADELEINE: Not jealous. Afraid, for all of us.

MOLIERE: You're not making sense.

MADELEINE: I shouldn't have returned with Armande because she isn't my sister. She's my daughter.

MOLIERE: I don't believe it.

MADELEINE: It's true, Jean, I swear it is.

MOLIERE: You're telling me I married my own daughter?

MADELEINE: I don't know.

MOLIERE: Is she your daughter or not?

MADELEINE: You may not be the father. There were others.

MOLIERE: You never told me that. *(She doesn't respond. Moliere will become furious.)* Why didn't you tell me that?

MADELEINE: Jean, I—…I didn't think it was any of your business.

MOLIERE: Not my business!

MADELEINE: We were so young.

MOLIERE: Not you, apparently, oh no, not sweet innocent Madeleine. Well, if I'm not the father, then who is? Did you sleep through the whole goddamn company or what? Is Charles the father? *(Calling off.)* Charles!

MADELEINE: Jean, for God's sake, don't you understand what I'm saying?

MOLIERE: Very well. Charles!

(La Grange hurries in.)

LA GRANGE: Yes?

MADELEINE: Jean, please…don't do this…

(A beat: La Grange is tense, wondering what is going on.)

MOLIERE: Have you ever gone to bed with Madeleine?

(La Grange is confused by the question. He turns to Madeleine.)

LA GRANGE: Is he serious?

MOLIERE: I do not ask questions unless I mean them! Have you or not?

MADELEINE: He has—but he is not…a candidate.

LA GRANGE: A candidate? For what?

MADELEINE: Let him go, Jean.

MOLIERE: You may go. *(La Grange, puzzled, hesitates.)* I said, you may go!

LA GRANGE: Yes, sir! *(And he hurries off.)*

MOLIERE: Then who are the candidates?

MADELEINE: It doesn't matter. The point is, you are one, in fact the most probable one. I think that's why little Louis was taken from you. I think—

MOLIERE: Providential retribution?

MADELEINE: For the sake of your own soul, Jean, don't ridicule the possibility.

MOLIERE: Louis died because the doctors couldn't save him! Because all they know how to do is drain blood and give enemas! Children are dying all the time!

MADELEINE: I'm her mother. And you may be her father. I swear it's true.

MOLIERE: I can't believe you never told me.

MADELEINE: It didn't matter at first. I never dreamed you'd one day marry her. When you did, I knew it was wrong, I knew it was sinful, but when I tried to tell you—

MOLIERE: We don't know that! That I'm actually the father. How many candidates are there?

MADELEINE: Including you, three.

MOLIERE: Three!

MADELEINE: I would think you'd wish there were dozens.

MOLIERE: I don't know what to think.

66 men's and women's scenes

MADELEINE: I pray you're not her father.

MOLIERE: I can only be sure of what I absolutely know. One, that I'm her husband. Two, that I'm the father of her…Christ, I don't even know if I can be sure of that. If you can lie to me so easily, live a charade so easily, perhaps she can as well.

MADELEINE: After so many years, I didn't know how to tell you.

MOLIERE: In words that speak the truth!

MADELEINE: I know I should have. I know I'll pay the consequences for not telling you. But all that's past and can't be changed. The only thing I can change now is the present, my life now and in the future. Which is why I'm quitting the company.

MOLIERE: Don't be ridiculous. What else could you do?

MADELEINE: I can pray for my soul.

(Moliere just stares at her.)

MOLIERE: I don't know whether to laugh or cry.

MADELEINE: I think you should pray as well.

MOLIERE: Have you told anyone else about this?

MADELEINE: Of course not.

MOLIERE: You must not, ever. You must promise me that.

MADELEINE: I shall tell a priest, I think.

MOLIERE: Where it will remain in confidence. But no one else. Ever. You must promise me.

MADELEINE: I barely had the strength to tell you.

MOLIERE: You don't have to leave the company. You can still attend to the books. You don't have to go on stage.

MADELEINE: No, I have to listen to my spirit, Jean, troubled as it may be. *(A beat. Moliere is at a loss for words.)* Will you tell Armande?

MOLIERE: No. And you won't either.

MADELEINE: I'll pray for both of you.

MOLIERE: I'm sure you will.

MADELEINE: I can't save your soul, Jean. Or Armande's. I can only save my own—if it's not too late.

MOLIERE: Then save it, Madeleine. Get out of here and save your soul. *(A beat: and Madeleine turns and leaves. Moliere kicks a chair, and lights fade to blackout.)*

SEVEN STRANGERS IN A CIRCLE

Eric C. Peterson

serio-comedic, 1 Man, 1 Woman

Masha (30s) recently divorced and Robert (30s) the man she meets on the rebound.

Scene: a hotel bar in Las Vegas

> *Although prickly Masha does her best to discourage Robert's advances, the two become hopelessly attracted to one another.*

○ ○ ○

(A casino bar in Las Vegas. Only two barstools are visible to us. One is occupied by Masha, a woman in her early thirties. Robert, a round-faced, friendly-looking man, enters and sits next to her.)

ROBERT: Hi. *(Nothing.)* Er…hello.

MASHA: *(Icily.)* Are you talking to me?

ROBERT: Yes.

MASHA: Don't.

ROBERT: Oh…okay. *(Pause.)*

MASHA: You think I'm a bitch. *(Short pause.)*

ROBERT: *(Taking a drink.)* The thought had crossed my mind. *(Pause.)*

MASHA: I'm not a bitch.

ROBERT: If you say so.

MASHA: But I didn't come to Vegas to sit around a table and gamble all my money away, and I didn't come here to watch a bunch of anorexic showgirls gently remind me that I'm thirty-two years old—

ROBERT: Uh-huh.

MASHA: And I certainly didn't come here to get picked up by strangers in bars.

ROBERT: I see.

MASHA: This isn't a pleasure trip for me. So I'm not obligated to enjoy myself.

ROBERT: No…

MASHA: I'm not a bitch. You should know that. You're one of those people who you meet in a strange place and will probably never meet again anywhere, but nevertheless, you should know that…I'm a very nice person.

ROBERT: I underst—

MASHA: I just don't want to be talked to right now.

ROBERT: Okay. *(Pause.)*

MASHA: And I'm not drunk.

ROBERT: What?

MASHA: I know it may look like I'm drunk because I'm sitting at a bar with a drink in my hand and I'm sort of slumped over and slurring my speech. But I'm not drunk. I've just had a very shitty day and I don't have the energy to keep up appearances. I think that if people weren't so obsessed with what everyone else thought about them, everyone would look drunk, almost all the time. But just because they looked drunk, it wouldn't mean that they were drunk. It would just mean that—

ROBERT: You know, for someone who doesn't want to meet strangers in bars, you talk a lot.

MASHA: Well…yeah.

ROBERT: How long had you been married?

MASHA: What?

ROBERT: Married. How long had you been married?

MASHA: None of your goddamn business.

ROBERT: Okay. *(Pause.)*

MASHA: Three years. Not that it's any of your business, but…three years.

ROBERT: If it makes you feel any better, you beat me.

MASHA: What do you mean?

ROBERT: Two and a half. You're not the only one who came to Vegas for a quickie divorce, you know.

MASHA: How did you know that?

ROBERT: I saw you down at city hall. You were three people ahead of me.

MASHA: Oh…And misery loves company, is that it? Well, don't waste your time on me. I'm really not in the mood to hear your sob story and I can make a pretty safe bet that you don't want to hear mine.

ROBERT: A pretty safe bet…you said you didn't come here to gamble.

MASHA: I didn't.

ROBERT: What's your name?

MASHA: Frank.

ROBERT: Your name is Frank?

MASHA: What? Oh. *His* name was Frank.

ROBERT: Your husband.

MASHA: My ex-husband. He was a pig.

ROBERT: I'm sure he was.

MASHA: Don't get me wrong. I don't think that all men are pigs, but Frank was definitely a pig. I don't think he ever—

ROBERT: I thought you didn't want to talk about your husband.

MASHA: My ex-husband. And I didn't say that I didn't want to talk about him. What I said was *you* didn't want to *hear* about him.

ROBERT: Six to one. What's your name?

MASHA: What's yours?

ROBERT: I asked you first… *(She's not budging.)* …Robert.

MASHA: What was *her* name? Your wife.

ROBERT: My ex-wife, you mean. Sharon.

MASHA: Robert and Sharon. It has a nice ring to it. That's important, I think. A marriage at least has a fighting chance if the names sound good together. Robert and Sharon. Robert and Sharon. It's like fate.

ROBERT: It didn't help us out too much, I'm afraid.

MASHA: Why did you split up?

70 men's and women's scenes

ROBERT: She was sleeping with her boss.

MASHA: That's a good reason.

ROBERT: As good as any.

MASHA: And what was her boss' name?

ROBERT: Mark.

MASHA: Sharon and Mark, Sharon and Mark. See, there you go. It has a better ring to it. It's all in the names. Was he married?

ROBERT: Who?

MASHA: Mark.

ROBERT: Yes.

MASHA: What was her name?

ROBERT: Danielle.

MASHA: Mark and Danielle. Nope. Doesn't cut it. He had no choice. It was written in the stars that he should pork your wife and make your life hell.

ROBERT: You still haven't told me your name.

MASHA: And I might not, ever.

ROBERT: That's your choice. *(Pause.)*

MASHA: Masha.

ROBERT: Excuse me?

MASHA: Masha. That's my name.

ROBERT: Are you Russian?

MASHA: My mother was an actress. I was conceived by a stage-hand during a production of *The Seagull*.

ROBERT: Anton Chekhov.

MASHA: Mother was playing the role of—

ROBERT: Masha.

MASHA: Bingo.

ROBERT: That's very interesting.

MASHA: Huh…You think that's bad. When she was playing Miss Julie, she became pregnant with my brother.

ROBERT: Another stagehand?

MASHA: *(A little sad.)* No…Same stagehand. *(Forgetting why she was sad, now brighter.)* She just assumed it would be a girl, and of course she planned on naming it Julie. When she found out he was a boy, she almost sent him back.

men's and women's scenes 71

ROBERT: What did she name him?

MASHA: *(She smiles.)* August.

ROBERT: After Strindberg.

MASHA: But we always called him Gus. It…suits him. *(A short pause.)*

ROBERT: Masha's a beautiful name, though.

MASHA: Ick.

ROBERT: What?

MASHA: Whenever people, men especially, although I don't like to stereotype, but men especially, run out of things to say to me…they tell me that I have a beautiful name.

ROBERT: They're right.

MASHA: Don't try to backpedal by flattering me. It doesn't work. "Masha" is not a beautiful name. It doesn't…suit me.

ROBERT: If you say so.

MASHA: When I was going through my awkward phase, all the kids used to call me "Masha Potatoes." *(Robert laughs.)* It's not funny…I hate it. I've always wished that Mother would have been doing Shakespeare when my brother and I were conceived. I could have been…Ophelia—

ROBERT: Who goes crazy and kills herself.

MASHA: Yes. It would suit me…I suppose you're wondering why I split up with Frank.

ROBERT: He was a pig.

MASHA: Did I already say that?

ROBERT: Yes.

MASHA: Oh. Well, that about covers it, I guess. He was a pig…and a louse…and a lying, womanizing, good-for nothing sack of shit.

ROBERT: So I gather…

MASHA: *(Letting some sadness in now.)* And what's worse…he was too good for me…

ROBERT: *(Not knowing how to respond to that.)* So…are you sorry you got a divorce?

MASHA: Hell, no.

ROBERT: I guess what I meant to ask was…Are you sorry you got married?

72 men's and women's scenes

MASHA: What do you mean?

ROBERT: I mean…if you had it to do all over again…would you have married him?

MASHA: I don't know…Probably not…well, maybe. I mean…It wasn't all bad, you know? And if I hadn't married Frank, who knows what I'd be doing by now? I hate hypothetical questions.

ROBERT: Why?

MASHA: Because they make you crazy, that's why. If I could go back; well, you can't go back, can you? I married him, and there are three years of my life that I'll never get back again, and I can't change that. No sense making myself sick thinking about it. *(Pause.)* Leave me alone.

ROBERT: I don't want to leave you alone.

MASHA: *(Calmly.)* Fuck you.

ROBERT: *(Just as calm.)* Fuck you back…I think I'm falling in love with you.

MASHA: Ha! You're crazier than I am.

ROBERT: I'm serious.

MASHA: So am I.

ROBERT: I'm in love with you. That's it.

MASHA: *(Seemingly indifferent.)* Boy, you don't waste any time, do you?

ROBERT: No.

MASHA: Is this how you fell in love with Sharon?

ROBERT: Yes.

MASHA: She ended up sleeping with her boss. Maybe you should learn to take your time with these things in the future.

ROBERT: I can't help it. I love you.

MASHA: What on earth makes you think that?

ROBERT: Because you need me. *(Pause.)*

MASHA: Listen, Romeo…I can promise you…that the last thing you want to do right now is fall in love with me. *(Going back to her drink.)* I'm damaged goods.

ROBERT: I'm a handy guy.

MASHA: *(Looks him square in the eye.)* You're in love with me.

ROBERT: I'm in love with you.

MASHA: You're nuts.

ROBERT: I agree with you.

MASHA: Look, just stop it, okay? You're giving me the creeps.

ROBERT: God, I love you.

MASHA: *(Suddenly very angry.)* Fuck off. *(Robert is silent.)* Jesus, you people will say just about anything, won't you?

ROBERT: What are you talking about?

MASHA: You just got a divorce from "Sharon," your wife of two and a half years. She was banging her boss. You're lonely. You're humiliated. You're basically pathetic. You think that it might cheer you up to find some broad in a bar whose life is just as screwed-up as yours, take her back to your hotel room, hump her 'til dawn, and then fly back to wherever it is you come from and never see her again. And if you have to make up some outrageous love-at-first-sight bullshit to do it, then that's fine; that's what you'll do. You make me sick.

ROBERT: You don't believe in love at first sight?

MASHA: Apparently not…Look, Robert, if that's even your real name, if you want some action that badly, I'm sure there are plenty of women in this bar who will give it you. If nothing else, you can always look outside, although it's considerably less expensive to shop indoors, if you know what I mean.

ROBERT: You think that? That I'm just trying to pick you up? For sex?

MASHA: Oh, don't look so stunned. It has happened to me before…once.

ROBERT: Did you do it?

MASHA: Did I do what?

ROBERT: Have sex with him?

MASHA: What do you think? *(No response from Robert; she rolls her eyes.)* I married him.

ROBERT: Oh…What do I have to do?

MASHA: What do you mean?

ROBERT: To prove to you that I love you, Masha; what do I have to do?

MASHA: Just leave me alone.

ROBERT: Wrong answer.

MASHA: Look, I'm not listening to you anymore. I want you to go away.

ROBERT: Then why don't you leave?

MASHA: Excuse me?

ROBERT: If you want to get rid of me that badly, why don't you get up and walk away?

MASHA: I was here first.

ROBERT: Infantile evasion.

MASHA: Besides, you'd just follow me around…Oh, I don't know. Just move, will you?

ROBERT: What do I have to do to convince you that I mean what I say?

MASHA: You don't have to do anything, Robert, okay? Because I don't give a shit.

ROBERT: I don't believe that.

MASHA: Look…say you really do mean it; say you're really and truly in love with me—

ROBERT: Which I am.

MASHA: It's just an aftershock from your divorce. Do what I'm doing. Kick back a couple of stiff drinks until the room spins and pretty soon you'll forget what whatshername looks like.

ROBERT: I've already forgotten.

MASHA: You're too much, you know that?

ROBERT: You said you weren't drunk.

MASHA: What?

ROBERT: Five minutes ago, you said you weren't drunk. You talked at some length—

MASHA: I lied. Besides, what's it to you? I can hold my liquor. I've had a shitty day, I'm entitled to get a little drunk. I came to this town to get a divorce. I didn't come here all the way from New York City to take *shit* from *you*.

ROBERT: You're a New Yorker?

MASHA: Yeah, so what?

ROBERT: So am I.

men's and women's scenes 75

MASHA: What, as if that's supposed to mean something? It's a big town, in case you haven't noticed.

ROBERT: Tell me, Masha, what I have to do.

MASHA: To prove to me that you love me?

ROBERT: To prove to you that I love you.

MASHA: Marry me.

ROBERT: What?

MASHA: You heard me.

ROBERT: But we barely know each other.

MASHA: And yet you've suddenly fallen head over heels in love with me.

ROBERT: That doesn't mean I want to marry you…yet.

MASHA: I called your bluff, didn't I? Ha! Nice try, Robert. You had me goin' there for a while. If it makes you feel any better, I actually enjoyed it…until it got creepy. But I knew I'd trip you up sooner or later. You see, Robert…you couldn't marry somebody like me. You wouldn't last a week.

ROBERT: Oh no?

MASHA: Not a chance.

ROBERT: Where and when?

MASHA: Where and when what?

ROBERT: Where and when do you want to get married?

MASHA: You're serious.

ROBERT: I am.

MASHA: You're fuckin' nuts.

ROBERT: I am.

MASHA: You really want to get married?

ROBERT: I do. *(Pause.)*

MASHA: Okay; let's do it. Tonight.

ROBERT: Alright.

MASHA: You're going to marry me tonight?

ROBERT: Why not? It's as good a time as any.

MASHA: We don't even know each other.

ROBERT: That's what I said. Didn't seem to bother you.

MASHA: You scare me.

ROBERT: I adore you.

76 men's and women's scenes

MASHA: You really *are* frightening.

ROBERT: Yes, I know.

MASHA: I'm sorry, but I can't very well marry a man that I've never slept with.

ROBERT: We can fix that.

MASHA: I've never even kissed you.

ROBERT: We can fix that, too.

MASHA: You are the oddest man. We just got divorced, you and I. Don't you want to be single again for at least twenty-four hours before you— *(He is kissing her. Her face rests in his hands. His kiss is gentle and slow but passionate nonetheless. It seems to last for some time. When he draws back he looks down, as if embarrassed.)* Oh my God…

ROBERT: Robert and Masha. It's got a nice ring to it.

MASHA: Uh-huh…

ROBERT: Masha…Will you marry me?

MASHA: Uh-huh…

SMOKE & MIRRORS

Eric C. Peterson

serio-comedic, 1 Man, 1 Woman
Simone (20–30) a sexual predator, and Gary (20–30) her date.

Scene: here and now

> *When Simone first espied Gary, she knew she had to have him. When she moves in for the kill on their first date, Gary surprises her by announcing that he's gay.*

○ ○ ○

(Simone's apartment exterior, Simone's apartment interior.)
SIMONE: I'm glad you could make it tonight.
GARY: I'm new in town. I'm glad you called.
SIMONE: Where do you come from?
GARY: Phoenix.
SIMONE: Is that where your family is?
GARY: No. Before Phoenix, I was in New York, and before that, I lived in Seattle. I'm not the stable type.
SIMONE: Oh. So…where is your family?
GARY: I don't have one.
SIMONE: Oh… *(She takes out her keys.)* …Before we go in, I should probably warn you. I don't have a lot of furniture yet, so it looks a little bit like…
GARY: Like a place without a whole lot of furniture?
SIMONE: Something like that…
   (The lights fade on Simone and Gary and rise on the "Interior Simone's Apartment" set, which at this point in the play is little more than bare stage. Simone and Gary walk into her apartment.)
SIMONE: Well, this is it. Like I said, it's kind of bare…I haven't decided exactly how I want to furnish it yet, but I figure…I'll know

it when I see it. I want art all over the walls, though, I know that.

GARY: Who's your favorite artist?

SIMONE: Oh, I don't know…Matisse, Salvador Dali…Picasso…

GARY: I would have guessed Picasso.

SIMONE: Why?

GARY: He's very bold…very contradictory…very sexual.

SIMONE: Huh. I've never discussed art with a man before…I've never discussed art with anyone before, except Jessica…although I s'pose she's close enough. Who's your favorite? Oh no, let me guess. This is so cool…Classic, right? Italian? Umm…Michelangelo.

GARY: Very good.

SIMONE: And I want a black leather couch right here. Have you ever made love on a black leather couch?

GARY: As a matter of fact, I have.

SIMONE: Oh. I haven't. Always wanted to try it, though. Ever made love on a waterbed?

GARY: Yes, I've done that, too.

SIMONE: Did you enjoy it?

GARY: Sure, it was kind of fun.

SIMONE: I've got a waterbed. Right through there. It's about all I *do* have in this place, but…it's functional. Hey, what's the matter?

GARY: Maybe this isn't such a wonderful idea.

SIMONE: What's wrong; gotta headache?

GARY: Oh, it's a little bit more than a headache.

SIMONE: Do you have a…wife?

GARY: No, a little less than a wife.

SIMONE: Your balls were blown off in combat.

GARY: What combat?

SIMONE: I don't know; who cares? You don't screw on the first date.

GARY: That's usually not a problem.

SIMONE: But you don't want to with me.

GARY: No.

SIMONE: You're gay. *(A long pause. Simone and Gary just stare at each other humorlessly for almost ten seconds.)* Oh my God, you *are*. Oh God…umm…Well…do you like it?

GARY: Compared to what?

SIMONE: Oh. I see what you mean. Do you have a boyfriend?

GARY: I don't believe in long-term commitment. I'm lucky that way.

SIMONE: Me too. I've never been out on a date with a gay guy before.

GARY: Are you sure?

SIMONE: Fairly certain, yes.

GARY: I see.

SIMONE: Have you ever done it with a woman?

GARY: No.

SIMONE: Ever think about trying it?

GARY: Don't waste your time on me, Simone.

SIMONE: It's not a waste of time—

GARY: It's a challenge. *(Pause.)*

SIMONE: How did you know what I was going to say?

GARY: I've heard it before. Often.

SIMONE: You are really full of yourself, you know it?

GARY: Pardon?

SIMONE: You know, most girls would have kicked you out on to the street the minute they heard you were gay.

GARY: Well, now *that* makes me feel much better.

SIMONE: I was just trying to be polite.

GARY: Simone. I'm gay. Gay.

SIMONE: I know what "gay" means.

GARY: No, no, no you don't. It means that I fuck men. You seem to think it means that I *used* to fuck men, but that would all change if I were to fuck *you*.

SIMONE: How do you know it wouldn't?

GARY: Suppose some lesbian didn't understand you, and started coming on to you…I suppose you would give in and just do it with her because she was so *polite*.

SIMONE: Look, I'm sorry! I'm sorry, okay? I'm sorry. I've never been in this situation with…someone like you before. I guess I don't know how to act. Usually if I'm having problems relating to a guy, I just seduce him. It usually works. I really do want to be sensitive to your…situation.

GARY: It's not a disease. You don't have to be sensitive to it.

SIMONE: I heard it's genetic.

GARY: The interview is over. I'm outta here.

SIMONE: No…wait. Why did you go out with me tonight?

GARY: You asked.

SIMONE: No…You knew I was interested, and you played along like I had a chance with you. What, were you trying to teach me some goddamn lesson? Well, go to Hell. I've always had an open mind about being gay or straight or black or white or…Arab, or…anything else, and I don't need to be told how prejudiced I am by some asshole who goes around practically hunting for it! Fuck you and get the hell out of my apartment!

(Gary stands looking at Simone. For one single moment, nobody moves. The Exterior Set is lit. Then, slowly, Gary turns around, walks to the Exterior, and begins to walk off when Simone stops him.)

SIMONE: Wait! Look……I'm sorry. I don't want you to leave. I'm not angry anymore. I just had to vent.

GARY: That was one hell of a vent.

SIMONE: Yeah.

GARY: I'm sorry, too…I *was* trying to…teach you a lesson…or something. Way out of line…Sorry.

SIMONE: Friends?

GARY: Fine.

SIMONE: So, is Michelangelo really your favorite?

GARY: I haven't the faintest idea.

SIMONE: *(Disappointed.)* Oh. Come on back inside; I'll make you a drink.

(Simone and Gary walk back into the apartment. Simone immediately exits in the direction of her "kitchen.")

GARY: So, what is it you do for a living?

SIMONE: *(From off-stage.)* Officially…I'm an aspiring actress.

GARY: Unofficially, then.

(She re-enters with two drinks in hand.)

SIMONE: Unofficially…Every week I have lunch with my very handsome, very charming, very *rich* father, and I tell him about all the auditions that never happened. And he gives me money to live on in the meantime.

GARY: Wouldn't you rather be taking care of yourself?

SIMONE: I *do* take care of myself—

GARY: I mean about the money…

SIMONE: *(Pause.)* Life is a maze of illusions, a hallway made of smoke and mirrors.

GARY: Who said that?

SIMONE: I did.

GARY: So what does it mean?

SIMONE: I don't know, it just…I really don't know. Nobody knows, I guess. You live your life, and I'll live mine, and everyone's happy…Can I ask you just one more question?

GARY: Shoot.

SIMONE: Well… *(She laughs at herself for having the nerve to continue this conversation before asking the question.)* How…do you meet guys? I mean…how do you know…?

GARY: You don't. You can't just look at a guy and know that he's gay. You hear it through the grapevine, or you hang out at a gay bar. And you carry a condom in your wallet at all times in case the unexpected happens.

SIMONE: Is it true that most male hairdressers are gay?

GARY: *(Without hesitation.)* Yes, that is true.

(Lights fade.)

THE SOUVENIR OF POMPEII

Sari Bodi

serio-comedic, 1 Man, 1 Woman

Jennifer (20s) a young woman with definite ideas about life, and Charlie (30s) a man who thinks he looks like John Kennedy; women love his arrogance.

Scene: here and now

> *Jennifer, a writer, has made up her mind to have a baby and is actively searching for the right man to assist her in this endeavor. Charlie is a literary editor who is attracted to Jennifer and here does his level best to sweep her off her feet…mytho-poetically.*

JENNIFER: Name the three protagonists from James Joyce's Ulysses.

CHARLIE: No problem, darling. I was an English major. (It was the best way to have lots of women in your classes.) There' s ah, Leopold Bloom. Stephan Dedalus, and uh, uh. Damn. I know it's the name of that sexy babe. Just like you.

JENNIFER: Sorry, Charlie. This isn't an essay question.

> *[Jeremy: I know the answer, Jennifer. Why didn't you ask me? Is it because with me, the image comes to mind of Mr. Rogers?]*

CHARLIE: Hold on, Jen. Don't go home yet. It's uh, Judith, Angie, Marilyn.

> *(Jennifer laughs.)*

JENNIFER: No. What are you doing? Naming the women who've had affairs with Jack Kennedy?

CHARLIE: Sure. Hey, did anyone ever tell you that you look like Marilyn Monroe? Come on, sing for me. *(As Marilyn Monroe.)* "Happy Birthday, Mr. President. Happy Birthday, to you."

JENNIFER: Did anyone ever tell you that you look nothing like a Kennedy?

CHARLIE: I don't? Well, I resemble the Kennedies where it counts. You'll see, Darling.

JENNIFER: Why do you idolize a cult of manhood that forces women into two categories—long suffering wife, and sexual play-mate?

CHARLIE: No, no, no. You don't get it. The Kennedies were myth-makers. Civilization needs myth in order to shape the desires of a people into a unified culture. Otherwise, we might as well be animals. Joseph Kennedy was as creative a myth-maker as James Joyce.

JENNIFER: But now those myths are starting to disintegrate.

CHARLIE: That's the problem with contemporary culture. We're always trying to destroy our gods.

JENNIFER: Then where does the ordinary human being fit into all of this?

CHARLIE: They must create their own myths for themselves.

JENNIFER: And your myth is that you are a long-lost Kennedy.

CHARLIE: It works for me. What will yours be?

JENNIFER: I'm not sure. Got any ideas?

CHARLIE: Sure. I'll create a myth for you. Jennifer Priestley was a woman who prided herself on her beautiful, tight flat stom-ach. Every summer she would strut the beach in her leopard-skin bathing thong, creating manly bulges in every pair of heterosexual bathing trunks she passed. Until this one partic-ular summer, as she was strutting the beach, she tripped on the sand, and suddenly came eye to eye with this adorable little child. The kind with the bright purple eyes, and the ringlets of hair which wrap themselves around your heart. She was in love. She had to fling herself into the ocean to cool down. And as she floated on the sea, proudly feeling her flat stomach, she suddenly felt herself pulled down into the ocean by the thong of her bathing suit. And she came face to face with this strange sea creature, he was half Lochness monster, half lifeguard. And then she noticed that he had bright purple eyes and ringlets of hair which wound tightly around her heart. She was sunk. Her thong floated off, as did his red Speedo. And when he showed her his imitation of a whale spouting water through its blow-hole, the ocean moved. And, well, now she has a little Lochness monster growing inside of her. And when she goes to the beach, she has to wear an ugly maternity bathing suit.

JENNIFER: Very good. I like that myth. And I suppose you have bright purple eyes? Let's see. Oh, you have something floating in your right eye?

CHARLIE: It's a mark of distinction passed down to me with a lightning bolt by my father, Zeus. Are you ready for the Lochness monster slash lifeguard?

JENNIFER: Maybe.

CHARLIE: Then tell me the name of the third protagonist in James Joyce's " Ulysses."

JENNIFER: Well, that would be cheating. But I will give you a hint. It's the name of Jeremy's cat.

[Jeremy: Oh no.]

CHARLIE AND JEREMY: *Molly Bloom!*

JENNIFER: Yes! Yes. I say Yes. *(Jennifer grabs Charlie and they kiss.)*

THE SWEET BY 'N' BY
Frank Higgins

dramatic, 1 Man, 2 Women
Babe (40–50) the outspoken widow of a coal miner, Libby (16) her outspoken daughter and Owen (20s) the young coal miner who loves Libby.

Scene: Glen Daniel, WV, a contemporary coal mining town

> *Babe will be damned before she allows her daughter to marry a coal miner. Here, she confronts Libby and Owen with her resolve.*

BABE: Libby!…I got this sewin done for old Mrs. Foley. You take it to her.
OWEN: I'll give you a ride up.
BABE: She got a bike. N come right back.
LIBBY: It's not what you think.
BABE: I told you go.
LIBBY: Mama—
BABE: *Go!*
LIBBY: I can explain.
BABE: I don't need it explained.
LIBBY: You can't treat me like this! I'm a woman!
BABE: You git on your bicycle n go, woman.
LIBBY: No! I do my own life! I'm not your little *girl* anymore!
BABE: Don't you never say that to me! Now git out!
LIBBY: No!
BABE: *(To Owen.)* My girl is virgin, or was.
LIBBY: Mama!
OWEN: She's virgin.
BABE: Swear.
LIBBY: I can't believe you!

BABE: Swear to me!

OWEN: She's virgin! Coz I told her we shouldn't do it.

BABE: He had to stop *you? (Babe slaps Libby.)*

LIBBY: Stop it!

OWEN: Nothing happened.

BABE: What have I told you? When sex gits started, things git crazy! You wanna wind up knocked up n on welfare?

LIBBY: That won't happen to me.

OWEN: I want Libby.

BABE: Libby's sixteen.

OWEN: You was sixteen you married.

BABE: Libby's not gonna marry a coal miner.

OWEN: *You* married a coal miner.

BABE: Yeah n he got his dumb butt killed in a cave-in.

LIBBY: That won't happen to him.

BABE: He's got no say what happens to him! Even when every miner in town is covered in coal dust I can recognize who's who from what's *wrong* with 'em. Woody Coombs with only two fingers n a thumb on his left hand; Gopher Davenport from how he limps on right knee; N then there's… *(Knocking on Owen's chest several times.)* young Owen Flynn. Easiest of all to spot, with nothing wrong with 'im, still waitin for his first accident. *(Owen coughs.)*

LIBBY: He's careful.

BABE: You think they weren't? N listen to him cough. He's gonna cough the rest of his life from the dust down there. You want somebody for a husband who's gonna cough all over you in bed?

OWEN: I'm good to her.

LIBBY: He treats me like a lady.

BABE: All these fools was good to their girls. Then the girls pop out another kid every year, they work their butts off, they wind up hags before they're twenty-five.

LIBBY: I won't let that happen.

BABE: You stay with him you're gonna wind up draggin your dumb, tired, fat ass to the bowlin alley so you can watch him bowl; you'll have bad teeth coz you can't afford fillings n that's gonna make your breath stink like you swallowed somethin dead.

LIBBY: Shut up!

BABE: You'll disgust him.

LIBBY: You're the one who's disgusting! I hate you! *(Libby takes the dress and stomps out.)*

BABE: I told you what I were gonna do to you.

A TOUCH OF SPRING

Keith M. Donaldson

serio-comedic, 1 Man, 1 Woman

Marni (46) a college professor being pursued by one of her students and Brad (24) the young man in question.

Scene: a college campus

> When Marni bumped into one of her old students, the last thing she expected was for sparks to fly between them. Here, she does her best to check Brad's ardor.

○ ○ ○

(Night. Outside the Boathouse. Brad pacing as Marni approaches.)

BRAD: I didn't think you were coming.

MARNI: Sorry I'm late.

BRAD: Your husband?

MARNI: *(Shaking her head.)* I almost didn't come. *(He starts to talk.)* No. Let me—your attention is flattering. You're sweet, and I want to help you—

BRAD: I didn't ask for your help. Just to be with me. *(She is silent.)* What ever I thought I was looking for, was trashed when I met you. I figured, when I found perfection in a woman: looks, brains, personality; I would experience the highest form of love. It didn't happen. Nobody's perfect. You showed me that. *(She reacts.)* No. No. This isn't coming out right. What I mean is, my ideas of perfection were way off. That love is a whole bunch of abstract things, and the perfection is in us, our feelings—

MARNI: Relationships are very complex. It's seeing the other for who they are. Recognizing when to do, and when not to do. Forgiving horrible thoughts, balancing your wishes with theirs. I'm sure you love Caytlin. Haven't you ever—

BRAD: I'm a long way from making a commitment to her.

MARNI: Oh?

BRAD: I'm lousy at making promises, because I'm not very good at keeping them.

MARNI: And you are now?

BRAD: Yeah. I've never felt this deeply about anything, or anybody.

MARNI: We hardly know—

BRAD: I have a passion inside me, I've never known before.

MARNI: I'm flattered. A handsome young man, is willing to give up a beautiful young woman, for me.

BRAD: Why not?

MARNI: Is your relationship—are you never vulnerable with Caytlin?

BRAD: I don't know. We have a good time, are both serious about our work, and stuff—help each other out. I love her, but I'm not *in* love with her.

MARNI: And the sex is great?

BRAD: The best! *(Stops himself.)* I mean —

MARNI: That's all right. May I offer some advice?

BRAD: Sure.

MARNI: Caytlin appears to be bright, hard working and full of life. I bet she's crazy about you. She's a treasure you don t want to let slip through your fingers.

BRAD: You're my treasure. *(Marni holds up her hand.)*

MARNI: And you say all the right things. But, if you let her go, you will find that no matter how many loves you have after, you will always be looking for her, but she'll be gone, and you won't be able to bring her back. You'll end up going from one unsatisfactory affair to another.

BRAD: Maybe it's you I should hold onto— *(She shivers, and pulls her jacket tighter. she looks up, as though she could see the clouds in the night sky.)* —not her.

MARNI: It feels like rain.

BRAD: We can go inside.

MARNI: *(Matter-of-factly.)* We could.

90 men's and women's scenes

BRAD: I've got the key. *(He shows her. Marni shakes her head.)* Just for a while?

(She looks toward the boathouse almost longingly.)

MARNI: It's a lovely idea. And don't think I haven't thought about it, but we have some thinking to do before we take that step.

BRAD: I want to hold you—talk with you. Stay—

MARNI: You're not making this easy.

BRAD: We've only been here a few minutes.

MARNI: I didn't think we would get this—

BRAD AND MARNI: Serious?

MARNI: —more a passing fling.

BRAD: We could have that too!

(She smiles at him. Touches his face.)

MARNI: You are a very sweet boy. *(She takes his arm.)* We really have to leave.

(They slowly exit. Lights fade.)

TUESDAY

Paul Mullin

dramatic, 1 Man, 1 Woman
Audie (30–40) a man suffering from a memory disorder, and Sister Fran (30–50) a nun.

Scene: a psychiatric hospital

> *Audie has been diagnosed with Korsakoff's Syndrome. Every morning when he wakes up, he has forgotten everything that happened the day before. Here, a nun takes him for his first walk outside the hospital since he was admitted.*

○ ○ ○

(Lights up on Audie sitting exactly where he was a moment ago. Sister Fran stands center.)

SR. FRAN: Hello, Audie.

AUDIE: Hello…you.

SR. FRAN: I'm Sister Fran.

AUDIE: You're my sister.

SR. FRAN: No. That's just a title I have because of some of my beliefs.

AUDIE: Belief?

SR. FRAN: Yes…So I come here every day and I see you. It's sort of my job to do fun things with you.

AUDIE: You're not a doctor.

SR. FRAN: Nope. Not a doctor.

AUDIE: 'Cause they don't seem very fun.

SR. FRAN: Shall we go?

AUDIE: Sure.

(Blackout. Lights up. The stage is empty. Sister Fran and Audie enter from upstage.)

AUDIE: Oh…what's this place called?

SR. FRAN: Outside.

AUDIE: Oh…outside…It's big. *(Looking up.)* um…

SR. FRAN: Sky.

AUDIE: Sky. *(Looking down.)* um…

SR. FRAN: Ground.

AUDIE: *(Smiling, nodding.)* Right. That's what I was gonna say. Ground. That's the perfect word for it. *(Looking out.)* Oh…oh…what is that? …Blue beyond the—

SR. FRAN: Trees.

AUDIE: —Trees?

SR. FRAN: Why don't we go and see?

AUDIE: Oh…it stretches…out…far.

SR. FRAN: Come on.

AUDIE: Oh…um…I'm a little…um…I don't know.

SR. FRAN: It's ok. Everyone feels something…sublime…the first time they see the ocean.

AUDIE: Ocean. *(They walk towards the audience.)* Oh…as it comes in it gets big, and then curls and then falls on itself and breaks. Breakers.

SR. FRAN: What?

AUDIE: What?

SR. FRAN: What did you say?

AUDIE: Breakers?

SR. FRAN: You remembered the word.

AUDIE: I did?

SR. FRAN: Strange. *(Pause.)*

AUDIE: How long have I known you?

SR. FRAN: A couple minutes.

AUDIE: No. I mean…Ok, how long have you known me?

SR. FRAN: A few years.

AUDIE: Do you like me?

SR. FRAN: Strange question.

AUDIE: Do you?

SR. FRAN: Of course. I mean—

AUDIE: Not "of course." Do you?

SR. FRAN: Yes. I do. Like you. Very much, Audie.

AUDIE: I love you…What?

SR. FRAN: How could you possibly know that?

AUDIE: It's not something…you know.

SR. FRAN: No?

AUDIE: I…feel. I feel it.

SR. FRAN: Sick is something you feel. Or tired. Or horny…You're just horny.

AUDIE: You think.

SR. FRAN: Or sick.

AUDIE: Or tired.

SR. FRAN: Right.

AUDIE: I think I'm tired.

SR. FRAN: No.

AUDIE: No?

SR. FRAN: It's still early.

AUDIE: I think…

SR. FRAN: Yes.

AUDIE: You love me.

SR. FRAN: How could you possibly know that?

AUDIE: I think…

SR. FRAN: Yes.

AUDIE: You're lonely…That's why you come…spend time with me…I'm some sort of saint.

SR. FRAN: Of loneliness?

AUDIE: Right.

SR. FRAN: Right.

AUDIE: I'm not responsible for your loneliness.

SR. FRAN: I never said you were. I never said I was lonely.

AUDIE: No.

SR. FRAN: Audie…

AUDIE: You should love me.

SR. FRAN: Audie, you have an illness. I…I—

AUDIE: You should. You could do worse.

SR. FRAN: We should go.

AUDIE: Ok. Let's go. Bye, breakers. So long, ocean.

(They walk upstage and exit. Blackout.)

94 men's and women's scenes

THE VISIBLE HORSE

Mary Lathrop

serio-comedic, 1 Man, 1 Woman
Scott (12–15) a young boy trying to cope with his father's death and Meg (30s) his mom.

Scene: a condo

As the first anniversary of his father's death approaches, Scott struggles to make sense of his feelings of loss and anger, and is helped in this sad enterprise by Meg.

(Scott is lying on his stomach on the floor of his room, holding some action figures. He's speaking for the action figures as he manipulates them.)

SCOTT: …I'm gettin outa here…Anthony, you're dead, you buttwad…Kerpow…Ahhhhh…Kerpow…
(Meg enters and hands Scott a pair of pajamas. The pj's are old, faded, and have a cartoon character on the chest. Scott pointedly ignores her and continues to make battle noises as he focuses on his action figures.)

MEG: Here, put these on, Scott. I really mean it tonight—you're not sleeping in your clothes again.

SCOTT: You'll never take me alive…

MEG: And just so you know: I know that you haven't changed your underwear for a minimum…

SCOTT: Surrender, you asshole…

MEG: …Of two days, so in the morning, you're starting from the skin out. You got it?

SCOTT: Captain, the escaping prisoner has been captured…

MEG: Scott?

SCOTT: …Good work, men…

MEG: Please?

SCOTT: Sergeant, I'm ordering extra rations for your men.

MEG: Or, if you really must sleep in underwear again, you can, but you have to put on clean ones. Okay?

SCOTT: I don't have any clean underwear. Captain, we're ready in interrogation…

MEG: Scott, you have a drawer…

SCOTT: …Prepare the prisoner…

MEG: …Full of clean underwear.

SCOTT: No Mom, what I got is a drawer full of jockey shorts with GI Joe on them…

MEG: What if we buy you more boxers this weekend? I bet you'd like that.

SCOTT: It's not going to be easy to break him, Captain… *(Meg has run out of patience, and she grabs the action figures away from Scott.)* Don't!

MEG: That's enough, Scott. Get in bed.

SCOTT: I'm doing something.

MEG: Scott, I've had it—it's late; I'm tired. *(Meg herds Scott into bed.)*

SCOTT: Can I stay home tomorrow?

MEG: Bedtime's always such a pleasure, isn't it?

SCOTT: Is my throat red?

MEG: No.

SCOTT: You didn't look. *(Scott gets in bed, clothes and all. Meg tucks him in.)*

MEG: Your throat isn't red, and you're going to school.

SCOTT: I don't feel good, Mom. For real.

(Meg kisses Scott's forehead checking for a fever.)

MEG: You're fine. You've got to go—school's your job.

SCOTT: Then I quit!

MEG: You don't get to quit.

SCOTT: Right, like you didn't quit your old job?

MEG: I quit my job so we could move to this happy place. We're done with this argument, Scott. Go to sleep.

SCOTT: Okay then, I'm just blurting this out, right?

MEG: Goodnight, Scott.

96 men's and women's scenes

SCOTT: Mom!

MEG: Will you stop?

SCOTT: This is important…It's really important. *(Meg gives Scott the floor.)* Okay, it's only fair if you're prepared, right?

MEG: Can we wrap this up?

SCOTT: You want me to go to school? I'll go to school, hey, I'll even go early, but the office is gonna call you tomorrow, because sometime, before school, morning break, sometime, I have to beat the crap out of Anthony.

MEG: Really?

SCOTT: Yeah.

MEG: Why?

SCOTT: Because he's a jerk.

MEG: Great reason.

SCOTT: He's a butt wipe.

MEG: Oh, well, a butt wipe. Of course! A butt wipe!

SCOTT: What are you mad at me for?

MEG: What am I supposed to say? Goodie gumdrops—crap beating! That all-American after-school activity!

SCOTT: Not after school. After school I come home. *(Scott puts his head under the pillow and snores loudly.)*

MEG: Scott!

SCOTT: I'm trying to sleep.

(Meg pulls the pillow off Scott's head. She sits him up and looks him straight in the eye. She isn't going to let him off the hook.)

MEG: Do I even want to know what happened to you today?

SCOTT: Nothing. Forget it. *(Pause.)* He said something he shouldn't.

MEG: What in the world did he say that made you want to hit him?

SCOTT: I don't want to; I have to. Didn't you hear me? I have to, which is not "I want to." I. Have. To.

MEG: You have to?

SCOTT: Yes. And I would of beat him up right then, but it was after school and he ran onto his bus, which he was standing beside, and which he knew I couldn't get on because you need a bus pass and I ride my bike.

MEG: Would you like to talk to Grandpa about it? Do you want to call Grandpa Ray?

SCOTT: Leave me alone.

MEG: Scott, what did he say?

SCOTT: Something bad.

MEG: Something bad.

SCOTT: Trust me, okay?

MEG: Trust you?

SCOTT: Oh, Jeez…Mom, he said something bad about…you.

MEG: About me?

SCOTT: Do you get it now?

MEG: People say all kinds of things.

SCOTT: People shouldn't say bad stuff about other people's mothers and if they do, then people have to stick up. Kids were laughing.

MEG: They were laughing at him.

SCOTT: No, Mom, they weren't laughing at him. So if I don't stick up, everybody calls me a wus for the rest of my life.

MEG: Come on, Scott, I don't really care if some boy in your class insulted me.

SCOTT: He didn't insult you, Mom.

MEG: Hey, I don't care if he said I was a green witch with snot for brains and bad breath.

SCOTT: Yo, Mom, he said you had sex.

MEG: With him?

SCOTT: Duhhhh.

MEG: He actually said that?

SCOTT: Don't smile.

MEG: Just so you know: he was lying.

SCOTT: This isn't funny.

MEG: What kind of jerk is this kid?

SCOTT: Anthony—he's a massive jerk, and a wus. And he has to take it back.

MEG: Scotty, my reputation was completely ruined long before you were ever born, so nothing that Anthony says can make it any worse…That's a joke.

SCOTT: Am I laughing?

MEG: No, you're not laughing.

SCOTT: I'm sorry if you don't like, Mom, but I gotta stick up. I gotta.

MEG: Jumping some kid a day later in the playground isn't sticking up.

SCOTT: Mom, look, it's like a rule.

MEG: A rule? There's a rule at your school that if someone says they "had" your mother…

SCOTT: …Mom!…

MEG: …You are required by this school rule to beat them up?

SCOTT: You gotta be tough.

MEG: Another school rule?

SCOTT: It's a man rule.

MEG: Oh, listen to you: a man rule.

SCOTT: You gonna tell me there aren't any of those?

MEG: Oh, no, there are definitely man rules.

SCOTT: I didn't start this!

MEG: Always lower yourself to the other person's level.

SCOTT: He called you a whore!

MEG: Whenever someone picks a fight, jump at the chance.

SCOTT: I'm defending you.

MEG: Always take the dare, pretend you know everything…

SCOTT: He said he fucked you!

MEG: My God! Isn't it bad enough that some twelve year old creep is talking dirty about me?…I couldn't stand it if you got hurt.

SCOTT: Hey, a really, really famous man rule is don't fight guys if they're way bigger than you are, and Anthony's little.

MEG: Well, then, great; no sweat!

SCOTT: Okay!

MEG: No sweat.

SCOTT: Okay, I won't fight him.

MEG: Look me in the eye, and you promise me, Scott.

(Scott thinks about it.)

men's and women's scenes 99

SCOTT: My dad would tell me to fight him.

MEG: No, he wouldn't.

SCOTT: No, he would. He would say, "You better get ready, Scott, cuz you're gonna take that guy down."

MEG: Some thug would maybe say that.

SCOTT: He would say to fight, but he would say to not tell you, also.

MEG: Oh?

SCOTT: He would say, "Humor her."

MEG: He would not.

SCOTT: He would say that people have to draw a line and stand on it, Mom.

MEG: Yes, he probably would.

SCOTT: I said I wouldn't fight him.

MEG: It's really late, Scott.

SCOTT: Mom?

MEG: Close your eyes.

SCOTT: Oh jeez, here we go—you're gonna cry.

MEG: I'm not sad.

SCOTT: Don't treat me like I'm a baby

MEG: I know you're not a baby.

SCOTT: Because I understand a lot of things. Like, example: in two more days, well, it's late, in one day and a half, will be exactly one year.

MEG: Oh?

SCOTT: I hate when you do that, Mom.

MEG: Yes, Scott, I know what day it is.

SCOTT: And surprise!, that one year after your husband got killed you would cry…

MEG: Well, I'm not crying, and you're going to sleep.

SCOTT: Mom, what would of happened if my Dad had got in the car later? Even one blink later?

MEG: I don't know, Scott.

SCOTT: Or that drunk guy who hit him—what if he was early? Or if he passed out and couldn't drive?

MEG: You know, you could make yourself go crazy.

100 men's and women's scenes

SCOTT: Mom? When it's really late at night, and you're in bed, and you can't sleep, right?, and you're just lying here, I mean lying here…

MEG: Yes?

SCOTT: Do you worry?

MEG: Absolutely.

SCOTT: What about?

MEG: All kinds of things.

SCOTT: Yo, Mom!

MEG: Yo, Scott, I worry about bills, I worry about getting fat…

SCOTT: You're not fat.

MEG: I worry about work, worry about that funny squeak that the car makes in the morning. I worry about you…

SCOTT: Hey, I'm tough.

MEG: I worry that I'm not much of a mother.

SCOTT: Really? Can I have more allowance?

MEG: I don't worry that much. Good night.

SCOTT: But this is creepy, isn't it? It's late and quiet, and your body's tired, but your brain thinks like it's now or never, right? I call this worry time.

MEG: What's your worry, Scotty?

SCOTT: What if I got kidnapped into a parallel dimension, where everybody looked the same, only they had evil souls, right?, and I'll never find my way back to my own world where people love me?

MEG: That sounds terrible.

SCOTT: It could happen.

MEG: No, Scott.

SCOTT: It could.

MEG: If you go into a parallel universe, I'll come get you—I promise.

SCOTT: But see, there'd already be an evil mother in that parallel universe ahead of you.

MEG: We'll make a password—so you can be sure it's me.

SCOTT: No. Because anything you know here, she knows there.

Like, if I'm in this parallel universe right now, the evil you is tricking me into a password. See what I mean?

MEG: How can I prove that I'm me, instead of someone who looks like me?

SCOTT: And acts like you, and sounds like you, and is you except on the inside.

MEG: Heh, heh, heh…

SCOTT: Don't.

MEG: My little pretty.

SCOTT: Mom, don't!

MEG: Scott, I'll do whatever you want to prove to you that I'm your real mother. Just tell me what to do.

SCOTT: No, that's good; that could be it. See, an evil, parallel mother, you know how she'd go?

MEG: No. How would she go?

SCOTT: Well, she wouldn't go, "How can I prove?" like you just went. No! She would go "yo, Scott, relax, you're perfect, you're perfect," deep inside my ear until I fell into a trance and then she'd pull my soul out of my mouth.

MEG: Oh, honey…You had a nightmare.

SCOTT: Do you ever have a dream when you think you wake up and everything seems normal and then you go, "Oh no, I'm still asleep", and then you dream that you wake up again, until you scream and scream without any sound, and finally you wake up for real and you're all twisted in the covers?

MEG: Yes, actually.

SCOTT: Mom, I feel like I dreamed my dad was killed in a car crash, and I wake up every morning, knowing he's in the kitchen, standing by the sink, eating corn flakes and bananas, only he's never in the kitchen, he's always dead.

MEG: Scott, it wasn't a dream.

SCOTT: If you could have Dad back for one day, what would you do? And you can say sex if you want to, I don't mind.

MEG: Would this be a day that I would spend alone with him, or would this be a family day with all of us together?

SCOTT: I would want a day alone, no offense, but you can ask for a family day if you want.

MEG: Oh, I would. I would definitely ask for a family day. I would ask to wake up in the morning, freezing, because, remember what a cover hog your Dad was? I would wake up and I would yank the covers, and just then, you would run in and jump on the bed. And your Dad would sit up and he would say, "Good morning, everybody."

SCOTT: No, he wouldn't. He'd go, "Where's my coffee?"

MEG: Right! So you and I make coffee, and it's a sunny morning so we sit on the deck, and Dad comes, just cleaned up, with wet hair, and smelling like shampoo and aftershave and toothpaste. And his skin would be cool, and the sun would be warm on our heads and the coffee mugs in our hands, hot.

SCOTT: And I would go, "Yo, parents, let's go for a picnic."

MEG: Oh yes, a picnic!

SCOTT: And Dad would make tuna fish. No offense, you use too much mayonnaise.

MEG: My tuna fish is great.

SCOTT: I'm just being honest.

MEG: Okay, Dad's horrible, dry tuna fish sandwiches.

SCOTT: And potato chips, pickles, cookies, apples, juice boxes.

MEG: And a good bottle of red wine for your father and me.

SCOTT: You know, I wouldn't really wish for a picnic day.

MEG: What would you really wish for?

SCOTT: I would wish for a regular day.

MEG: Oh?

SCOTT: I would wish for a day that started with my Dad going, "Get up, it's time for school." A day when I couldn't find clean socks, a day when I missed the bus, and my Dad takes me, so I get the big lecture about dawdling. I would wish for a day with nothing special after school and nothing great for dinner. I would wish for a day that, in the evening, you have a meeting, and Dad's too busy to help with homework, although I would wish we watch TV together and stay up

men's and women's scenes 103

late. No, I take it back, I wouldn't wish for that at all. I would wish that he makes me go to bed right on time, maybe even forgets to tuck me in.

MEG: Sounds dismal.

SCOTT: I would wish for a day so plain that I could forget myself right into it.

MEG: Sweetheart, a whole year's gone by—what do you think your Dad would want for you?…Do you think he wants you to pretend that your life isn't real because he isn't here? He wants you to have fun, to make friends, to grow up happy into a wonderful future…

SCOTT: What do you call a guy when his dad is dead?

MEG: When both parents are dead, you call that being orphaned.

SCOTT: Right. An orphan.

MEG: You're not an orphan, Scott.

SCOTT: Sure, no sweat.

MEG: You have me, both the grandmas, your Grandpa Ray. You're not an orphan.

SCOTT: Right.

MEG: Scott, you're not an orphan; you're not in a parallel universe; you're not in a bad dream.

SCOTT: Yeah? Maybe someday, someday, I'll wake up for real real, and my Dad, he'll be sitting on my bed, going "shhhhhh, you're in your own bed, Scott, everything's fine, and I'm right here."

MEG: Sweetheart, I'm sorry, but that's not ever going to happen. A car ran a red light and hit your dad's car from the side. It was a horrible accident, he never saw it coming, and he died right away. We didn't want him to leave us, but it really happened.

SCOTT: I want to go home, Mom.

MEG: I know.

SCOTT: Come on—can't we just go home?

MEG: Scott, we are home. Now, this is home. We moved here because maybe it wasn't going to hurt so much someplace else.

104 men's and women's scenes

SCOTT: You mean we ran away.

MEG: I can't change it now. I'm sorry. I can't change anything…

SCOTT: …We ran away from my dad.

MEG: My god! You are so mad at me!

SCOTT: I have to look at his picture to make sure it's his true face inside my brain.

(Meg puts her hand on Scott's heart.)

MEG: No Scott, your dad is right here, inside.

(Scott knocks her hand away. He is infuriated.)

SCOTT: That's a lie!

MEG: As long as you remember him…

SCOTT: But I wanted to say one more thing to him! You wouldn't let me. So answer me this, this one easy thing. Answer me why you didn't let me say goodbye to my Dad.

MEG: Of course you said goodbye. We said goodbye to him together.

SCOTT: I wanted to go to the funeral.

MEG: You were at the funeral.

SCOTT: No, I wasn't! You wouldn't let me go! You wouldn't let me go!…

MEG: Scott, listen to me! I promise you, from the bottom of my heart, you were at the funeral. We were all at the funeral. Joe Gresham and Uncle Al both spoke about Dad. I really want you to remember this, Scotty. Uncle Al told the bike race story from when they were little boys, and even though we were crying, we were laughing, too. And remember riding in the limousine?

SCOTT: No.

MEG: You really liked that part. You sat backwards all the way from the funeral home to the cemetery. And remember the motorcycle cops? You had a big conversation with one of the motorcycle cops when we got to the cemetery.

SCOTT: It all sounds like fun and such, but it's some dream of yours, because I don't remember, because I wasn't there.

MEG: Why would I make this up?

SCOTT: How should I know?

men's and women's scenes 105

MEG: Scott, don't you remember anything?

SCOTT: I remember when you came to school…

MEG: I told you first, Scott…

SCOTT: …Hoo, I remember that.

MEG: I told you before I told anybody else. And then we called the Grandmas and Grandpa Ray. And remember how everybody came to our house? And Grandpa Ray wouldn't go home— remember? And he wouldn't even stay in the spare room; he slept in the living room. And remember all the food that people gave us? Things we'd never eat…

SCOTT: Potato salad!

MEG: Yes! Several bowls full. And we picked out Dad's blue blazer and his red Donald Duck tie and took them to the funeral home. We did that together. And then we went to the Disney Store at the mall and we found a matching one in yellow for you. That's your Donald Duck tie, Scott. It's right in your closet, right now. And at the funeral home, at the funeral, remember how we sat in that little side room with the curtain, and you said you liked being able to spy on everybody?

SCOTT: No.

MEG: Yes. And when we got to the cemetery, we all stood under a big tent because it was raining. And about ten old aunties all came over and said that heaven was crying, until we rolled our eyes at each other. And I had a red rose and you had a white rose, and we laid them on the casket. And then later, when we got back home, I told you how brave you were, how much you had helped me, and I told you that Dad would live in your heart and we would never leave you.

SCOTT: The biggest lie of all!

MEG: It's how parents feel, Scott.

SCOTT: Why did you promise that? You shouldn't have promised that.

MEG: You're right. I shouldn't have promised that. But I really am telling you the truth. You were there, Scott.

SCOTT: Well, there's one thing.

MEG: What's that?

106 men's and women's scenes

SCOTT: It explains that lame Disney tie in my closet.

MEG: Of course, your father was famous for his ugly ties…Don't you remember anything? *(Scott shrugs, but won't answer Meg or look at her.)* You know, Scott, whatever that last thing you didn't get to say to him, you ought to just say it. I'm pretty sure he'll hear you.

SCOTT: I don't know.

MEG: I love you, Scott.

SCOTT: Can I be by myself?

MEG: Yo Scott, sweet dreams, right?

(Meg exits. Scott gets out of bed and gathers together his magic rock, an old t-shirt, a framed photograph, a star-shaped candle, and a book of matches. He sits on the floor, places the objects around him, and lights the candle. End of scene.)

WHEN STARBRIGHT FADES...

Sandra Marie Vago

dramatic, 1 Man, 1 Woman

Laura (18) a young woman trapped in an abusive marriage, and Marty (20s) her husband, about to be sent to Vietnam.

Scene: Augusta, GA, early 1960s

> *Stalked by fear of combat and haunted by ghosts of his own unhappy childhood, Marty has become increasingly more violent with Laura. Here, a quiet evening at home turns ugly.*

MARTY: Shoulda seen ole Gussy today. Gonna get himself killed one'a these days...Up there without a belt, hangin' half assed, watchin' some broad in tight shorts crossin' the street...almost falls right offa the damn thing... *(He takes a drink and looks in the glass.)* Laura, what'd you put in here?

LAURA: Ice water, honey.

MARTY: Hell, I need a drink, get my bourbon, will ya? So much shit goin' down.

LAURA: Marty, you said you wouldn't...

MARTY: Come on, the ice is meltin'. I'm only gonna have one, that's all. Where's my Jack Daniels? *(She puts the chalk down.)* And Laura, would ya look at your hands, ya got that chalk shit all over the ice. *(He hands her his glass.)*

LAURA: Oh, sorry, honey, here take my glass. (She goes for the bourbon and he moves to the table. After she gets the bourbon and pours him a drink, he lights a cigar and sits back to relax. While he talks he has several glasses of bourbon.)

MARTY: Okay, now tell me why ya couldn't get the ice box back. Did ya tell that ole lady what I said?

LAURA: I did, honest.

MARTY: No you didn't or we'd have it! I told ya, dammit ya gotta be firm with that ole broad. Ya let people walk all over ya. Can't let nobody walk on ya, ya hear me?

(She watches him drinking two more shots, then turns to the pantry and starts nervously looking for something to fix for dinner.)

LAURA: What should I make for supper, honey? I got chili, and I got beef stew in a can.

MARTY: Fuckin' fantastic.

LAURA: We'll have the ice box back tomorrow for sure. Then I'll get some things from the store 'n fix a real supper, I promise.

MARTY: Just gimme some more ice.

(She looks back at the pantry and is delighted with her next idea.)

LAURA: I know! I could make ya a sandwich, honey, I got some a that Cheeze Whiz in a jar!

MARTY: I'll get somethin' at the club.

LAURA: *(Excited.)* Are we goin' out tonight, Marty?

MARTY: *(Beginning to slur his words now.)* No. We ain't goin' out tonight, I am.

LAURA: Please don't drink anymore, honey.

MARTY: What?

LAURA: I, uh…don't go out, stay here tonight with me, please.

MARTY: I already got plans. Gonna play some cards with Gussy. I won't be out long.

LAURA: I don't wanna be alone. We could sit out on the porch'n I'll put some music on the radio, we can dance, just like before…

MARTY: Before what? Before I got busted, before the constant fuckin' fights?

LAURA: Before when we were happy.

MARTY: Not tonight.

LAURA: Not any night.

MARTY: D'you say somethin'?

LAURA: No.

MARTY: I'm meetin' the guys. Man wants to play a little cards, have a couple'a drinks with his friends once in a while. That too much to ask?

LAURA: No. I know ya need that sometime. It's just, I guess the nightmare…it scared me. I didn't wanna be alone.

MARTY: You wanna hear about a nightmare? It won't be long, we're goin' to, hell only knows, in the stinkin' rice paddies…it ain't hot 'nough here, shit…

LAURA: Marty, you're gettin' shipped out?! When? No!

MARTY: Hell, Laura, why you think we been doing so many fuckin' maneuvers? There's big time shit comin' down 'n I'm supposed to worry about your goddamned nightmares!?

LAURA: You're right, honey. It's not your fault about the nightmares…it's just, sometimes they seem so real.

MARTY: Gimme a clean shirt, will ya? *(She goes quickly to the dresser, brushes her hair and pulls it back with a ribbon. Then grabs a clean shirt from the dresser and takes it to him. He turns pushing his face into her stomach and caressing her.)* I didn't mean… *(As he pours another drink, she goes on.)*

LAURA: I know you can't stop the nightmares, but sometimes I get confused, honey. I don't know if I'm here or back home. If you're here or I'm with daddy.

(He pushes back now, angry.)

MARTY: I ain't your goddamned daddy! *(He steps back and moves to the window.)* How ya think it makes me feel? I got enough goin' on. Okay? *(She doesn't answer.)* I wanna have a few laughs, sometimes.

LAURA: We used to laugh, me and you.

MARTY: Yeah? I don't remember.

LAURA: I wish I knew what happened. *(Pause.)* It's me. I ain't smart like you. I get things all screwed up. *(She kisses him from behind and rubs his neck, relaxing him.)* Things'd be different if we had a place of our own, a house, honey, like mamma and daddy had, ya know? One with real stove 'n a big ole ice box. I'd have a little garden in the backyard. We could have vegetables and lots of flowers.

MARTY: But I can't give ya no house, right? I ain't good enough, I'm just…

LAURA: No! You're good to me, honey, you can't help it that you get mad sometimes, I know that. You ain't like daddy…I mean we ain't like them… *(She puts her arms around him, soothing him.)* not exactly like them, I mean. *(She brushes his hair back as he closes his eyes as she rubs his pounding temples.)* We could be happy, I know we could. You'd come home from work at night and I'd have real stew made…or chicken, fried chicken. I know how much you love that! I'd make apple pie and fresh coffee after supper and we'd sit out on the porch and talk to all our neighbors…Good evening Mrs. Randall, my, how the baby's grown… *(She's lost in the fantasy.)* and how's the store, Mr. Randall?

MARTY: *(Suddenly pulling away.)* No babies! *(She looks at him suddenly with real fear.)* You live in a dream world, Laura. I'm a career man, United States Army. Ya knew that when ya married me, 'n we ain't sittin on some damn porch sippin' coffee while the neighbors parade by like one a them Doris Day movies you're always watchin'. We're here in Augusta, G.A. Savvy? This is me, Marty Randall. I'm doin' the best I can. Don't go expectin' me to change. I can't change.

LAURA: No, honey, I love you, you know that.

MARTY: Do I?

LAURA: But, you don't have to stay in the Army. You're smart.

MARTY: You're damn right I'm smart. I don't need this bullshit. *(He finishes dressing.)*

LAURA: I just mean that you don't gotta prove nothin' cause a your pappa, 'n stay in the Army. That ain't got nothin' to do with you.

MARTY: Don't you start up again with that shit about my ole man, ya hear?

LAURA: What I mean is, ya don't have to prove nothin' to nobody. Just cause he… *(She catches herself.)* I mean, just cause you ain't got no high school, that don't mean…

MARTY: *(Getting really angry now.)* I got just as good a job as any

men's and women's scenes 111

a them jerks finished high school! I'm a communications expert, ya know?

LAURA: Course you are, that's why I know you could do anything you wanted, Marty. You are so smart.

MARTY: *(Visibly upset.)* I am doin' what I *want.* I need another drink.

LAURA: Sure honey. *(She makes him another drink and pours some ice water in her own glass.)* I'm sorry. I'm always sayin' the wrong thing.

MARTY: Just keep my ole man outta things. Always the same fuckin' bullshit. First them now you.

LAURA: I didn't mean to upset ya, honey. I know ya don't like to talk about your pappa. *(He pulls away from her, shoving her.)* I won't argue no more I promise.

MARTY: I got people to see. *(He gets his wallet from the dresser.)*

LAURA: *(Suddenly yelling.)* Daddy, don't get drunk and hurt mama again! *(She stops, covering her mouth with her hand she starts to laugh, nervously.)* I wadn't sayin' that to you, honey, I wadn't…I do not know where that came from… *(She goes to the table and tries to immerse herself in the drawing in front of her.)* You go ahead. I know you wanna see Gus and play cards.

MARTY: Don't you yell at me. Not ever, Laura. You don't tell me what to do, ya hear?

LAURA: I'm sorry.

(He picks up the drawing she's working on, tearing it in half.)

MARTY: Livin' in these cartoons you draw…You don't need me. Ya got your pi'tures 'n the friggin' dykes next door.

LAURA: You don't know them. They're just nice ole ladies.

MARTY: Fuckin' lesbians. I caught 'em holdin' hands, this morning…ain't that precious?

LAURA: Don't make fun of them cause you're mad at me.

MARTY: They make me sick.

LAURA: Why do you get so angry? You don't have to be afraid…

MARTY: What?! Afraid?

LAURA: Please. You're not really like this, you know you're not.

112 men's and women's scenes

MARTY: I'm not, huh?

LAURA: No…Besides, they don't hurt no body. Look, they gave us the ice.

MARTY: If you'd gotten the damned ice box back, you wouldn't be gettin' ice from them freaks.

LAURA: Please, honey. *(She goes to the box of drawings under her bed and starts rummaging through them in a desperate attempt to change the mood.)* Here, lemme show ya another drawing I did today, honey. This one, it's Jackie Kennedy, can ya tell?

MARTY: I don't wanna look at no pi'tures. I never shoulda come home, I shoulda just stayed on the base.

LAURA: Marty, come on. I don't wanna fight no more.

(But he's angry now, too angry to turn back.)

MARTY: Fuckin' bullshit! Arguin' all the time, hangin' around the fruits next door. Never doin' anything I tell ya to do.

LAURA: I try to do everything you tell me. It's just, sometimes it don't work out like it's supposed to but it ain't cause a Mitzi and Louella, I hardly ever even talk to them.

MARTY: You know their fuckin' names!

LAURA: Just now…she just now told me when I…

MARTY: Bullshit. I see how they look at you.

LAURA: *(Laughing, she touches his hand.)* Honey, you're imaginin' that.

MARTY: *(Grabbing her.)* You stay away from them!

(She pulls away.)

LAURA: Marty your mama told me, she didn't leave you cause'a… *(Pause.)* Let's quit this fightin', honey. I didn't mean to yell at ya. I'm sorry.

(He looks at her, pushes her away.)

MARTY: My mama's dead!

LAURA: She ain't, honey. She wants to see you. She told me she loves you, she didn't mean for you to…

MARTY: Shut up! *(Picking up his smoking cigar, suddenly throws it in her glass of ice water as she picks it up to take a drink.)* Now I'm sorry.

men's and women's scenes 113

(Silence. She looks at the cigar, then at him, then back at the cigar. She gets nauseated, drops it and it splashes, drenching his clean shirt. She jumps back, grabs a towel from the bed and begins frantically wiping him off.)

LAURA: Oh, god! I didn't mean it, honey, I didn't…

(He yanks the towel out of her hand.)

MARTY: Sonofabitch! *(He slaps her, knocking her to the floor. He starts tearing his shirt off and she gets up. He turns as she comes toward him, crying, and he hits her again, harder than he ever has in the past, knocking her across the room this time. She slides down the wall, dizzy from the blow. He continues to change clothes without looking back as he is screaming at her.)* Ya happy now? Huh? Look what ya made me do… *(He turns and sees her lying there.)* Talkin' about my ole man, talkin' about that…she's dead, ya hear me? She's…Laura? *(She doesn't answer. He goes to her, shaking her roughly.)* Laura, answer me, dammit….Laura! *(She looks at him. He pulls away and starts to the door.)*

LAURA: Don't leave, Marty, please. Don't leave.

MARTY: *(Defiant now.)* Get outta here, ya hear me. Get outta here before it's too late. Go back home. *(He throws some money at her.)* By a fuckin' bus ticket and run back to daddy.

LAURA: No. *(She reaches for him and tries to get up.)* I love you.

MARTY: No you don't! Go on, just get out!

WICKED GAMES

Paul Boakye

serio-comedic, 1 Man, 1 Woman

Leo (34) an attractive sports instructor, black, and Helen (27) a lusty Irish social worker, white.

Scene: a bar

Here, Leo and Helen seduce one another over many Margaritas.

○ ○ ○

HELEN: My mother and Kofi's mother were great friends back in our home town when he was still Henry and I didn't have to cope with his black trip. His mother is Irish, his father is Ghanaian, and he got no input from him. He ain't even black. He's mixed.

LEO: Let's not talk about Kofi.

HELEN: Okay then let's talk about us.

LEO: Yeah. So what do you say you do again? Don't you have one where you eat the worm?

HELEN: The worm? Yeah but that's when you get expert. You're an apprentice here. You have to excel to that.

LEO: So what do I do first?

HELEN: Slam it. Knock it back. Lick the salt. You get tingles all over. It's just like Mmmmm. And then bite the lemon. Okay. got your lemon?

LEO: Okay.

HELEN: When I say go.

LEO: If I start talking rubbish after this…

HELEN: You've never done this before, have you?

LEO: Don't believe a word I say.

HELEN: Have you?

LEO: No, I haven't.

HELEN: Okay, a Tequila Virgin, alright. Go!
(They slam the glasses, knock back the drinks, lick the salt and suck the lemons.)

LEO: Fucking hell. Oh. Oh! Bas-tard.

HELEN: Ah! Pheeeew! Yes! See.

LEO: Jesus.

HELEN: Outstanding.

LEO: Wah! Do you wanna another one?

HELEN: Yeah. Lets get another one.

LEO: That's amazing. (Aside.) Two of the same, please.

HELEN: It's the lemon, you see. The lemon is the best bit cos each segment.

LEO: But I hate it.

HELEN: It just burst in your mouth and the juices flow…

LEO: Why can't you use oranges?

HELEN: And…It hits the roof of your mouth like an explosion. Better than sex.

LEO: You've obviously not had very good sex.

HELEN: It's all relative.

LEO: To what? How good the Tequila is?

HELEN: Well, I would bet… (Pulls out a cigarette and lights it to smoke.) That three Tequila Slammers are probably equivalent to one incredible orgasm. But…I would almost bet…

LEO: No, is that, go on…

HELEN: I'd also bet that bad sex isn't even equivalent to one Tequila Slammer. Tequila Slammer is still better than bad sex.

LEO: Have you tried Sambuka?

HELEN: Yeah. It's the fire.

LEO: But you have to put it out first. I don't understand why they light it?

HELEN: So you get a richer flavour. You're not a drinker, are you?
(Leo takes the new drinks.)

LEO: Are we going for this? I'll say it this time. Hold on.

HELEN: That's right, you're no longer a virgin.

LEO: Experience talking now.

116 men's and women's scenes

HELEN: Hold on. I love salt, don't you? *(She touches the salt and licks her finger.)*

LEO: Yeah. In my cooking.

HELEN: Do you cook?

LEO: Sometimes.

HELEN: You must invite me over.

LEO: You just drink, don't you?

HELEN: No.

LEO: After three. One, two, three. *(They do it together again.)* Fuck!

HELEN: Hmm. Mmmhmm! Nearly orgasmic. One more and I'm orgasmic.

LEO: Do you wanna go for that orgasm?

HELEN: Too early in the night. Slow. I like to take things slow. Have you ever had Guinness?

LEO: Yeah I have.

HELEN: Cos you're talking about Sambuka. So you're talking about rich flavour.

LEO: It gets caught in your beard, though.

HELEN: What Sambuka?

LEO: No Guinness.

HELEN: Yeah and then you just lick it off. Well, you don't have to lick it off yourself.

LEO: I suppose not. I'm a spirits man myself.

HELEN: Are you?

LEO: I like Rum.

HELEN: Do you know what I like about you? You like all those really really textured drinks. I mean, we're talking about drinks that have flavour, that have atmosphere, like a country.

LEO: What?

HELEN: Like a woman.

LEO: Tequila?

HELEN: Yeah. You're talking about a whole personality. What's Vodka? Vodka is a bimbo. There's nothing going on.

LEO: I hate Vodka.

HELEN: Vodka is a fucking bungalow.

LEO: You drink gin?

HELEN: What?

LEO: Gin?

HELEN: Only for medicinal purposes.

LEO: An ex-girl-friend of mine, her dad used to say, "don't go having any-a-them leg-openers."

HELEN: Gin?

LEO: Gin and Tonic. Apparently.

HELEN: Do you think it's a leg-opener?

LEO: It didn't work for me and her but her dad thought so.

HELEN: No, no. I think for a really…Brandy. I think Brandy is the exception. For a really really exotic feel. God, I'm getting a blister.

LEO: Look at your feet, man. What have you been doing?

HELEN: I know. Brandy. Brandy in cotton wool.

LEO: In cotton-wool?

HELEN: There are two things here, okay? You dip the cotton wool in the Brandy. And you just soak it on your toes. And you get someone to lick it off, and they're in heaven. They're in ecstasy. And they get drunk too. The second thing Is pineapple.

LEO: You prefer them drunk, don't you?

HELEN: What? No, no, no. Just warmed.

LEO: Yeah?

HELEN: The second thing is Brandy and Pineapple. You pour Brandy on the pineapple chunks and then you eat the pineapple chunks. And then the pineapple is like the lemon. Each segment burst in your mouth and fill you with thick creamy juices just rolling down your throat. It is so exciting…and it is so delicious…and you get no rot in your stomach because it's in food. I mean, Vodka jelly, it's the same. You know, it's cheap, and it's shallow but this…this is a country. We're talking a whole new horizon.

LEO: So what country is Pineapple and Brandy then?

HELEN: Caribbean. The West Indies. Mountains. Have you ever been there?

LEO: I was born in Jamaica.

118 men's and women's scenes

HELEN: Oh, so you know what I'm talking about. I'd like to go to Jamaica. In fact, I'm maybe planning to go to Africa soon.

LEO: I thought rum was the Caribbean.

HELEN: Yeah but this is a particular…

LEO: Brandy…is that French?

HELEN: Brandy goes worldwide. You don't drink enough, man. You do not drink enough.

LEO: You like your drink, don't you?

HELEN: If it's used for the correct purposes.

LEO: So it always has to revolve around sex?

HELEN: Did I say sex was the correct purpose?

LEO: No. But it just seems that way.

HELEN: Are you telling me that after a few drinks you're not feeling a little more?

LEO: Yeah.

HELEN: Well, see.

LEO: 'Course. But I ain't saying it's the only purpose for drinking.

HELEN: No. No. It's not. Course not.

LEO: Or that to have sex you have to have drink. For me, I like to know where the action's at! *(He slams the table with his fist.)* You know what I mean? So I can control. And be controlled.

HELEN: So you like it both ways, do you?

LEO: Hmm.

HELEN: You're kind of dominant but…

LEO: Not necessarily.

HELEN: But not…

LEO: It depends on the person. Anything goes really.

HELEN: So you were submissive there a minute ago when you had your Tequilas.

LEO: I just felt like doing it.

HELEN: Is that cos I told you to?

LEO: Yeah.

HELEN: And if I told you to have that third orgasmic Tequila, would you?

LEO: I started out a virgin tonight, didn't I?

HELEN: Yeah. I seduced you. *(She laughs.)*

men's and women's scenes 119

LEO: I feel abused.

HELEN: I hope so.

LEO: I should have saved it for a better person.

HELEN: *(Laughs.)* No you should not! *(Pause.)* Yeap. You're my first. It was worth it. Are you gonna order?

LEO: Hmm?

HELEN: You're scared, are you? You don't wanna order?

LEO: I find you very attractive. *(Helen giggles.)* How about dinner?

HELEN: Maybe. *(They take the orders; slam the glasses, kick back the drinks, lick the salt and suck the lemons.)*

LEO: Do you wanna dance?

HELEN: I don't mind if I do.

WHITEOUT

Jocelyn Beard

dramatic, 1 Man, 1 Woman

Candy (28–30) sole survivor of a plane crash, and Elihu (45–50) member of a white separatist militia.

Scene: a remote mountain cabin belonging to a white supremist group

> When Candy's plane crashes in the Tetons during a record-setting blizzard, she is saved from certain death by Elihu, a member of the Brethren, the largest private militia in the country. Trapped together in a tiny cabin while the storm continues to rage outside, these two very different people find absolutely nothing to like about one another.

(The Cabin. Early the next morning. Dim morning light manages to provide limited illumination to the cabin, whose windows are covered with snow. Elihu stands at the kitchen counter preparing tea. The door bursts open and Candy stomps in, accompanied by swirling snow.)

CANDY: That is the most amazing thing I've ever seen! Ever! *(Elihu pauses and regards her without expression.)* I mean, I've been in heavy snow before, but nothing—*nothing* like this! How long has it been going on?

ELIHU: Four or five days.

CANDY: Jesus…I mean, *shucks,* that's a lotta snow, Elihu. It's almost up to the windows! Thank god you kept digging all night, or we'd be buried in this shack.

ELIHU: Tea?

CANDY: Sure, thanks. *(She takes the offered mug and sips.)* Thanks. *(Elihu takes his own mug and goes to the window.)* Not much to see.

ELIHU: No.

CANDY: What's it called? A whiteout?

ELIHU: *(Shrugging.)* Sure.

CANDY: Pretty weird when all you can see is white. *(Elihu makes no reply. Joining him at the other side of the window.)* It reminds me of my Dad's favorite movie…what's it called? With Sean Connery and Michael Cain? They're British army guys looking for a lost kingdom in the…

ELIHU: "The Man Who Would Be King."

CANDY: That's it! "The Man Who Would Be King!" Daddy just loved that movie. I guess I did, too, but especially when I watched it with Daddy. He'd get so excited. About a week before it was going to be on TV he'd announce: "Hear Ye! Hear Ye! On Tuesday next, our Cathode Ray Temple will be graced by the intrepid Rudyard Kipling's greatest of tales: 'The Man Who Would Be King!' No other programming will be permitted between the hours of whatever time it was going to be—You have all been dully warned!" So for a week, that movie would become the lodestone of our daily lives; you know, 'Sorry, you can't come over Tuesday, Daddy's watching "The Man Who Would Be King."

ELIHU: It's a good movie.

CANDY: *(Agreeing.)* Very romantic.

ELIHU: Romantic.

CANDY: Well, in the truest sense of the word. Two men storming off into the unknown to claim a lost empire. Very romantic.

ELIHU: Hmm.

CANDY: Sean Connery and Michael Cain. *Very* romantic.

ELIHU: *(Almost smiling.)* I'll take your word for it.

CANDY: Anyway, the scariest part of the movie for me was when they get lost in the blizzard, and Michael Cain goes snow-blind. *(Looking out the window.)* That's what made me think of it. *(They both stare out the window. Candy, moving to cot.)* It's got to stop soon, right? It just can't keep snowing for a whole week.

ELIHU: Can.

CANDY: Really? A whole week?

ELIHU: Longer, sometimes.

CANDY: *(Trying not to panic.)* Longer than a week?

ELIHU: Sometimes. Think this one's going to blow out soon. Snow's getting wet.

CANDY: How can you tell?

ELIHU: Smells wet.

CANDY: So, when it blows out you'll try and get down to the Brethren for help?

ELIHU: *(After a moment.)* Yes.

CANDY: *(Collapsing on cot.)* Dan must be shithouse by now. *(Elihu busies himself in checking the straps on his snow shoes.)* I mean, we just went down, you know? Wham! Nailed by Thor's hammer. That's another one of Dad's expressions. From his Airforce days. *(Pause.)* You know, all the way down I kept thinking: just like Patsy, just like Patsy. *(When Elihu doesn't respond.)* Patsy Kline.

ELIHU: I know.

CANDY: Yeah, well. It was a miracle that I was strapped-in. Usually I'm all over the place. Can't stand being cooped-up. I hate to fly. But Dan said, Sun Valley, so I said okay.

ELIHU: Dan is your husband?

CANDY: *(Turning away.)* No.

ELIHU: Daniel.

CANDY: *(Quickly.)* He's not Jewish!

ELIHU: No?

CANDY: Neither am I. We're both one hundred percent northern European white trash just like you, so ix-ne on the racist bull-shit.

ELIHU: Racism is the purest expression of the white soul.

CANDY: I'm telling you, don't start.

ELIHU: America will never be whole until it has cleansed itself of the Talmud-reading devil worshippers in Washington.

CANDY: Racist jerk-offs like your John Creek stab America in the back every time they blow up another Federal building, gun down another officer of the law…

ELIHU: Who's law? The law of God? Or the law of the Satan-loving Jews?

CANDY: The law of common decency!

ELIHU: And what would you know about that, Harlot?!?

CANDY: Excuse me?

ELIHU: You heard me, whore. *(He pulls a small plastic folder out of his pocket and tosses it onto the cot.)*

CANDY: What the hell is this?

ELIHU: Registration papers.

CANDY: Of what?

ELIHU: Of the plane. The plane that crashed on its way to bring you to the arms of your lover, Senator Daniel Tattinger, negro democrat from the Zionist Empire of Westchester County, New York. Senator Daniel Tattinger, corporate officer of CADEX International, registered owner of one downed Jetstream.

CANDY: *(Quietly.)* If you already knew, why did you make me lie to you?

ELIHU: To see if you would.

CANDY: Well, now you know! I *will* lie! I'll say *anything* that I think you want to hear because I don't want to die in the middle of nowhere because I said the wrong thing and pissed off a terrorist.

ELIHU: I am not a terrorist!

CANDY: Yes, yes you are. Terrorism is your great equalizer.

ELIHU: Whose equalizer?

CANDY: All you hate groups. Terrorism is what binds you together. Lose your farm? No problem! Go blow something up! Aww, you got shit-canned? Go torch that black guy's church!

ELIHU: You talk too much.

CANDY: *(Flopping back onto cot.)* Get used to it.

ELIHU: And all you talk is trash! Ignorant, stupid trash!

CANDY: *(As in, I'm really scared—not.)* Oooooh!

ELIHU: What, did you write a paper on "racism" in college? Read a bunch of those books? Parrot the lies and get an "A"? Did you memorize all the names of all the "hate" groups? Call up the Southern Poverty Law Center and get a bunch of xerox-ed articles sent to you? Learn all about Elysium Fields from a bunch of Jews in Seattle? Or from an article in the Jew York Times? Or is this all re-mouthed bullshit from the desk of your Jew-loving nigger boyfriend?

(During the above, Candy has slowly risen to her feet. She now confronts Elihu with steely reserve.)

CANDY: No, Elihu. This isn't re-mouthed bullshit, and I didn't write a paper. All I had to do to learn all about you and your kind was to go to a funeral.

ELIHU: I've buried more than you'll ever know.

CANDY: Sgt. Francis Barrett, retired, United States Air Force. Two tours in Nam before a bullet finally took out his spleen and sent him home. That was fine with Mom, she was sick of liv-ing on base; having someone measuring the grass in the front yard, the two AM nuclear attack drills, all the stupid parties at the Colonel's house…she hated it. So when Daddy was released from the VA and got a job with the LAPD, Mom was downright ecstatic. Their own house in Toluca Lake, grass too long, no more sucking up to officer's wives, a baby on the way…it was great. We lived a *great* civilian life. Until August 14, 1984.

ELIHU: *(Immediately recognizing the date, in a whisper.)* Judgment Day.

CANDY: *Don't you dare call it that, you stupid, stupid man!* August 14, 1984 was the day that my father, Detective Francis Barrett and his partner, Detective James McBride were gunned down in cold blood by Wayne Bolson; *member,* Aryan Fortress; *member,* three state militia groups; *member,* Christian Identity Movement; *member,* the Hand of God and mastermind of the counterfeiting ring that was bankrolling the hate agenda from LA to Dusseldorf. Wayne Bolson: a gutless coward who took my father hostage *(She strides quickly to the closet and pulls out a Mini-14.)* and then emp-tied one of these into his head until he had no head! *(She drops the gun to the floor.)* A man who spent his life serving the citizens of this country! Who wanted nothing more than to do his part to keep the women and children on his beat safe. This was the man who your Wayne Bolson butchered!

ELIHU: He was a brilliant man! A martyr!

CANDY: *Wayne Bolson was an asshole!* Oh, his death was very dramatic, there's no lie in that. Seems like you all go up in fiery blazes. Why is that?

ELIHU: The Lord embraces his warriors in the flames of righteousness.

CANDY: Yeah, well, I hate to deprive you of one of your movement's big heroes, but the warehouse fire that took out Wayne was started by sparks from an old electric panel.

ELIHU: What…?

CANDY: That's right, Elihu, an old panel that your brilliant martyr never thought to fix. A spark from the panel flew into an open container of dye that Wayne had been using in his counterfeiting and started a fire that had been burning for at least fifteen minutes before the cops and the Feds chased him back to the warehouse after the shoot-out. The explosions that looked so good on CNN were caused by the fire spreading to Wayne's stored munitions, *not* by the gas canisters that the Feds lobbed in the windows. Of course, that's just a sidebar item, isn't it? After all, your leaders got whatever fifteen minutes they could out of Wayne Bolson's death and he was declared "martyr." Forget about any sort of ongoing investigation into the fire and the truth! Truth is the one thing that people like you never seem interested in. When Wayne Bolson, his three "soldiers" two wives and four children died in that fiery blaze, it wasn't the Lord's righteousness that took them, but Wayne's own stupidity. *(She pauses to take a breath.)* So, you're right, Elihu: it was Judgment Day. It was the day that my father was judged too good for this world and the day that Wayne Bolson was judged too stupid.

(The wind has picked up and howls around the cabin, sounding like a pack of wolves.)

ELIHU: *(After a moment.)* We each have our Truth.

CANDY: That's right, we do. At least my father died trying to make sure that all of us—even people like you—get to keep living in a world where we're allowed to have our own truths. What do your people die for?

(This hits Elihu hard. He has suffered a great personal loss. He turns away and peers out the window.)

ELIHU: Storm's picking up again.

CANDY: Your people die for nothing. Just like the boy who died right here *(Indicates blood stains.)* For nothing.

ELIHU: You…talk too much.

CANDY: *(Evenly, each word precisely placed.)* Get used to it.

(The sounds of the storm intensifies as the lights fade to black.)

WORKING CLASS

Richard Hoehler

serio-comedic, 2 Men, 1 Woman
Michael (40s) an English teacher, Igor (20s) a student and Svetlana (20s) another student.

Scene: the English School at Hudson Manufacturing

Here, Michael finds that teaching isn't always as easy as he'd like it to be.

○ ○ ○

(A man wearing a cardigan sweater stands center with an opened folder. Note: There are five brief scenes; a bell sound separates each. The voices of Igor and Svetlana are live, miked, from the booth.)
(Bell.)

MICHAEL: *(Reading a pre-written statement to his class.)* 'Welcome to the English school at Hudson Manufacturing. It is important that you understand our methods and our rules… Learning a new language is a step-by-step process. It takes hard work, commitment, and enthusiasm. You are not the first immigrant to be faced with the task of learning English. Relax! Don't worry if you don't understand television, radio, people in the street, or even your own children! It is normal to feel confused and overwhelmed. Try to have a positive attitude. Worrying about your level, your age, or making mistakes only impedes your progress.' "Impedes?" Who wrote this? 'If you don't understand something, relax, listen and repeat. You can ask your teacher for help after class or on the break…'

IGOR: Break? *(The rustle of papers.)*

MICHAEL: No. No. It's not break. We understand break. Okay. Let's get started. Let's find out a little about everybody, okay? My name *is* Michael Jacobs. What is your name? *(Silence.)* My name *is*…Michael Jacobs…

IGOR: My name *is*…Michael Jacobs.

MICHAEL: No. *My* name is Michael Jacobs. What is *your* name?

IGOR: Your name *is*…

MICHAEL: No, no, no. My name is… *(Points to student.)*

IGOR: My name is…Gabovich Igor.

MICHAEL: Good. Good. But not Gabovich Igor. In America—Igor Gabovich. My name is Michael Jacobs. Your name is Igor Gabovich. Repeat.

IGOR: Your name is Igor Gabovich.

MICHAEL: No. No, no, no, no. My name is Igor Gabovich. Repeat.

IGOR: My name is Igor Gabovich.

MICHAEL: Excellent. Excellent. Okay, I am from New York. Where are you from?

IGOR: Are you from…

MICHAEL: No, I am from…

IGOR: I am from is Ukraine.

MICHAEL: No, I am from Ukraine. No is.

IGOR: I am from Ukraine.

MICHAEL: Beautiful, Igor. Beautiful. Okay. Now, listen. My name is Michael Jacobs and I am from New York. What is your name and where are you from?

IGOR: My name is from Gabovich Igor and are you from is Ukraine.

MICHAEL: Mother of God.

(Bell.)

MICHAEL: Svetlana. Do you cook?

SVETLANA: Yes, I am cook.

MICHAEL: No. I cook. No 'am.'

SVETLANA: I no am cook.

MICHAEL: I cook. Repeat.

SVETLANA: I cook.

MICHAEL: Do you like to cook?

SVETLANA: Yes, I like cook.

MICHAEL: No. Do you like *to* cook?

SVETLANA: Yes, I like to cook.

MICHAEL: Very good. Do you like to cook for your family?

SVETLANA: Yes, I like my family.

MICHAEL: No.

SVETLANA: Yes.

MICHAEL: Okay, I understand. You like your family. I like my family. But that's not the question. Listen. Do you like to cook for your family?

SVETLANA: Yes, I like to cook my family.

MICHAEL: No, no, no, no, Svetlana.

SVETLANA: I like to cook my family! Every day I cook my husband, my daughter…

MICHAEL: *For, For…*

SVETLANA: Every day!!

MICHAEL: Okay. Svetlana, relax. Remember, relax. Let's try a different verb. Igor. Do you come to class every day?

IGOR: Yes, I come in class every day.

MICHAEL: No. Listen. Do you come *to* class every day.

IGOR: Yes, I come in class every day.

MICHAEL: Igor, Igor. To, To, To. I come *to* class every day. Never in, never come in. In English this is not…this is not good English. Trust me. Svetlana, does Igor come to class every day?

SVETLANA: Yes, he is come to class every day.

MICHAEL: Svetlana…

SVETLANA: *To* class. I am speak *to*.

MICHAEL: Does.

SVETLANA: Ah…Comes.

MICHAEL: Riiiight.

SVETLANA: Yes, he comes to class every day.

MICHAEL: Good. Does he come to class with his wife?

SVETLANA: Yes, he comes in his vife.

MICHAEL: Svetlana!!!

SVETLANA: He comes in his vife in class.

MICHAEL: No, Svetlana, no.

SVETLANA: *To* class?

MICHAEL: No.

SVETLANA: *In* class?

130 men's and women's scenes

MICHAEL: No.

SVETLANA: *Is* class?!

MICHAEL: No! No! No!

(*Bell.*)

MICHAEL: Igor, What is today's date?

IGOR: Today's date is February third.

MICHAEL: Excellent Igor. Svetlana, what *was* yesterday's date?

SVETLANA: Yesterday's date vas…is…

MICHAEL: Was-is? What is that, a time warp? Is—present. Was—past. Today's date is…Yesterday's date was…

IGOR: Tomorrow's date vill be.

MICHAEL: That's right, Igor. But we usually don't say tomorrow's date will be…We usually say tomorrow's date is…

IGOR: Vill be—future!

MICHAEL: Yes. I know future is 'will be.' And you can say that, but most people don't. They say tomorrow's date *is,* like the present, but it's really the future.

SVETLANA: Present is future?

MICHAEL: Sometimes…you know how when Present Continuous is future? Well, sometimes the simple present is future also.

SVETLANA: Present Continuous?

MICHAEL: You know: I am teaching now. Present Continuous. But if I say, I am teaching tomorrow. Then it's future. We usually say…What are you doing tonight? It's really the short way of saying: What are you going to do tonight? Remember, 'going to' as future.

IGOR: 'Going to' is past…

MICHAEL: Yes. 'Going to' is also past…and we are *going to* learn that lesson in a few weeks. Future. Because past would be, we were going to learn that lesson a few weeks ago…We were going to do something that we didn't do. (*Beat, considers.*) Unless you said, we were going to learn that lesson in a few weeks, which would mean that we are not *going to* do what we *were going* to do at some time *in* the future…I think that has something to do with conditional speech but… *(Students groan.)* oh the hell with it…anyway, what is tomorrow's date?

(Bell.)

MICHAEL: Okay. Now when we make the Present *Perfect* tense, we use 'to have' plus the past participle of the main verb, right? For regular verbs, the past participle is the same as the past form, the verb plus 'd', and irregular verbs whose past participles don't end in 'n' are just like the regular verbs in that the past participle is the same as the past form. Okay? It's easier if we just do it. Igor, where do you live?

IGOR: I live in Brooklyn.

MICHAEL: Good. Now Present Perfect. How long *have* you *lived* in Brooklyn?

IGOR: I have lived in Brooklyn…three months ago.

MICHAEL: No. Well, yes. That's correct. That's Present Perfect, but that's the reference for simple past. I lived in Brooklyn three months ago. Done. Finished. Present Perfect. How long…

IGOR: I have lived in Brooklyn…is three months.

MICHAEL: No. No. You love that 'is.' What is it about 'is?' For.

IGOR: Three.

MICHAEL: What?

IGOR: Three months.

MICHAEL: *For* three months.

IGOR: Three!!

MICHAEL: For, F-O-R, not four, 4. I have lived in Brooklyn *for* three months. Repeat.

IGOR: I have lived in Brooklyn for three months.

MICHAEL: Good. Now, Svetlana, how long have you spoken English?

SVETLANA: I no speak English.

MICHAEL: I no speak English? I no speak English?

SVETLANA: I do not speak English.

MICHAEL: Do you speak a little English?

SVETLANA: Yes…

MICHAEL: Okay. How long have you been speaking a little English?

SVETLANA: Shto?

132 men's and women's scenes

MICHAEL: Oh, I'm sorry that's Present Perfect Continuous.

IGOR: Present Perfect Continuous?

MICHAEL: I meant to say, how long have you spoken a little English.

IGOR: Vhat is this Present Perfect Continuous?

MICHAEL: It's not important right now.

IGOR: Please, vhat is this Present Perfect Continuous, I vant to…

MICHAEL: Igor, It's just like Present Perfect but instead of 'to have' plus the past participle of the verb, it's 'to have' plus the past participle of 'to be' plus the present participle of the main verb. How long have you been speaking English…but don't even try it. Let's get the Present Perfect down first.

SVETLANA: I have head pain.

MICHAEL: Headache.

SVETLANA: I have headache.

MICHAEL: *A* headache.

SVETLANA: I have *a* headache.

MICHAEL: *(Beat.)* How long have you had a headache? *(Laughs, to himself.)* See, *that's* Present Perfect…

IGOR: Repeat question.

MICHAEL: Igor, I was joking. I'm sorry, I'm sorry. I didn't mean to…We're getting a little bit ahead of ourselves here…

IGOR: Repeat. Please.

MICHAEL: Igor…

IGOR: Pleeeease.

MICHAEL: How long have you had a headache?

IGOR: I…I have…had a headache…for six months…shas…shas… because…I have…been…studying English…for six months!

MICHAEL: That's right! That's right! Present Perfect and Present Perfect Continuous. Igor, how did you know that?

IGOR: I is lucky for guess you know homework my vife everyday help for me.

MICHAEL: Oh…I see.

    (Bell.)

MICHAEL: Okay. Today's Friday, you ask *me* the questions. See if I make…maybe *I* will make a mistake.

SVETLANA: Michael no make mistakes.

men's and women's scenes 133

MICHAEL: Michael *does not* make mistakes.

IGOR: Da?

MICHAEL: You know what I mean. I make mistakes. You make mistakes. We all make mistakes. Svetlana, why is it okay to make mistakes?

SVETLANA: It is okay to make mistakes because I learn for mistakes.

IGOR: From.

MICHAEL: That's right. Igor, what would happen *if* you did not make mistakes?

IGOR: If I did not make mistakes…I vould not learn many English.

MICHAEL: Can you count English, Igor?

SVETLANA: Much English.

MICHAEL: Right. What *else* would happen, Svetlana?

SVETLANA: If I did not make mistakes, my teacher vould not—have job.

MICHAEL: Svetlana…

SVETLANA: *A* job. *A* job. My teacher vould not have *a* job.

MICHAEL: That's right. Okay, Igor, ask me a question…uh…work.

IGOR: Vhere do you vork?

MICHAEL: I work…is New York.

IGOR: On.

MICHAEL: On New York?

SVETLANA: In!

MICHAEL: Uh-huh. I work in New York. Svetlana, ask me about my English.

SVETLANA: How is your English?

MICHAEL: My English is very badly.

SVETLANA: No. My English is very bad.

MICHAEL: No!

IGOR: My English is getting better every day!

MICHAEL: That's right Igor. Remember Svetlana? Positive. Positive. Repeat.

SVETLANA: My English is getting better every day. *(Beat.)* Present Continuous.

MICHAEL: That's right. Present Continuous. Pretty slick, Svetlana. You guys are doing really well. Remember the first day…

134 men's and women's scenes

you've come a long way from then. But of course this is a very good class.

SVETLANA: The best class.

MICHAEL: Well, yes. But we don't want the other classes to find that out. So let's keep it under our hat. Do you know that idiom? When something is secret we say we keep it under our hat.

SVETLANA: Mikhail?

MICHAEL: Yes?

SVETLANA: It also is under my hat.

MICHAEL: What is also under your hat?

SVETLANA: A secret.

MICHAEL: What secret?

SVETLANA: Ve very like you.

MICHAEL: Oh, thank you…but, 'very like?'

IGOR: Ve like you very much.

MICHAEL: That's right Igor. Repeat, Svetlana.

SVETLANA: Ve like you very much.

MICHAEL: Good. Repeat…

SVETLANA: Ve like you very much.

MICHAEL: *(Beat.)* Repeat.

    (Music builds as lights fade slowly.)

SVETLANA: Ve like you very much.

MICHAEL: Repeat.

IGOR AND SVETLANA: Ve like you very much.

MICHAEL: Repeat.

IGOR AND SVETLANA: We like you very much…

    (Blackout.)

WOMEN'S SCENES

BURNING DOWN THE HOUSE

Jocelyn Beard

dramatic, 2 Women

Claudia (40s) a woman whose life is out of control, and Heddy (40s) her best friend, whose life is equally chaotic.

Scene: Provence, France

> *When Claudia and Heddy vacation in the south of France, an unexpected mistral begins to blow, driving them both to the edge of their sensibilities. Many years' worth of feelings of hurt and guilt quickly surface in the shrieking wind. When Claudia falls in love with Alex, a local man on whom Heddy does not approve, a heated discussion and shocking revelations follow.*

○ ○ ○

HEDDY: *(After a moment.)* Well, that was some show.

CLAUDIA: *(Starting.)* Jesus Christ, Heddy!

HEDDY: You look like shit.

CLAUDIA: It's the wind. Did you get out at all today?

HEDDY: Juliette took me shopping in the village.

CLAUDIA: Ah yes, fresh flowers. Very pretty. I thought Juliette hated Americans.

HEDDY: She does.

CLAUDIA: Hmm.

HEDDY: Hmm? That's it?

CLAUDIA: What do you mean?

HEDDY: I mean two sentences and you terminate the topic—any topic. Where the hell are you these days, Claudia?

CLAUDIA: I'm right here.

HEDDY: No, you're not.

CLAUDIA: I'm not?

HEDDY: You're not! You're not here. You haven't been "here" for the last six months.

CLAUDIA: What are you talking about?

HEDDY: I've been watching you, Claudie. Day after day I've watched as you've started to fade away; from me, from Jess, from Ray. Don't deny it. Something powerful is dragging you away from us, and it isn't this place or that boy you're screwing…

CLAUDIA: I'm not…

HEDDY: You are.

CLAUDIA: Okay, I am.

HEDDY: What's happening to you?! Is this some weird kind of mid-life crisis? I mean, cheating on Ray! You never would have done that a year ago!

CLAUDIA: No?

HEDDY: No! *(Claudia does not respond.)* Claudia, please. Why can't you talk to me anymore?

CLAUDIA: Because there really isn't much to say.

HEDDY: You stroll in here, fresh from the sack, and have the nerve to tell me that there isn't anything to say?? You, the girl who took twenty minutes to describe Matthew Reilly's lips?

CLAUDIA: That was another place, another time and another Claudia. Unlike you, Heddy, I've changed. The years have changed me. Fundamentally. I'm sorry, but I can't be the person you want me to be. Not anymore.

HEDDY: *(After a moment.)* Well, that's a kick in the ass.

CLAUDIA: I'm sorry.

HEDDY: You're so full of shit. No one changes, Claudia. We're born the same people that we die. *(Scornfully.)* Fundamentally. If you're not Claudia, who the hell are you?

CLAUDIA: What do you want from me?!

HEDDY: Talk to me about Ray, Claudia. What the hell do you think you're doing?

CLAUDIA: It's none of your business, Heddy. Leave it alone.

HEDDY: You're making a huge mistake, Claudia.

CLAUDIA: I won't discuss this with you!

HEDDY: You will! Don't you think I know that this thing with Alex is more than a crush? I know you're falling in love!

CLAUDIA: What if I am? Is that my business or yours?

HEDDY: What do you really know about him?

CLAUDIA: Everything I need to!

HEDDY: No! You don't!

CLAUDIA: Really? What don't I know that I need to know?

HEDDY: Oh, Christ, I don't know…what if he's got a wife somewhere?

CLAUDIA: His wife is dead.

HEDDY: *(Incredulously.)* You know about Soja?

CLAUDIA: How do you know her name?

HEDDY: I can't believe it! I can't believe that you would knowingly enter into a love affair with a man under these circumstances!

CLAUDIA: What circumstances?

HEDDY: *(After a pause.)* You don't know. He didn't tell you.

CLAUDIA: Tell me what?

HEDDY: About Soja. About the way she died.

CLAUDIA: She died in Sarajevo.

HEDDY: Uh-huh, and did he tell you that she was buried in a shroud in a communal grave? *(Claudia is silent.)* Did he tell you that he stopped eating and drinking for days after her death, until his parents had him hospitalized?

CLAUDIA: Stop it…

HEDDY: Did he tell you that he spent six months on anti-depressants, but still woke up screaming in the middle of the night?

CLAUDIA: Heddy, stop it. Alex has put this all behind him.

HEDDY: Yeah, right.

CLAUDIA: He's dealt with it.

HEDDY: Oh, grow up, will you? Did he tell you about this house?

CLAUDIA: What about it?

HEDDY: This was *their* house! Did you know that?

CLAUDIA: So what?

HEDDY: So, he hasn't set foot in it since she died!

CLAUDIA: Oh, for the love of Mike, Heddy! You're making nothing out of nothing!

HEDDY: *(Fiercely.)* All right, Claudia. Just now, when the two of you were humping in the door jam, do you remember what he said to you in French?

CLAUDIA: I don't speak French!

HEDDY: He said: *(French.)*. Do you remember? Up against the door? Do you remember? *(French.)*

CLAUDIA: *(Furious.)* Yes! I remember!

HEDDY: I don't remember too much, but I can tell you this, it was a simple sentence. A child could translate. *Fait que ce soit elle:* Please be her, please be her. Over and over again. Please be Her! Please be Soja!

(Claudia is now white with fury.)

CLAUDIA: *(Quietly.)* You bitch.

HEDDY: Yell at me all you want, but get over Alex, Claudia. Get over him now! You've got a good man waiting for you at home. Ray doesn't deserve this!

CLAUDIA: You *bitch!* Is there *nothing* you would leave me?

HEDDY: *(Thrown.)* What do you mean?

CLAUDIA: You've taken it all now, haven't you? It's just like when we used to play Monopoly when we were kids. You weren't happy until you owned every god damn piece of property on the board! You megalomaniacal *bitch!*

HEDDY: *(Suddenly nervous.)* Claudia, I…

CLAUDIA: Shut up! Just shut up, Heddy! Do you think I didn't know, that I wouldn't find out? Did you think I was so busy…what was it? Fading away? Did you think I'd be so busy fading away that I wouldn't notice when you started fucking my husband?

(Heddy collapses into a chair.)

HEDDY: *(Exhausted.)* You knew.

CLAUDIA: Oh, please. Exactly how stupid do you think I am? Just because I didn't go to work after college—just because I don't have a career like you, that doesn't mean that my brain atrophied!

HEDDY: How long have you…

CLAUDIA: From the first night, Heddy. I knew the very first night. Remember? That beautiful night in late May when I was supposed to go to the movies with you, but you had to work late with the judge? The "big deposition" that had to be "transcribed"? The night that Ray "had to stay late" at the marina? Someone was coming in to look at that stupid yacht he hadn't been able to sell in three years? Remember? Well, when I found myself stuck all by my lonesome that night, do you know what I did? Not what you and Ray expected me to do, obviously. I went to the movies by myself. Can you imagine that? Me the mousy little hausfrau with a condo in Boca? I drove to the multiplex and sat through a movie all by myself.

HEDDY: Claudia, you don't…

CLAUDIA: Shut up! You wanted to know! You *demanded* to know what strange force has been dragging me away from you— so now you just shut up and listen. After the movie, I was hungry—just like I always am after a movie. So I decided to go to the Brightside for a corn muffin and a cup of coffee.

HEDDY: Oh, god…

CLAUDIA: That's right, Heddy. The Brightside Diner. The diner we *always* go to after a movie. Where I always get a corn muffin and a cup of coffee. Right across the street from the Coachman's Inn Motor Lodge, where your Honda and Ray's BMW were parked side by side. Right in front of the door to room 212….

HEDDY: *(A weak attempt to forestall the inevitable denouement.)* 212…?

CLAUDIA: *(Viciously.)* That's right, 212. Knowing Ray as I do, I doubt that night was special enough for you to have committed the room number to memory, so just take my word for it, Heddy. The room was 212. 2-1-2. The door was scratched-up metal painted forest green and 212 was stenciled on it in gold paint. It was room 212. Right next to the ice machine. When I saw your cars, parked right there in the open, right in front of room 212, do you know what the first thing I thought was? Do you?

HEDDY: No.

CLAUDIA: I thought: *How fucking arrogant.* My best friend and my husband go to the Coachman's Inn Motor Lodge to screw, and they have the *arrogance* to park their cars side-by-side, right in front of the door to their room? I mean, why bother spending money on a hotel room? Why not just do it right there in the parking lot?

HEDDY: *(Resigned.)* What do you want me to say?

CLAUDIA: I don't want you to say anything. I know you, Heddy. You'd never apologize. You're not sorry for your actions. That would violate your most basic ethical tenants. "Guilt is a synthetic emotion." Isn't that what you always told me?

HEDDY: Claudia, I'm not…

CLAUDIA: Well you can be very proud of me, because that very same night I did something specifically to never feel guilty about.

HEDDY: What did you do, Claudia?

CLAUDIA: Well, after I watched you stagger out for a bucket of ice, I figured that Ray was in for the long haul, so I went right to the pay phone there in the Brightside and called Mark.

HEDDY: Mark? You called…oh my god, Claudia! You told Mark?!?

CLAUDIA: Don't be ridiculous, Heddy. Why would I want to make poor Mark suffer like I suffered in that half hour I sat in the window booth at the diner? I like Mark…which came in handy.

HEDDY: What are you talking about?

CLAUDIA: I called up Mark, and I told him he could finally have the one thing he'd always wanted. Me.

HEDDY: You? You mean…

CLAUDIA: Mark took me to the Park Plaza, Heddy. That very weekend. Remember? I had to go to a seminar on primitive American art up in Cooperstown and Mark had to go pick up a friend in Atlantic City who'd gotten himself in trouble with a loan shark? Remember? Well, while you and Ray were probably marking territory like cats all over my house, Mark and I were sipping Piper on the twenty-sixth floor of the Park Plaza, on a nice big bed in a nice big room with a mini-bar.

HEDDY: *(Slowly.)* You know, I wondered what it was. These past few years. You were so distant. I wondered…

CLAUDIA: Heddy, I just told you…

HEDDY: I know what you just told me.

CLAUDIA: And all you care about is putting the last missing piece in the puzzle. You finally get to prove your "Claudia's Fading Away" Theory. You have the confirmation you needed and you're satisfied.

HEDDY: It's not like that, Claudie.

CLAUDIA: No? What's it like, then?

HEDDY: I can't…I can't talk about this now… *(Heddy turns and heads for the door. Without thinking, she yanks it open and The Mistral hits her dead on. She stands in the wind Claudia makes no move to stop her. Heddy shouting.)* You're right, Claudie: if you stand in this wind long enough, it'll blow your mind clear. All the bullshit that's trapped up here will turn into Sahara dust. *(She turns to face Claudia.)* I lost my soul a long time ago, Claudia. The first day I hated you for having the kind of life I wanted. That was the day I lost the first big chunk. You had the man I wanted and the life that went along with him. *I* wanted the big house in Cathedral Park. *I* wanted to join the museum societies. *I* wanted to be able to go back to school to take a course whenever I felt like it. *I* wanted a kid like Jessica. *I* even wanted the condo in Boca. I wanted all these things, Claudie. Wanted them bad. And the day I realized that you didn't give a shit about any of them— except Jessica—was the day I started hating you. Every day I drove to work, carpooling because I couldn't afford to drive alone, I hated you. Every time you called me up to tell me that you just saw the greatest exhibit at the Metropolitan, I hated you. I hated you for all the little mother-daughter trips you and Jess took. And most of all, I hated you because you turned the man I wanted more than anything right out of your heart. But all this hating has cost me, Claudie. It's cost me big and now it's costing you. I can't believe you whored yourself to Mark just to punish me for taking something I wanted and you didn't. I can't believe it.

CLAUDIA: *(Incredulously.)* You whiny little bitch! *You* hated *me?* For what? For living a boring life? For having free time?

HEDDY: I suppose you think having to go to work every day is better, somehow.

CLAUDIA: At least it fills in the hours!

HEDDY: Having to deal with idiots—day in and day out…

CLAUDIA: At least you're dealing with *people.*

HEDDY: What, there are no people in your life?

CLAUDIA: No, there are not.

HEDDY: What about Ray?

CLAUDIA: Ray's an asshole. You want him, be a woman and take him, but stop sneaking around like you're…oh, what the hell was that stupid little girl's name?

HEDDY: Amy Fischer.

CLAUDIA: Right! Stop sneaking around like you're Amy Fischer and Ray's Joey Butta-whatever!

HEDDY: Fuoccio.

CLAUDIA: *Whatever!* You love Ray so much? *(Struggles to remove her wedding ring.)* Here! *(Throws ring at Heddy.)* Take the ring! *(She grabs her purse.)* You want some leisure time? *(Gets her wallet and starts removing credit cards which she hurls at Heddy.)* Take his credit cards and buy yourself a year off! *(Fishes a set of keys out of bag.)* And here! *(Throws keys.)* Here are the keys to the god damn condo in Boca! You want my life—*Take it.*

(Heddy sinks to her knees and begins to gather the thrown items. Claudia pushes past her to the door. At the door, she turns.)

CLAUDIA: Until this very moment, Heddy, I loved you. Despite *everything,* I've loved you. You've been my best friend…my soulmate for over forty years. Forty years, Heddy! And I've idolized you. You've always been my hero. You always stood up for me, even when I wouldn't. But now...seeing you down there on your knees, trying to....forget it. You're not worth it. *(Claudia exits into the wind.)*

A GIRL'S TIE TO HER FATHER

Sari Bodi

serio-comedic, 2 Women

June (30s–40s) an alcoholic, and Claire (12) her long-suffering daughter.

Scene: a bathroom

As she bathes Claire in Bombay Sapphire gin, June tortures the poor girl with yet another creative retelling of the alleged circumstances that led to her conception.

○ ○ ○

(A young Claire is in the bathtub. Her mother, June, is washing her hair.)

JUNE: Gin will bring out the highlights.

CLAIRE: But it smells terrible, Mother.

JUNE: Your hair will look wonderful. You'll be the most popular girl in school.

CLAIRE: Everyone hates me. They think I'm weird. At least, my hair has grown back.

JUNE: You looked lovely without it.

CLAIRE: Please don't shave it off again, Mother.

JUNE: We'll see. When the creative urge strikes to make you over, I can't control it. And now for the rinse, I'll use my best gin—Bombay Sapphire—with just a little splash of vermouth.

CLAIRE: Are you going to your parent-teacher conference tonight?

JUNE: Of course not. Your teacher's bound to tell me the sorts of disagreeable things I try to keep out of my life.

CLAIRE: But I told her you would come. She made me promise.

JUNE: Well, I'll give you a nice gift-wrapped bottle of Bombay Sapphire to take to her and my recipe for a martini. That should make her happy. Now, are you ready for your bedtime story? It's the story of how you were conceived.

CLAIRE: No, Mother. I don't want to hear that story again. I want to talk about my teacher. Mrs. McKnight will be sitting in the classroom waiting for you. She wanted you to be punctual.

JUNE: But I've just remembered another detail. Once upon a time, your mother was a young woman with tight buttocks, and curls that cascaded down her back driving every virile man within a fifty-mile radius absolutely mad with desire.

CLAIRE: Mother. My teacher needs to talk with you. She's worried about me with my strange haircuts, and the stupid clothes you make me wear and the kids make fun of me, and…

JUNE: Claire, you're interrupting. Don't they teach you manners in school? Your clothes set you out as an individual. I am not raising my daughter to be a slave to every fashion trend Seventeen magazine throws at you young girls.

CLAIRE: They're all your old clothes. They're too big on me.

JUNE: Nonsense. Those clothes served me well in my youth. And they'll do the same for you. Anyway, one day, your mother was walking down 57th Street and First Avenue when someone whistled at her. Mommy turned to give the man a "Don't fuck with me" stare, when she noticed that the man was missing an arm.

CLAIRE: Daddy didn't have an arm? You never told me that before.

JUNE: This wasn't Daddy.

CLAIRE: Oh.

JUNE: So Mommy hitched up her skirt to reveal her shapely legs to the man because she felt sorry for him, when another man came running out of the grocery store and knocked into her. Mommy would have been very angry except that she noticed he had a seeing eye dog.

CLAIRE: Daddy?

JUNE: No, not yet.

CLAIRE: Mother. Please. Mrs. McKnight wants to send me to a foster home. If you don't go tonight…

JUNE: Nonsense. She's threatened that before.

CLAIRE: Yes, and I did go.

JUNE: And so you did. But you're back. Now where was I? You're confusing me.

CLAIRE: The seeing eye dog?

JUNE: Right. So Mommy yelled, "Watch it, Buddy" to the man with the seeing eye dog, and he, liking the sound of her sassy voice, handed her a card on which was written, "If you need a change of luck, see Malcolm."

CLAIRE: Malcolm was my father?

JUNE: No. Now, Claire, if you think by speeding up this story, I'll finish washing your hair in time to see Mrs. McKnight, you're sorely mistaken.

CLAIRE: But, Mother. She already has a family picked out. And they have a big dog. And I hate dogs that slobber.

JUNE: She's not going to take you away. So Mommy took the card, and knocked on the door. And who should answer?

CLAIRE: Malcolm?

JUNE: No, Samuel. And he took her hand and escorted her up three flights of stairs. At the top of the stairs, she noticed that he was missing…

CLAIRE: Three fingers.

JUNE: Right. Which he had lost in a…

CLAIRE: Poker game.

JUNE: No, a lightning storm while he was playing golf.

CLAIRE: Was that the detail that you just remembered?

JUNE: No, you'll see. So, Samuel led her into the room where there was a long line of people waiting to see Malcolm because…

CLAIRE: Luck was scarce in those days.

JUNE: Exactly. But while she was holding Samuel's two-fingered hand, she realized that perhaps her luck had already changed so she lead him to…

CLAIRE: the stairwell where someone had thrown out an old-tattered plaid pillow. Mother pulled Samuel down on the pillow and unzipped his overalls, and pulled up her tightly fitting black skirt which showed off her shapely thighs to good advantage. Samuel undid her stockings from her garter belt, and that was it. I was conceived.

JUNE: Oh, you're leaving out the best part.

CLAIRE: I don't want to hear it. It's smutty. Other kids don't have to hear the excruciating details of their conceptions. They were conceived in comfy suburban homes by Mommys and Daddys under clean sheets with the lights off.

JUNE: Other kids live in a puritanical world ruled by reactionary customs brought over by the Pilgrims. You should be happy that your mother is a progressive woman. Sex is beautiful, and if I were still young with tight buttocks, I would spend every waking moment engaged in sexual activity.

CLAIRE: You told me every body is beautiful when engaged in the act of love-making.

JUNE: I was wrong. I believed that until I started to sag. Get it while you can, Honey.

CLAIRE: I'm only twelve years old.

JUNE: It's never too early to enjoy the fruits of the flesh.

CLAIRE: But Mommy. This is why Mrs. McKnight wants to take me away. She doesn't think you're a fit mother.

JUNE: Darling, I gave you an auspicious beginning. Why you even had an audience with applause. The curtains parted and you were begun.

CLAIRE: How embarrassing. Everyone was watching while you and Samuel, my father…

JUNE: Actually, it wasn't Samuel, after all.

CLAIRE: But I thought Samuel was my father.

JUNE: That's what I thought, too. But then today, I was gazing into my martini glass when suddenly I saw what happened. You see, Samuel and I were panting with delight—As I've told you…

CLAIRE: It's the anticipation that's the most exciting part.

JUNE: And all the people from Malcolm's gathered around us, cheering us on, and screaming, "Take it off." So I pulled off Samuel's overalls. But that's when I realized that the golf accident had taken away more than his three fingers.

CLAIRE: No, Mother. You're making this up. You're so cruel to men.

150 women's scenes

You say awful things about them. Daddy had a p…He had to have one. Or I wouldn't be born.

JUNE: Daddy had one. He had a lovely one. As smooth as baby's skin and with a motion as liquid as motor oil.

CLAIRE: But.

JUNE: Samuel wasn't your father. As soon as the crowd realized what I realized, they pushed another man forward to take his place, and that man is your father.

CLAIRE: What?

JUNE: That's what I just remembered.

CLAIRE: How could you just remember such an important detail?

JUNE: Sometimes details get mixed up when passion is involved.

CLAIRE: Then who is my father?

JUNE: I'm afraid I don't remember very well. I certainly don't know his name or how he happened to be at Malcolm's, but I guess like me, he was looking for some luck. And you my dear, are that luck, for both of us.

CLAIRE: Oh my god. All these years, I've been imagining that I would run into a two fingered man, and I would yell out, "Father," and he would be so happy to see me he would take me home to meet my brothers and sisters, and we would drink lemonade on the front porch, and play stickball until it turned dark.

JUNE: Well, I'm sorry, dear. Now, out of the bath. *(June wraps Claire in a towel, and kisses her on the head.)* The story will be continued on another night. But it's off to bed for you.

MANY COLORS MAKE THE THUNDER-KING

Femi Osofisan

dramatic, 3 Women

Oya (20–30) first wife of King Shango, desperate to have his child, Osun (20s) second wife of the king and Yeye Iroko (any age) a tree goddess.

Scene: the kingdom of King Shango

> *Here, the desperate Oya begs the tree goddess to grant her a child.*

○ ○ ○

(Forest grove. Night. Moon up. Oya and Osun by a huge iroko tree. They are dressed in white, with white chalk stripes on their faces and around their eyes. Their attendants wait close by. Osun kneels and rings a bell.)

OSUN: Iroko! Mother of the forest!
We call on you!
We've brought your sacrifice,
Poured out your favorite drink!
Let me not be disgraced tonight!
Please answer our supplications!
(A song starts, from the belly of the tree. It opens like a door, and a female figure, resplendent, appears.)

YEYE IROKO: Who has chosen this hour to call?

OSUN: Yeye! I am happy to see you again! It's your daughter, Osun!

YEYE IROKO: Oh Osun. It's you! I heard you were married.

OSUN: Yes, Yeye. And this woman here is my senior wife, Oya.

YEYE IROKO: Oya, daughter of the river?

OYA: Yes, Yeye. I greet you.

YEYE IROKO: You are as beautiful as they say! Even more beautiful!

And so of course are you, my daughter, Osun. But did you just say one man, one single man, has been lucky enough to capture both of you in his household?

OSUN: Yes, Yeye, he is a man worthy of ten of us. His name is Shango, the king of Igbeti!

YEYE IROKO: The empire-builder! The one who would be greater than Oronmiyon, father of our people!

OSUN: You know him very well then!

YEYE IROKO: News of him has spread far, my daughter.

OSUN: We are here because of my iyaale. She has a problem which only you can solve. She's come to speak to you.

OYA: Yeye, please help me! I've known such suffering, such pain as I never imagined anybody in this world could experience, and it has turned me bitter. Yeye, I've come to you to rescue me. I'm a hollow husk! My husband has forgotten the way to my room.

YEYE IROKO: You want him back.

OYA: I'll give you anything you ask! The most precious things I own. If I can have him back, even for one night, and carry his seed, I'll give you the child itself. Just for one tender moment if I could look at this child, hold it to my breast, and tell myself that it is mine! You'll have anything you wish, Yeye, for a moment of such fulfillment!

YEYE IROKO: Careful now! Careful, my daughter! When you speak to Iroko, every word you utter is taken in all seriousness. Every promise becomes impossible to retract. Don't be reckless.

OYA: No, please, Yeye! Every word I just said is in dead earnest! I mean it all, as long as—

OSUN: Wait, Oya! You're making a promise you'll not be able to keep!

OYA: I'll not take a word back! Yeye, let me just have the child! A child of my own! Let me show it to my husband, let the palace see at last that Oya is not just an empty husk. Then, you can ask for the child back. Or even take my life itself! It wouldn't pain me any more! Even if several more wives filled

the palace, my place of eminence could never again be chal-
lenged! Yeye, that's all I want!

YEYE IROKO: Well, my daughter, so be it! Follow me.

(They go into the belly of the tree.)

THE RED ROOM

S. P. Miskowski

dramatic, 2 Women

Alma (30–50) a wanderer, and Martha (30–50) her sister.

Scene: rural Georgia

> *Alma has recently returned to her childhood home after many years away. Here sisters, Martha and Louise, have been keeping up with the farm as best they could following the execution of their mother, a convicted murderer. On a stormy night, Louise suffers an emotional breakdown, and Alma does her best to convince Martha to send for a doctor.*

(Night. A crash of thunder, followed by the sound of voices in confusion. Another roll of thunder, and another, growing more distant as the voices become more distinct. Flashlight beams cut the dark, as Martha and Alma enter.)

ALMA: Why would she wake up?

MARTHA: The storm's so bad, that's all.

ALMA: You sure you gave her enough medicine?

MARTHA: I gave her the same as always. I better give her another dose.

ALMA: Not supposed to.

MARTHA: What else can we do? She won't sleep at all, otherwise.

ALMA: Just excited's all. Thunder in the middle o the night, the smell o the rain.

MARTHA: You stayin up all night with her?

ALMA: Martha.

> *(Light comes up, upstage, on Louise. She stands staring up at an unseen object. As scene continues between Alma and Martha, Louise slowly raises her arms over her head. As she does so music rises then levels off and continues. Louise*

clenches her fists as if seizing bars of a cage. She shakes the "bars" while silently mouthing the line "Mother, wake up," over and over.)

MARTHA: Say?

ALMA: You stay up. You're better at it.

MARTHA: Alma, I stayed up with her most o the night.

ALMA: You sayin what…?

MARTHA: Nothin. I'll give her another dose o medicine.

ALMA: Two doses? Martha, you can't.

MARTHA: She won't sleep at all. What else are we gonna do? Alma!

ALMA: I'll stay up. If she's still bad tomorrow, you can call in Dr. Bell.

MARTHA: What for? We don't need that quack comin in here with his "remedies."

ALMA: Think about Louise.

MARTHA: I'm thinkin 'bout Louise! The hell you think I'm thinkin about? What else do I think about? She's fam'ly. No call to bring an outsider over here. We can take care o Louise.

ALMA: I only said to call Dr. Bell if she's still bad tomorrow. I said, just if she's still bad tomorrow.
(Martha considers this.)

MARTHA: No.

ALMA: Not unless she's doin bad.

MARTHA: We don't need help from that fool.

ALMA: He's got a license, an' a degree.

MARTHA: What difference does that make? Annie Swann's cousin Lamar's got a degree, an' he's dumb as a chicken.

ALMA: You won't call Dr. Bell?

MARTHA: No, I won't.

ALMA: No matter how sick Louise gets?

MARTHA: Don't do it. Don't try lyin to me. I can't have him over here, and you know why.

ALMA: Why? Why, say?

MARTHA: Alma, he's the doctor to every fam'ly in this part o the county.

ALMA: Uh-huh.

MARTHA: Everybody knows him. He's not stranger.

ALMA: You need to think about it.

MARTHA: I need you to stop tellin me what to do.

ALMA: I didn't ask to come back to this house.

MARTHA: You—couldn't wait! You made me leave everything the way it was, in your room.

ALMA: I was done with it. I was too busy to think about it.

MARTHA: Yeah, gin kept you awful busy.

ALMA: You know so much, sister! You know me inside and out. I said, I was done with it.

MARTHA: I can tell. You're not done. You'd be sittin in a motel room by yourself if I didn't come after you. You wanted to be back here, with all her things, you said. You had to come home! You're not done. And I'm not callin that doctor out here, for Louise or for you.

(The flashlights go out. Shadows cut across the stage.)

TRANSFORMATION SCENE

Jo J. Adamson

dramatic, 2 Women
Geraldine (30s) a small, plain woman and Sissy (30–40) her aggressive sister.

Scene: here and now

> *Here, two sisters visit, and as usual, are mystified, provoked, challenged and inspired by their differences.*

GERALDINE: We called it cheat grass then, brought it home sticking to our anklets with little spears penetrating the socks an puncturing the foot. It was hard getting it out of the cotton. Especially if you broke it off at the top, trying to get it out. *(Sissy turns toward her, but does not speak.)* What?…No, I *can't* be more specific. Cheat grass. We called it that because mother told us that was what it was. Like Piggypies and Grasswidows, flowers that can't be found in any botany books. Cheat grass, she said, because it "cheated" and hitched a ride on running feet.

SISSY: Quaint.

GERALDINE: *(Ignores her.)* When mother talked, I forgot my fears and took comfort in words I couldn't find in dictionaries or reference books.

SISSY: Your *fears?*, Geraldine.

GERALDINE: They numbered a thousand and one.

SISSY: Perhaps your "cheat grass" was some variety of bunch grass that grew in the bottomlands along the river. You lost your best friend to a drowning in that river. Remember Alice The girl who drew profiles of herself in bridal veils?

GERALDINE: No, I don't remember Alice. *(Beat.)* The drawings were full face.

SISSY: *(Bored.)* Whatever

(Geraldine turns to face Sissy.)

GERALDINE: Come *on.* You lived by the river Why don't you remember the cheat grass?

SISSY: I was more interested in cloud formations.

GERALDINE: Remember mother standing over that old woodstove? She'd rest her hands on top, lean down into the into the heat. Sometimes her face would get as red as an apple. She forgot we were even there.

SISSY: I had to gather the wood. *You* got to stay inside where it was warm.

GERALDINE: The stories she told us! All about life on other planets. She believed that people lived there, just like you and me.

(Sissy picks up magazine.)

SISSY: Creatures on other planets would be totally different from us. Evolution proceeds in thousands of small and unpredictable steps. The variations would be incredible There may be, *beings* Geraldine. But they would in no way resemble *us.*

(Sissy sits in wing back chair.)

GERALDINE: The heat from the stove made blotches on the underside of her arms. *(Geraldine holds up arm, looks.)* Blotches on her arms: and face as red as an apple. In our lifetime she said, we would travel to distant planets.

SISSY: It would take our present space craft some tens of thousands of years to go the distance to the nearest star: several tens of million of years to the nearest civilization.

GERALDINE: It just stood to reason, she said, that others would think as we do.

SISSY: Optimistic estimates puts our nearest civilization at a hundred light-years.

GERALDINE: It was so warm in that little corner by the woodstove. I used to crouch in that little space every morning. I could feel the heat clear to my bones. I resented it when I had to get ready for school.

SISSY: A light year is almost six trillion miles. Six *trillion* miles.

GERALDINE: Electric heat does not open children like flowers. It doesn't make them sleepily secure.

SISSY: Beware of security, Geraldine.

(Geraldine winces. She gets up slowly, (Walking is "unnatural" for her.) Geraldine goes over to Sissy, takes magazine from her. Drops it.)

GERALDINE: *Look* at me when I'm talking.

SISSY: I can't take my eyes off you.

GERALDINE: Mother told me that I wouldn't have to leave home. I could stay with her forever. Her house was kept warm all year Just like this one! All she required was that I stay with her.

SISSY: You didn't. Stay, I mean.

GERALDINE: Mother never forgave me for marrying. She thought I was destined for something better.

(Sissy makes snorting noise.)

SISSY: That robe looks ancient, Geraldine. Don't you ever take it off?

(Geraldine turns from her, hunches shoulders.)

GERALDINE: Don't be critical, Sissy I can't bear it when you're critical.

SISSY: You look as if you're wrapped in dirty skin.

GERALDINE: Why are you always picking on me. Pick, pick, pick. You never let up.

SISSY: Do you know what will happen if you don't take that thing off?

GERALDINE: It's not time yet.

SISSY: It'll turn from gray to brown. Black, then moldy green. The material will become cracked and brittle. You'll have to crawl out of it. Tell me Dear, wouldn't it be more "hygienic" if you removed the robe to launder it? *(Sissy goes over to Geraldine.)* Here, give it to me. I'll just toss it in the washer.

GERALDINE: Don't touch me!

(Sissy puts her hands up in the air.)

SISSY: I was only trying to help.

GERALDINE: Don't help. Don't…do…anything.

SISSY: Why are you so touchy?

160 women's scenes

GERALDINE: *I'm* not the touchy one!

SISSY: Geraldine, I hardly know you. You're changing.

(Geraldine looks at her, apprehensive.)

GERALDINE: In what way?

SISSY: Well you *hair,* for one thing. It used to be blond. It's now drably…brown. And your skin has lost its natural pink tone. Moreover, you seem determined to attach yourself to… things.

GERALDINE: I suppose I should get out of the house more.

SISSY: You *cling,* Geraldine.

(Geraldine reaches for fruit. She selects an orange. Geraldine picks it up, sticks finger in it, making a hole. She puts orange to mouth and begins to suck.)

GERALDINE: Nothing interests me anymore. Take you, for example. You appeared and made yourself felt in my life this very morning. And already, I've taken you for granted. If you become obnoxious, block my food supply or something, I may be forced to climb over you. But other than that, your existence has no significance whatsoever. *(Loud sucking noise as Geraldine works orange.)*

SISSY: Don't you feel at all Queer?

GERALDINE: Not a bit.

SISSY: You've got to feel something! Love, hate, desire, sadness, anger, hunger, thirst. *Something.*

(Geraldine "thinks" for a moment. Then shakes her head.)

GERALDINE: Nope. Mostly I just like to suck.

SISSY: "Well, perhaps your feelings may be different…all I know is, it would feel very queer to me."

GERALDINE: "You!, who are you?"

SISSY: Don't you feel a little odd when you see the changes in your bathroom mirror?

GERALDINE: I haven't approached a mirror in years! Not since the day I saw the San Andrea's Fault forming along my cheek. When the cornea clouded, I adjusted my light tolerance. I know this room like the back of my hand, and there is nothing outside my window but rows and rows of houses.

(Geraldine thinks for a moment.) Silver bells and cockleshells I could live with.

(Sissy turns to go.)

SISSY: You're *weird,* Geraldine.

GERALDINE: *(Alarmed.)* Where are you going!

SISSY: Out of this cracker factory. They'll be coming after you in a butterfly net!

GERALDINE: Don't go. I need someone to…adhere to.

SISSY: You have your husband, Jay.

GERALDINE: I am lacking.

(Sissy comes over beside her. She sits next to her. Sissy takes Geraldine's hand in hers.)

SISSY: You're too preoccupied with yourself, Little June Bug. Remember Papa always calling you that? His little June Bug. *I* was Baby Huey. May he rest in Purgatory. *(Sissy squeezes Geraldine's hand.)*

GERALDINE: Ouch!

(Sissy releases grip.)

SISSY: Sorry Dear. Where was I?, oh yes. Preoccupation. You must direct your attention to events outside your window. Explore the world at large.

GERALDINE: The world at large?

SISSY: The universe!

GERALDINE: It took me one hundred thirty million years to develop the art of camouflage, and you expect me to silhouette the sun!

(Sissy starts to rise.)

SISSY: Well if you're going to think that way…

(Geraldine pulls her down.)

GERALDINE: No!, don't go. Look, it's the world at "small" that I inhabit. My skeleton's outside my body and I don't hear things the way you do. Through the years I've been able to live with Jay because I've developed a pleasant scent. When he's angry, I just brush against him and give off this aroma. If that fails, I approach him in such a manner as to make him think of other things. Other than these "tactics" my day is quite ordinary. I awake, forage for something to put in my mouth and stay out of harm's way. *(Geraldine looks hard at Sissy.)* When something or *someone* interferes with these steps, I go on to the next one…which happens to be… *(Geraldine puts her hand over her mouth, and yawns. She becomes drowsy, lies down. Sissy begins to shake her.)*

SISSY: You've got to think, Geraldine. Think, think, think! *(Geraldine mumbles something groggily. Sissy addresses audience.)* You want to know how she got into such a pitiable state of inactivity? Adaptability. Ever since she was a tiny one, Geraldine got along by getting by. When Papa got angry and focused his eagle-eye on her, she could do the most marvelous impression of a music box dancer. Geraldine would stand on her little toes as dainty as a butterfly and whirl around the room in a blaze of color! It was really quite a sight. When she finished her dance, Papa forgot why he was angry with her, and take her in his arms and give her a big squeeze. *(Turns to Geraldine, gently shakes her.)* Remember the dancing?, Geraldine. *(Geraldine makes some inarticulate sound. Back to audience.)* She danced a lot in those early years. And when she began to grow, she had to develop other talents of diversion. For example. Papa had an immoderate fondness for tobacco. And Geraldine, in some strange way, able to… *(Leans forward.)* Well, "manufacture" that scent. Papa tolerated her on the days she was able to smell like Old Velvet pipe tobacco. *(Turns to Geraldine.)* How *did* you manage that? *(Geraldine does not respond.)* And so she grew. A bit. But she never did achieve full height. And her basic body structure didn't change. Geraldine looks pretty much the same now as she did when she was in swaddling clothes. Come to think of it, she didn't change so much in looks as in color. She darkened like an apple without its protective skin. *(Gently shakes her.)* Geraldine?…Geraldine! Oh darn. She's out of it. It would take an earthquake to rouse her. *(Sissy picks up Geraldine's head, plumps the pillow beneath her. Sissy lets Geraldine's head fall back. She straightens a few things on the table, and then gets up and begins to moves about the room. She stops beside a plant.)* Every year I manage it. Come to Geraldine's aid.

WINDSHOOK

Mary Gallagher

serio-comedic, 2 Women
Ruby (18) the prettiest girl in town, determined to live out her dreams and Darlene (17) her best friend.

Scene: the Catskills

> *Ruby has become attracted to an enigmatic drifter, leaving her high school boyfriend out in the cold. Here, Darlene, a teen mother, expresses her concern over Ruby's behavior.*

DARLENE: Where'd you go last night? We thought you was coming out to the dirt track.

RUBY: Didn't feel like it.

DARLENE: Lance was looking for you. He looked good too, got his ear pierced in three places! Had little gold rings in, he looked so cool.

RUBY: *(Amused.)* That ain't gonna go over too good at the lumber yard.

DARLENE: Lisa was hanging on him, I'm serious. He won all his races too.

RUBY: *(Dismissive gesture like her father's.)* Aw hell, he always wins the quarter-mile, since he was twelve or something. Why don't he move up to the half-mile and go for it?

DARLENE: Why do you give him such a bad time? I wish Dale ever treated me half as nice as Lance treats you.

RUBY: I wouldn't take the shit you take from Dale, Darlene. And you don't have to, either.

DARLENE: Well…I got Ashley to think of now…

RUBY: You always took shit from him.

DARLENE: …He don't mean it…

RUBY: What *does* he mean?

DARLENE: He don't mean nothing. You know Dale. He don't think that much.

RUBY: One of these days he's gonna run you down in the parking lot in that stupid high-wheeler he went and bought.

DARLENE: Do you want Lance or not?

(Beat; Ruby starts playing with Darlene's hair, twisting it around various ways in front of an invisible mirror as Darlene lights a cigarette.)

RUBY: You ever read the wedding announcements in the *Banner?*

DARLENE: …We don't take a paper regular—

RUBY: *(Affectionate.)* Yeah, you only read the *Star.*

DARLENE: Hey, when I buy the *Star,* you read the whole thing—

RUBY: Yeah, but you believe it.

DARLENE: …Well, it's right there in black and white, why wouldn't it be true?

RUBY: Darlene…

DARLENE: Well, I spose you don't believe the wedding announce-ments either.

RUBY: I believe 'em, that's what's wrong with 'em. "The bride is a medical receptionist. The bridegroom is a shipping clerk at Sears. After a honeymoon in Florida, they are living in Lindaville."

DARLENE: I wish Dale was a shipping clerk at Sears.

RUBY: "The bridegroom is a plumber's assistant in Crawley. The bride is a clerk at the Crawley Laundromat. After a honey-moon in the Poconos, they are living in Crawley."

DARLENE: I bet I'll never in my whole life see the Poconos with Dale! But Lance would take you anywhere, if you'd just not spit on him—

RUBY: He *likes* it when I spit on him—but you're missing the point, Darlene. Is that all they're gonna get? Probably get pregnant on their stupid boring honeymoon, and forever after they'll be "living in Lindaville?" Don't that depress you?

DARLENE: Yeah, they depress me cause they're so much better off than me.

RUBY: …I give up.

166 women's scenes

DARLENE: …You're just spoiled is all.

(Ruby looks at her. Darlene nods wisely. Ruby smiles.)

RUBY: …Maybe.

DARLENE: Are you seeing somebody besides Lance?

RUBY: I ain't seeing Lance.

DARLENE: You know what I mean.

(Pause. Ruby drops Darlene's hair.)

RUBY: …I don't know what I'm doing yet…

DARLENE: *(Ponytails her hair.)* Well, you seem all stirred up to *me.*

RUBY: That's 'cause everyone around here is dead, and I'm alive.

MEN'S SCENES

ASK NOSTRADAMUS

R. J. Marx

comedic, 2 Men
Michel de Notredame (30s) a would-be seer, and Jean de Chevigny (30–50) his friend and biographer.

Scene: France during the sixteenth century

One successful prophecy has created quite a public groundswell for Michel that has reached the King himself. Here, the unhappy Michel agonizes over new prophecies with his best friend.

○ ○ ○

(Nostradamus in his private study, filled with arcana and mystical equipment with Chevigny.)

CHEVIGNY: Michel, the world is waiting.

NOSTRADAMUS: Let them wait, let them wait.

CHEVIGNY: But you took the advance. If you don't come up with some hot predictions, you're screwed.

NOSTRADAMUS: Let 'em re-read the first one. Margaret Mitchell didn't write anything after "Gone with the Wind."

CHEVIGNY: But they're tired of waiting! They want more! You must consult your oracle, Master…and conjure new predictions!

NOSTRADAMUS: Another day, Chevigny.

CHEVIGNY: But you signed a three-book deal. If you don't deliver…you'll have to give back your advance!

NOSTRADAMUS: Oh jesus—let's get to work, Chevigny!

CHEVIGNY: I'm ready, Master! Start predicting!

NOSTRADAMUS: Okay, okay…

CHEVIGNY: I'm ready, Master. You start talking, I'll start writing.

NOSTRADAMUS: Yeah. Just one sec. Hold your horses, I'm-a-comin'. Let's see. Mm hm, mm hm…I got lucky once, I can do it again.

CHEVIGNY: Think future, think far in the future. That way, we'll all be dead before anyone finds out.

NOSTRADAMUS: I'm trying! My mind's a blank.

CHEVIGNY: Here, try this, Master. (Chevigny passes Nostradamus an "astrolabe," a globe shaped object used for astrological readings. Nostradamus inspects it.)

NOSTRADAMUS: Nothing.

(Chevigny holds up a crystal ball.)

CHEVIGNY: Try this.

NOSTRADAMUS: *(Massive effort.)* I can see…I can see… *(Pause.)* It needs a cleaning. It's no good, it's hopeless, the world thinks I'm a seer, I don't even know what I'm going to eat for dinner tonight. The world wants to see the future and I just can't.

CHEVIGNY: Be obscure…"The wolf tracks the lamb…" "The seeds turn to musk…" "Clouds warp like muses." That kind of thing.

NOSTRADAMUS: I'm dry, Chevigny. I'm dry. *(He starts crying.)* I'm a phony, I'm a fraud. I deserve to be hung at the gallows. Burned at the stake. I'm no good.

CHEVIGNY: There there, Michel, it's alright. Your words do show a certain inspiration, remote though it may be.

NOSTRADAMUS: Don't shit a shitter. *(Suddenly hopeful.)* Please, Chevigny, you're my best friend. I need your help. Write them for me? Just this one time?

CHEVIGNY: Just this one time. *(Chevigny takes a pen and thinks.)* Let's see…how's this one…suppose in the Nineteenth Century there's a big fat French leader who almost conquers the world…but gets stuck in Russia. "The heavy one marches upon the Volga…he ends up in Elbe."

NOSTRADAMUS: Chevigny, you're brilliant, how do you do it?

CHEVIGNY: Here…"The land of the Indians becomes a new nation…gambling is legalized in Vegas…"

NOSTRADAMUS: Oh! The public will love it! *(Pause.)* What's "Vegas"?

CHEVIGNY: Hell if I know. But it'll keep 'em guessing.

NOSTRADAMUS: You're a genius Chevigny. I don't know what I'd do without you.

THE COYOTE BLEEDS
Tony DiMurro

dramatic, 3 Men
Hunt (50s) a NYC detective who has seen and done too much, Mitchell (25) his partner and Greene (20–30) a murder suspect.

Scene: the 124th Precinct, New York City

Here, the world-weary Hunt demonstrates to his young part-ner the best way to wring a confession out of a suspect.

(A small empty space. As the lights start to come up slowly, we see the set. There are no walls. In the middle of the space is an old beat-up desk. The desk is empty. Standing next to the desk is Mitchell dressed the same as in the earlier scene except he is wearing a blue wrinkled suit jacket. He is walk-ing in circles around the desk smoking a cigarette. Every few seconds he looks at Hunt, who is dressed the same as in the earlier scene, in the corner of the room, standing motionless with his arms folded. Hunt nods at Mitchell who continues to circle. Mitchell looks at Hunt again. Hunt nods back and rais-es his hand signaling to be patient. The lights are still dim until the door opens. When the man enters the lights should shoot to full intensity. The man is a light skinned black man. He is short, has short curly hair and is overweight. His face is as expressionless as an accountant's face in the middle of a work day. He has no identifiable characteristics. He is dressed in work pants with cheap sneakers and a flannel shirt. His name is McKinley Greene. As soon as he enters the room, he speaks.)

GREENE: Hello, my name's McKinley Greene. I got down here as soon as I could. Is there a problem?

MITCHELL: So you're McKinley Greene? *(Mitchell extends his hand*

and shakes with Greene. Hunt stays in the corner of the room.)

HUNT: Hello Mr. Greene. My name is Detective Moore, Hunt Moore and this is Detective Confer, Mitchell Confer.

GREENE: Hello, is there any problem? I was outta town stayin' at a friend's house and my Aunt called and told me she saw me on the t.v. screen and I was all excited. Me on the television. Then she told me I was on the City's Most Wanted show. I said, 'The City's Most Wanted show?' Everybody watches that. Man, I gotta get down there right away and take care a this. What goin' on? Is there any problem? I mean I know I got a lot of parking violations. Is that it? That damn meter maid at work always given me tickets. I can't leave my job to put money in the meter and I can't afford to put it in a lot so I gotta get the tickets. But I'll pay them. I swear. Am I talkin' to much, I always talk a lot when I'm nervous…

HUNT: Where do you work Mr. Greene?

GREENE: At the museum. I'm a maintenance man. Is this about parking violations?

HUNT: No, Mr. Greene, McKinley, can I call you Mac?

GREENE: Sure.

HUNT: No Mac, this is not about parking violations. In fact, after we're done, you give Mitchell your driver's license number and registration and he'll take care of them for you.

GREENE: Really. Thanks.

MITCHELL Our pleasure.

HUNT: We need your help, Mac. We need you to help us.

GREENE: Me help you? Well I don't know…

HUNT: Look Mac, Mr. Greene, lets cut to the chase. We know there's a warrant out for your arrest…

GREENE: Uh-huh…

HUNT: Driving with a revoked license…

GREENE: Uh-huh…

HUNT: Which is normally not a severe charge, but in your case with your record that could be a problem. We could make that go

men's scenes 173

away. And we can get you a new license. We just want to ask you questions and for you to be honest.

GREENE: Uh-huh. *(Pause.)* I'll do my best.

HUNT: I'm sure you will. Now, I don't know if you're aware, but last week a woman was murdered in your apartment building.

GREENE: Yeah. I know, the whole neighborhood knows. What a shame…

HUNT: And we, Detective Confer and myself would like to ask you some questions.

GREENE: Sure. I'll do my best because she was a nice lady, beautiful…

HUNT: Mr. Greene, she wasn't beautiful. She was ugly. Coyote ugly, but that's not the point. The point is she's dead. We have to find the person who did it. Do you know what Coyote ugly is, Mr. Greene?

GREENE: No.

HUNT: Well it's when you wake up in bed with a women under your arm who is so ugly that you want to chew off your arm to get out of bed rather than wake her up.

GREENE: Uh-huh?

HUNT: When a Coyote gets caught in a fur trap, Mr. Greene, the steel trap clamps shut on his leg and the coyote is trapped usually in three feet of snow to die a slow painful death. But that doesn't happen. Do you know why?

GREENE: No, I don't.

HUNT: Because the coyote chews his leg off. Because the coyote realizes that sometimes you have to sacrifice the limb to save the body.

GREENE: Uh-huh?

HUNT: Well, he realizes that in the long term, as horrible as it may seem, it's better to cut off your leg, than die.

GREENE: Oh…But I still don't understand what that has to do with me.

HUNT: Well, Mr. Greene, we need you to answer some questions, questions that could possibly lead to the capture of a murderer. Would you do that, answer some questions for me and Detective Confer?

GREENE: Sure.

HUNT: Mitchell, will you get Mr. Greene some coffee? Would you like some coffee, Mr. Greene?

GREENE: No. No thanks.

HUNT: Are you sure? It's no problem.

GREENE: No. I'm sure.

HUNT: Okay, Mr. Greene, as we already told you, we are in the process of investigating a murder. You look like a pretty swift guy. I mean, you ain't no dummy, right?

GREENE: No.

HUNT: Do you read, Mr. Greene?

GREENE: Sometimes, but I ain't too good at it.

HUNT: Do you read the newspapers? Keep on top of the news?

GREENE: No. I try to see the news on t.v., but…

HUNT: Good for you. The man who reads nothing is better educated than the man who reads only newspapers.

GREENE: I guess. Most days, I read the sports section.

HUNT: Really? So does Mitchell.

MITCHELL: Big Mets fan.

GREENE: Me too.

HUNT: Think they have a chance this year?

MITCHELL: They have a good chance every year.

GREENE: They got the pitching. But they always choke.

HUNT: Yeah. You're right. Middle of every season they go in the tank.

GREENE: I have a theory on that. You can have all the talent in the world, but if you don't have no heart, you got nothing.

HUNT: Well you seem like a pretty sharp guy, pretty observant. So tell me: We got this young girl. Everybody that she works with likes her.

GREENE: Uh-huh.

HUNT: No boyfriend. No lovers. She turns up dead in her apartment.

GREENE: Uh-huh.

HUNT: What do you think? Given those sets of circumstance, what do you think? I mean where do you even start. Where would you start on this one, Mr. Greene. *(Pause.)* Let me tell you something. We do one hundred twenty cases a month. The damn Post calls this Dodge City. They're wrong. It's worse. At least in Dodge City you could defend yourself. Here, you defend yourself, you're going to jail. Like you're the criminal. Geez. This city is the Alamo with street signs.

GREENE: Uh-huh.

HUNT: Well, in most of our cases we get help from the outside. Somewhere out there. Somebody calls up and says try this or do that, or a lot of times, I use my wife. Mitchell uses his girl-friends. Whatever one he happens to be with at the time. Know what I mean? *(They laugh.)* I might run something by my wife and she might say, "Didn't you ever think of this, or that." So, given our set of circumstances what would you look for?

GREENE: What did she die of? Can you tell me that?

MITCHELL: Cause of death was…

HUNT: Mr. Greene, there are a million ways of dying in this city, but only one way of being dead. You tell me what you think. You be the homicide investigator.

MITCHELL: Some theory.

HUNT: Give us your theory…

GREENE: But why? I'm not a cop. I don't know anything…

HUNT: Mr. Greene, that's exactly why we need you to help us. We need an outside perspective. Someone who knew her, but knows nothing about the case.

GREENE: Like a police dog.

HUNT: What?

GREENE: A police dog knows what he's lookin' for, but he don't know why.

HUNT: Exactly.

GREENE: Okay.

HUNT: Okay so given our set of circumstances, what would you say? What do you think happened?

GREENE: Well, I figure it has to be someone that knows her.

176 men's scenes

HUNT: Okay. That's good. That's a good theory. Why do you say that?

GREENE: 'Cause I didn't think she is, was the type of person to just bring anybody home. 'Cause I never seen her dates stay over.

HUNT: Good. You're giving us input that we don't have knowledge of, and this is good.

GREENE: But see, I might have a whole wrong opinion of her.

HUNT: You know her better than we do. We don't even know the girl, right? When you think about it, right?

GREENE: But you got all these other people's opinions too, the people she works with, right? So you know something about her, right?

HUNT: Aren't you different at work than you are at home?

GREENE: No.

HUNT: Same guy, huh?

GREENE: Pretty much. Oh, I bullshit a lot more at work.

HUNT: Everybody does. But the people we're talking to were her friends so they're giving biased opinions of her, really. Favoring her. They're not going to tell us if she had any bad sides to her…

GREENE: Well, I might be biased, too, because of the fact that I was attracted to her.

HUNT: Was that a fact?

GREENE: Yeah. And so I don't want you to think she was an angel because I was attracted to her. That's stupid, sick really because people ain't angels…

HUNT: That's for sure…

MITCHELL: Who's perfect?

HUNT: Who's perfect? That's why we're here on earth. *(They laugh.)*

GREENE: At first I thought it had to be somebody that knew her just because I wouldn't imagine that she'd bring somebody home that she didn't know. I know she wasn't like that.

HUNT: Okay. Good. Thank you. That's good. Thank you.

GREENE: The other part I heard, and I don't really know if I should tell you… *(Hunt and Mitchell turn around and stare at*

Greene. Greene stares back at them. Pause.) I don't know if it's true or not.

HUNT: Well why don't you tell us and we'll decide if it's true or not?

GREENE: Okay. I heard from one a her friends that she and her friends went out on Friday night and she wanted to go to someplace that the others didn't want to go to. Some concert, rock 'n' roll band. Hard rock band. So she went by herself. Maybe she met a guy there, right? She gets a date with him on Saturday night…

HUNT: Okay…

GREENE: No. This is stupid. This is really…

HUNT: Doesn't sound stupid to me…

MITCHELL: It's never stupid.

HUNT: We wouldn't be talking to you if we thought what you said was stupid.

GREENE: Okay, okay. Well as many people that come and go in this city…

HUNT: It's a transient city.

GREENE: Yeah. And this guy could have been from anywhere. He might have went back to her place with her. *(Pause.)*

HUNT: Okay. *(Pause.)*

GREENE: He could have, might have killed her and took her car to the airport and split.

HUNT: That's good. That's good thinking.

GREENE: I think it's stupid. *(He laughs.)*

HUNT: Why?

GREENE: 'Cause that's something you'd see in the goddamn movies, you know.

HUNT: Why would that be stupid? You know what? Those movies—some of them are actually pretty true. They hire on ex-cops as technical advisors.

MITCHELL: Some of them are actual cases. You ever see Quincy? Now that show, that guy don't talk no mumbo jumbo. If you sat there with a medical encyclopedia…

GREENE: Yeah. I guess.

HUNT: All right, so what do you think happened in the house? We know it's just your opinion, right? But tell us what you think might have happened.

GREENE: I don't think she fucked him. *(They laugh.)*

HUNT: But she certainly got fucked. *(They laugh harder.)*

GREENE: And then he killed her and left.

HUNT: Simple. Good. How? What is your opinion of what happened? So far it's good. Very good. So what do you think happened?

GREENE: What do I think happened? How he killed her?

HUNT: However. Whatever you think. I don't…you know.

GREENE: I don't know how he'd kill her. 'Cause you wouldn't have sex with a girl and then kill her unless you was crazy…

HUNT: Well it's not nutty. Happens more than you think.

GREENE: Really?

HUNT: Really. He was probably upset…

GREENE: Yeah. Really pissed off…

HUNT: That's right. He doesn't have to be nutty. She could have set him off wrong, you know. Don't have to be his fault.

GREENE: Yeah, yeah, right.

HUNT: Right? She could have caused the problem. *(Hunt leans over the side of the desk and puts his arm around Greene and quietly and confidently speaks.)* There have been several women in the past that have been known to piss off guys. *(They laugh.)*

GREENE: Yeah, right, okay. He's got the attitude I'm gonna get this bitch, right?

HUNT: Because he's been rejected.

MITCHELL: Rejected. Wow. That sucks.

HUNT: You're damn right that sucks.

GREENE: Damn right.

HUNT: Yeah. The guy probably spends the whole night talkin' to her about shit he don't give a damn about. About people he don't give a damn about. Spendin' money on food and drinks and whatever. Probably more than a hundred bucks. She's wearing an attractive outfit, right? The whole nine-yards and… *(Greene cuts him off.)*

GREENE: …and she rejects him. Right. Shit.

HUNT: Okay. Then what?

GREENE: So then he rapes her, but then he's gotta kill her or he's going to be put in court for rape.

MITCHELL: Right.

GREENE: But he likes her, so how can he kill her? How?

HUNT: Maybe it was an accident. A crime of deep passion.

GREENE: *(Slight doubt.)* Yeah, right, okay.

MITCHELL: Maybe it happened while he was trying to rape her. He was just trying to hold her still.

HUNT: Oh, I see. You're saying he strangles her, right? How does he strangle her? From the front, behind, or what?

GREENE: Front…

HUNT: So what would he use? One hand or two hands. What would your theory be?

GREENE: Two.

HUNT: Good. Stand up for a minute. *(Greene stands up and Hunt motions for Mitchell to come center stage.)* Okay, now I want to try something. He is her. All right…

GREENE: He is her?

HUNT: He is the woman that was killed.

GREENE: But why? I don't…

HUNT: I need you to show me your theory. To work out the logistics.

GREENE: But, really, this is stupid. I don't…

HUNT: Mr. Greene, Mac, we need your help. We have families we want to go home too. The quicker we clear this up, the quicker we can go home.

GREENE: Well, I guess…

HUNT: Okay, so he's facing her and using two hands, right?

GREENE: Right. *(Greene faces Mitchell and after some prodding puts his hands up to Mitchell's neck. He acts out each succeeding suggestion, at first reluctantly then with increasing enthusiasm and intensity.)*

HUNT: Okay, two hands, right? And what's she doing?

GREENE: Probably trying to claw his eyes out. *(He laughs.)*

180 men's scenes

HUNT: Now, how do you deal with that?

MITCHELL: Yeah. How do you deal with that?

GREENE: He would have to try to hold…

HUNT: Show me! *(Greene does it.)*

GREENE: …her back, or something with one hand while…

HUNT: Right. This is good. One hand, right?

GREENE: *(Voice strained while holding Mitchell off.)* Uh-huh.

HUNT: Very good. Let's keep going. So he's holding her from hitting him with one hand—and he's choking her with the other? Is that what you're telling me?

(Greene continues holding off Mitchell.)

GREENE: Uh-huh. *(Greene is starting to get into the action, forcing Mitchell over the desk.)* Uh-huh!

(Hunt moves in closer.)

HUNT: And then what happens! What happens? What if she kicks him?

GREENE: Kicks him in the balls!

HUNT: Yes!

(Mitchell attempts to kick Greene in the groin, but Greene blocks him.)

GREENE: You've got to knock her out, damn it!

HUNT: Yeah?

GREENE: Yeah! He's got to knock her out somehow!

HUNT: He's got to knock her out because she's resisting.

GREENE: Right!

HUNT: I think you're right. So he picks something up, right? And what does he do?

GREENE: He grabs something…anything…a vase…anything…

HUNT: A vase. Why? Why a vase?

GREENE: He has to hit her over the head. He's scared! He's got no choice.

HUNT: And then what happens? Where are they now?

GREENE: In the living room.

HUNT: Okay, keep working with me, now. They're in the living room. And then what happens? *(Greene has his back to the audience and Hunt while holding Mitchell over the desk with great strength.)* What happens next? *(No response.)* Come on! Don't stop, now! Work with me, baby! What happens next? *(Greene straightens up from the desk and slowly turns around to face Hunt and the audience. His physical and psychological appearance have changed and he is clearly caught up in the situation. Mitchell slowly gets up off the desk rubbing his head and neck. His clothes are even more disheveled. He walks to a corner of the room and sits down and lights a cigarette. Hunt walks over to Greene. More calm.)* What happens next?

GREENE: She's…dead.

HUNT: Right.

GREENE: And then…he realizes what he's…done and he takes her upstairs.

HUNT: Right. He takes her upstairs. Where does he bring her?

GREENE: To the bed.

HUNT: Good. Very good. What's he do?

GREENE: What's he do?

HUNT: Uh-huh. When he puts her in the…Does he put her in the bed? Does he put her on the floor? What does he do?

GREENE: Puts her on the bed. Puts her in the bed!

HUNT: Then what?

GREENE: Takes off all her clothes and puts the covers over her. *(Greene is now lost in acting out the situation.)*

HUNT: How does he put her in bed? What's she doing?

GREENE: She's sleeping…

HUNT: Okay. What would you put her on? Her si…

GREENE: Her back.

HUNT: On her back? On her…?

GREENE: In bed?

HUNT: Yeah. No. When you put her in bed, where would you put her? How?

GREENE: I'd lay her down.

HUNT: Where?

GREENE: Where?

HUNT: Yeah. On her side sleeping? Put her on her side sleeping.

GREENE: No. I'd put her on her back sleeping.

HUNT: Put her on her back sleeping?

GREENE: Don't you sleep on your back?

HUNT: No.

GREENE: *(To Mitchell.)* Don't you? *(Mitchell doesn't respond.)* Well, I don't sleep on my side. I sleep on my back.

HUNT: *(Patiently.)* Well, what other way would you put her? *(Pause.)*

GREENE: Face down?

HUNT: Right. Exactly. Face down.

GREENE: Yeah, but I really would put her on her back.

(Mitchell excitedly springs up from his chair and moves toward Greene. Hunt steps in front of him before he can reach Greene and stops Mitchell.)

MITCHELL: Would you really…

(Hunt stares Mitchell back into his chair and turns to Greene.)

HUNT: *(Calmly.)* Would you leave her battered face up? Think about it? Would you really want to look into the eyes of a dead person?

GREENE: Oh yeah.

HUNT: On her back? How?

GREENE: No. I'd definitely put her on her stomach.

(Hunt looks at Mitchell and then nods his head.)

HUNT: You'd put her on her what?

GREENE: Stomach.

HUNT: *(Calm.)* Sure. You'd put her on her stomach. Right. That's what you would do. Put her on her stomach.

GREENE: Yeah. You wouldn't want her looking at you. No way. Believe me.

HUNT: No, you wouldn't want a dead woman looking at you. No way. You hit the nail right on the head. Let me shake your hand. *(Hunt walks over to Greene and extends his hand. Greene is motionless.)* Shake my hand. *(No response.)* Shake my hand. *(Hunt shakes Greene's limp hand and then moves away from him and straightens out his suit. He looks at Mitchell who is standing in the corner. Hunt nods at him and smiles and then exits the stage. Greene looks around the stage and is lost. He stands up and then sits back down. He is lost. Mitchell walks over to the desk and sits on it. Lights out.)*

DETAIL OF A LARGER WORK

Lisa Dillman

dramatic, 3 Men

Ed (79) once a great artist, now suffering from Parkinson's and emphysema, Zach (27) an ambitious photographer and Duane (50s) an old friend of Ed's, now dead.

Scene: San Miguel de Allende, Guanajuato, Mexico

> *Duane allowed Zach to chronicle his slow and painful death from AIDS in a series of photographs. Now in Mexico on another assignment, Zach and his girlfriend pay a courtesy call on Ed and his wife, who live nearby. Zach becomes fascinated with Ed, and decides to do another series of photos on the twilight of the ailing painter's life. Here, Ed collapses in his studio and has an unexpected encounter with the deceased Duane.*

○ ○ ○

ED: These days I'm concentrating mostly on what you might call natural forms. *(Beat.)* I've been thinking a lot about those wha'da'ya'call'em trees down in the *el centro.*

ZACH: The laurels?

ED: Laurels, that's right. Thinking about sitting in that square down there and watching the world go by a while. And studying the laurels. There's things an artist sees from time to time. And they make clear something he's known for as long as he's known anything. Only he never knew before that he knew it. You following me? *(He coughs, spits into a hankie. Beat.)* Last time I was down there a bird pooped right on my head. Big old stream of bird-fling. Copious. I looked up and that bird was way the hell and gone up in the branches. Shaking her tail feathers at me. Couldn't see the top of her.

Just the ass end and the tail feathers. Funny feeling. Dense, those trees. Lot of…mystery up in there.

ZACH: I'm going to need a little more light here, Ed. *(Ed pulls a string, and harsh white light fills the area.)* Would you like to show me some of your work?

ED: Oh. Why, sure. *(He continues to stand there. Zach takes his picture.)* Now hold on there. No fair. I wasn't ready.

ZACH: I keep telling you, Ed, I don't want you to pose.

ED: You don't want a flock of pictures of some old jamoke with a dopey look on his mug.

ZACH: I want pictures of you and Vanessa in the environment you've built here. And whatever look you have on your mug at any given time is *fine*. As long as you don't put it there just for me. The first day I shot Duane he was mugging and prancing and winking and leering till I wanted to throw up.

ED: Well, now, do you know? That used to be my nickname for ol' Duane. Used to call him Prancer. But he liked it, so I had to give it up. Hah.

ZACH: I didn't think I'd ever get him to quit. But within forty-eight hours he'd got so used to me—to the camera—he completely stopped any kind of posing. That's what made the series effective. I need to become just another part of your life.

ED: You enjoy that, do you?

ZACH: Taking pictures?

ED: Moving into people's lives.

ZACH: *(Pulls away from the camera and looks directly at Ed.)* I do. Yes.

ED: That's important. *(Zach takes his picture.)* You have to find what you enjoy doing. And do that. Full out. Till you croak. Otherwise you turn into some kind of damn Mr. Magoo. *(Zach takes his picture.)* That's why I keep on painting. You don't know. You can't even imagine what it's like to get old. Hah. *(Clears his throat raspily.)* I've got the emphysema. Vannie tell you?

ZACH: No. She didn't. I'm sorry.

186 men's scenes

ED: Well. Don't ever get it. That's what I say to you. *(Ed goes on another brief coughing jag. When he is finished, Zach speaks.)*

ZACH: So. You want to show me some of your work?

ED: Why, sure. *(Beat.)* You want to see some of my older work?

ZACH: Whatever. *(Ed begins pulling some stretched canvases out of a storage unit. Zach watches through the camera. Takes a picture.)* Careful, Ed. Let me give you a hand there.

ED: That damn Vannie's been giving you the impression that I'm some kind of invalid, but there are a *few* things I still know how to do. *(Ed pulls out a large canvas. His breathing is very labored. He puts the painting down suddenly.)*

ZACH: Are you okay, Ed? You don't sound so good.

(Ed tries to answer, but instead goes into a violent attack of coughing. He gasps desperately for air and staggers against the table. Reverberated sound of the camera clicking wildly; then tinny music. The sound suddenly stops and a pool of red light comes up on Ed, leaning heavily against the table. On top of the table sits Duane. Zach is in darkness or heavy shadow, wherever he was standing before.)

ED: Say? *(Beat.)* Ahh, now dammit. I think I'm *hurt* here. *(Beat. Ed turns slowly and focuses on Duane, who steps down from the table.)*

DUANE: Well, old man.

ED: What the hell—?

DUANE: It's *me,* Ed.

ED: Duane. I don't want you here.

DUANE: Well, that's a heck of a note. Why not? We're friends, aren't we?

ED: We *were* friends. That's all done now.

DUANE: Why's that?

ED: Because. Ahh, come on, you. You *know* why it's done.

DUANE: Because I'm dead?

ED: Aren't you dead?

DUANE: Oh, I'm dead.

ED: See now? *(Beat.)* How *is* that?

DUANE: Being dead? Ah. It's not so bad. You get used to it. *(Beat.)* I always liked it here. I never got to spend enough time. With you two. You and Vannie.

ED: Well. Now's not a good time. We've got…we've got house-guests and…Zach? *(Ed peers around him.)*

DUANE: He's there. *(A white light comes up on Zach, frozen, his camera in front of his face.)* He can't hear you. *(The light on Zach goes out.)*

ED: What do you want? I think I'm hurt.

DUANE: You are. You're hurt. You're old and you're sick. And now you're hurt. Some day, huh?

ED: Vannie!

DUANE: God, I've missed you, Ed. Vannie too. I've *missed* you.

ED: Well, now, Duane, it's not that we don't—didn't—but, really now…

DUANE: It's time to relax, Ed. Relax and let go. *(Ed struggles for words but cannot speak.)* I know. You never thought it'd be today, did you? Well, listen. I thought it would be *every* day for almost two years and it *still* took me by surprise. But then, I didn't get an old age. Maybe you're more ready. *(He watches Ed a moment. Ed stares back at him, stricken.)* I guess not.

ED: You're a *memory.* Duane. That's all you are.

DUANE: What else is there? *(Laughs.)* When you woke up today, did you feel…something? Anything? It didn't feel like *the* day, did it? Or did it?

ED: I don't know…I—

DUANE: Same old morning breath, am I right? The sour teeth in a cup by the bed. The ache in the knees. Same old unrecognizable face in the mirror. Same every-morning questions. To shave or not to shave. When'd I get so *old?* Hearing yourself breathing like a seal. Nothing special…whispering to you. *(Beat.)*

ED: You had a painting of mine, didn't you, Duane?

DUANE: You're a terrific painter, my friend.

ED: Think so?

DUANE: Oh, God. *Terrific.*

ED: Which one did you have?

DUANE: *Valle Grande at Four P.M.* Do you remember? Deep greens and blues. So peaceful. You could almost pretend it was under water. If you didn't know, I mean. If you'd never seen Valle Grande.

ED: It was a good one, huh?

DUANE: That painting…It was the last thing I saw, Ed. It hung right in front of my bed. I opened my eyes as wide as they would go. I went *inside* that painting and I lay myself down in that shadowy valley. *Valle Grande at Four P.M.* And it was like coming home at the close of a too-long day. I'm going to tell you something. Everyone who's ever seen a painting of yours has got a little piece of you. Inside. *(Pats his chest; beat.)* But, you know…

ED: What?

DUANE: Those laurel trees. There's still the laurel trees.

ED: In the *el centro!* Oh, those trees, Duane. They've been there…for*ever,* don't you think? Before the primordial ooze, there those trees were. When I came through this little burg all those years back, and I got a look at those trees…And I *never* got them right. Must've painted them fifty times. More. You know, if I had to pick one thing…

DUANE: Well, then that's what's important.

ED: What is?

DUANE: Eternity, man.

ED: Come again?

DUANE: The laurels, Ed. The laurel trees.

ED: Well, what do you know. *(Slowly Ed's breathing becomes labored and raspy again. The red light fades as the studio lights pop on. The effect should be jarring. Duane has vanished. Zach moves toward Ed.)*

ZACH: Ed? Ed! *(He moves clumsily to the door and begins to shout.)* Vanessa! Chloe! I need help here! *(Zach again moves back toward Ed. Looks toward the door once, then takes several fast photographs. The lights fade. End of Act I.)*

THE ENDS OF THE EARTH
David Lan

dramatic, 2 Men
Daniel (30) a British geologist and Pintilje (40) a dentist-turned-freedom fighter.

Scene: Somewhere in the Balkans

> *When the peace of his valley is threatened by the construction of a large dam, Pintilje leads his people on a dangerous mission to destroy the construction site. Daniel has worked on the dam project in the past, but has returned to the Balkans in search of a seer whom he believes has the power to cure his terminally ill daughter. Pintilje captures Daniel during their raid, and here these two very different men discover that grief is the great equalizer.*

> *(Pintilje comes in. He wears camouflage and carries a rifle. He speaks to the soldiers. They go out. He looks at each of the men in turn. He sees Daniel.)*

Pintilje: Ah. *(He reaches into a pocket of his coat, takes out a mobile telephone, looks at it, laughs, takes off the coat. Of the coat:)* Whose is this?
> *(He speaks to the Guard who takes the coat and goes out. The telephone rings. He answers it—furious. He barks orders, then puts down the phone.)*
> They told me all you foreigners had run away. You are from where? From America?

Daniel: From England.

Pintilje: From the pastures and meadows of England.
> *(The Guard brings in a second coat. Pintilje takes it, puts it on, reaches into a pocket, takes out a pistol. He laughs, then shouts at the Guard who runs out.)*

(of the pistol:) This is from England. Very delicate, very light. So we pay big money. So we shoot, the trigger jams, we die. So I wish to ask you a question: in what do you people believe? Can you answer? *(He drinks from his hip flask.)* In what do you believe? We begged you: stop, stop, stop, stop, stop, stop, stop building this dam. What can we do? We climb the mountain, surround your camp. Your English, your Americans—a helicopter flies up, away they go. Who remains? These poor fools, these beasts of burden who dig your trenches and carry your stones. Do they care about land? No, they are herders of sheep. You flood a million of their acres, so what? But we, we who live below, we who will lose control of our water in our river, we cry to the government: you're our father, we are in pain, dry our tears. They are too far away to hear us. We don't wish to hurt anyone. *(The Guard has brought a third coat. Pintilje puts it on, reaches into a pocket, takes out papers.)*

(To Daniel:) Is it you who wrote these?

Daniel: Yes.

Pintilje: So it comes down to a simple question: is what you write true?

(The phone rings. Pintilje answers, speaks, puts it down. He reads Daniel's papers at random. A long moment passes.)

You were found wandering with a guide in the mountains. Were you told that place was outside the war zone? *(Silence. He tears up some of the papers.)* This is no good! None of this is any good! You must do it again! *(He reads.)* You have written why you came to our country the first time. Why did you return? Is it here? Show me. Where can I read it?

Daniel: I didn't have time to write everything.

Pintilje: You have it now. I am a generous man. I give it to you.

Daniel: The reason I came back was to find…

Pintilje: The old man.

Daniel: He isn't that old. I don't think he's much older than I am. Maybe he is.

Pintilje: You were following his orders?

Daniel: He didn't give me orders.

Pintilje: *(reads)* 'He ordered me to give up smoking.'

Daniel: I didn't write that.

Pintilje: 'He ordered me to come back to this country.' Wait. Don't speak. 'He ordered me to build the dam.' My friend, there are a hundred thousand rivers, there are a hundred thousand valleys. Why choose ours? Answer please.

Daniel: A survey carried out for your government suggested that was the best place for it.

Pintilje: 'Suggested'? You were not sure?

Daniel: We were quite sure.

Pintilje: 'Quite'?

Daniel: Absolutely.

Pintilje: Ah! 'Absolutely'. That sounds like our government. You see, my friend, the Hajda Valley is the most beautiful place God left his fingerprints on. It is our duty to protect it. It was in the Hajda Valley Anton Lubovic fought his extraordinary battle.

Daniel: You told me all about Anton Lubovic.

Pintilje: I did? *(He stares at Daniel, then hands him his flask.)* Your face I know. Orientate me.

Daniel: The square at Novi Mesto. You told me about the statue under the tree. You offered to take me to the airport. *(He sniffs the flask.)* We drank this.

Pintilje: And did you like it?

Daniel: Yes.

Pintilje: Then drink.

(Daniel drinks.)

What did I tell you?

Daniel: That Anton Lubovic wrote many fine songs. What a warrior he was. His sword. His horse. How you'd like to climb onto it, you and your sons.

Pintilje: My sons?

Daniel: It's all there.

Pintilje: You wrote about my sons? Show me. What did you write? *(He laughs.)* I told you nothing about them. How many do I have? Five? Or four?

Daniel: *(showing him)* Peter and Karoli.

(Pintilje reads. He speaks to the Guard who answers.)

Pintilje: He says you haven't eaten today. You've had at least a cup of coffee? *(He speaks to the Guard who answers.)* I'm sorry. These animals have drunk it all. Well, I did my best for you. *(Pause.)* I told you Anton Lubovic fought an extraordinary battle but what I didn't tell you is: he was defeated. He lost everything. Even so he went on fighting. Why? Do you know? Because he was a man. What else can a man do? Moreover, and this is what is hard for you to understand, sometimes you have to lose to win. Listen to me. There is a battle over a piece of land, you fight, you win. The land is yours. Time passes. Somwone offers a good price for it. You sell, why shouldn't you? Or, or there is a battle, you fight, you lose. You die. Your blood soaks into the earth. It's yours for ever. No one can ever take it from you. In the Hajda Valley thousands of our brothers were slaughtered.

Nico: Eight hundred years ago! You see? They're crazy, these people. This was eight hundred years ago!

Pintilje: Eight hundred years. How time flies.

Nico: Igor, these people, they're nothing to me. This man wanted to find an old fellow. I showed him the way. I help anyone. I help you. With food. I serve you food. Look. Brotik, sonno salvi. I serve anyone! Everyone!

Pintilje: *(laughing)* No, no, no, no, no. The Hajda valley. Dig its soil, your spade sticks. Why? The mud is my tears mixed with my skin.

(An explosion.)

Soon of your dam there will remain nothing.

Nico: Igor!

Pintilje: Sh! Look at this. this is interesting. yes. Here we are. Sally. Little Sally, your daughter. Yes, sh! Let me read. Interesting.

(After a moment, he speaks to the Guard who takes out a packet of cigarettes and a box of matches and hands them to Pintilje. Pintilje lights a cigarette, offers cigarettes and

matches to a man who takes them, lights up, passes them on. All the men light up except Daniel. They are passed to the Guard who lights up and hands them to Pintilje who chuckles. The men smoke. In the distance: a burst of machine-gun fire.)

In this country you could make very good tests of the dangers of smoking. For us thirty, fourty a day—nothing. *(He speaks to a man who answers.)* Sixty! And look how strong he is. That's how we are. We smoke, we drink, we die in the arms of our wives. Have one. *(Daniel doesn't move.)* So now I understand everything. He didn't order you to build the dam, he didn't order you to return, he didn't order you to give up smoking.

Daniel: I'd struggled for years to give up. When he said what he said I was able to. That's all.

Pintilje: So you are free to do as you choose? Good. then as an acquaintance, even a friend, I invite you. Join me.
(Daniel takes a cigarette, puts it back.)

Daniel: Alright. He ordered me to give up smoking.

Pintilje: At last we know who we are. One of our enemies gives you an order, you obey. Now I'm ordering you. *(Silence.)* How is little Sally? You don't know. You've had no news for one, two weeks. Let me see your eyes. Show them to me!
(After a moment, he speks to the Guard who offers Daniel a cigarette. Danile doesn't move.)

Daniel: Why are you doing this?

Pintilje: You believe if you smoke your daughter dies? Is that what you believe?
(Daniel takes a cigarette, lights it, coughs, chokes, stubs it out. Silence.)
And we are the ignorant savages. We behave without logic, without reason. Take one! Smoke it! Do it! *(Daniel takes a cigarette.)* Put it in your mouth! *(Daniel puts it in his mouth.)* Must I tell you everything?

Daniel: *(takes the cigarette out of his mouth)* I thought my daughter was dying. I could do nothing. The one time of my life I really needed to be strong—

Pintilje: You were weak. Be weak again. For me.

Daniel: I do not believe if I smoke she'll die.

Pintilje: It's what you wrote. Look! But if you don't believe it, do it! Why not!

Daniel: All he said to me…It was a metaphor. I was enslaved by a wrong way of looking at the world. By guilt. By habits of mind that were stale. I was blind. He showed me my life's in my own hands. All I have to do is take control of one, even one part, not do one thing I long to do, sacrifice even one thing…and I'll be free. He helped me. Why did I come back? To thank him. No. That's only part of it. I came because… *(Silence.)* What did I write there? *(Silence.)* Where's the fucking thing? *(He finds the cigarette in his hand. It has gone out.)* Cheap tobacco. (He relights it.) Oh God, I can do it. I'm free. *(He brings the cigarette to his lips, throws it down.)* You'll have to shoot me.

Pintilje: You? Not you.

(He speaks to the Guard who goes out. He comes in pushing a Prisoner with a sack over his head. Pintilje shouts at the Prisoner, shouts again. the Guard hits the Prisoner, shouts at him. The Prisoner exposes his upper body. Pintilje speaks. The Prisoner takes his shirt off. Pintilje speaks, then shouts. The Prisoner lets his trousers fall.)

God is great. Don't you think so? Look what he made. Strong. Beautiful. He is going to die for what he's done. Maybe you can save him. (He points the pistol at the Prisoner.) One, two three.

(He speaks. the Guard puts a cigarette in Daniel's mouth, lights a match.)

One. Oh, my friend, it would be just one tiny sin. Don't you know, a man can commit a thousand and even so God says 'Come over here, beloved, sit on the side of the sheep.' Two. These men, one of these, maybe this one, went to my village, killed my sons, my Peter, my Karoli.

Daniel: Why?

Pintilje: Why?

Daniel: Why did they kill them?

Pintilje: I'm only their father. Why ask me? You build a dam. There's fighting. They must die. Now so must be. Do you want to see him?

(He speaks to the Guard who pulls the sack off the Prisoner's head. It is Takic. He has been badly beaten. Gunfire nearby.)

Daniel: Jesus.

Pintilje: You know him? Is he a good man? What did he do in his life? Did he curse his mother? Did he envy his neighbour? Did he steal? Did he commit adultery?

Takic: *(to Daniel)* Hey! You! Rabbit! Rabbit! You like live in mountain? *(He laughs. He rubs his crotch.)* Old man. Old man. This is old man. What you got for him?

(Pintilje speaks to the Guard who lights a match.)

Pintilje: Myself I long to love everybody. In my heart is room for the world. Who do you love? Your daughter and that's it. *(The match goes out. The Guard lights another.)* One, two…One, two…Please. Do it. My sons are dead. They killed my sons! Your daughter is alive. Why should yours live and mine die? Let her die too. Let everyone die. Smoke. Help me.

(A long silence. Then Daniel takes cigarettes and matches from the Guard, lights one, gives it to Pintilje. He lights another. He smokes. The gunfire stops. The wind continues to blow.)

Now we're equal. We're both childless, both alone. Good. So, tell me about science. You are a geologist, yes? The earth will last for ever. Is that true? I think no. I think the earth is a piece of God's shit. Dry. Hard. Flying through space. Which is dark, which is empty. Except for the wind.

(The phone rings. After a moment the Guard answers it. He speaks to Pintilje. There is a joyful bubbub among the men. Takic begins to sing a jubilant song. Pintilje shoots him.)

FIRST ON LINE
Albert Verdesca

serio-comedic, 2 Men
Gar (20–40) a man waiting on line, and Bernie (60s) a man who wants to be first on line.

Scene: a line

> *Mild-mannered Gar is caught off-guard by the volatile Bernie, who will do almost anything to be first on line.*

> *(Lights up. Gar enters stage right. He is dressed casually in summer clothes. In one hand he carries a large cloth shopping bag. Under his other arm is a folded picnic blanket. He is listening to music through earphones. He walks directly to the sign-post, spreads the blanket on the ground and begins to lay out all the makings of a picnic from the bag, wine, bread, cheese, etc. After a brief time, Bernie enters rapidly from stage right. He is heavier than Gar and is dressed in what appears to have been a nice suit but is now worn and tattered. He wears a white dress shirt but no tie. He is out of breath and at the sight of Gar becomes agitated and starts to move and pace with intensity and impatience. After a few moments he speaks.)*

BERNIE: Hey. *(There is no response. Louder.)* Hey, mister. *(Still no response. He shouts.)* Hey! *(Softer and fired in rapid succession.)* Hey-hey-hey-hey-hey-hey-hey.
> *(Gar looks up at Bernie and removes his headphones. We can hear the choral movement of Beethoven's Ninth Symphony emitting from them. He reacts very calmly.)*

GAR: Are you speaking to me?
> *(Bernie shakes his head rapidly up and down in assent while plugging his ears with his fingers.)*

BERNIE: *(Shouting.)* I can't hear you. Turn that down or you'll be deaf soon.

GAR: *(Turning the volume down.)* Why are you shouting? I can hear you.

BERNIE: Are you an anti-Semite?

GAR: What?

BERNIE: You're listening to German music. That Nazi son-of-a-bitch.

GAR: Beethoven wasn't a Nazi.

BERNIE: *(Shouting.)* Not him, you putz! *(Gar turns the volume up, puts the headphones on and continues with his picnic, ignoring Bernie. A few moments go by. Louder.)* Excuse me!
(Gar looks at him but doesn't respond. Loud.) Pardon me, you palindromic poop. Hey! *(Gar removes his headphones.)*

GAR: What is it? What do you want?

BERNIE: You're in my place.

GAR: Excuse me.

BERNIE: My place in line. You're sitting in my spot.

GAR: Your spot? There was no one here. I took my place in line, so here I am.

BERNIE: *(Trying to be calm.)* I can see that but there has been a mistake. I'm always first in line. I'm sure you wouldn't mind switching. I'm always first.

GAR: I'm sorry. Today I'm first.
(Bernie starts to become agitated.)

BERNIE: I had no control. It tocked but didn't tick. I lost track. It flew out the window. I don't know where it went.

GAR: Would you like a plum?

BERNIE: Oh, sure What is it this time? Dates of the allied troops movements? Anna Frank's hiding place? What is your reward for this information? Free passage for your family? A few crumbs of bread? I despise you and your kind. Cowards—and where are you now. Huh. Tell me Mr. Symphony in d minor—Mr. Pathetique I'll tell you were you are. You're on this side of the line; when what you really want is to be in there. You're a nobody! A putz!

GAR: What about you? Why are you here?

BERNIE: I'm here for a different reason I'm here to be first. I never go inside when my number is called. I have no desire to enter, ever. I only come to be number one. I have to be first. I've always been first. I never settle for second. I was the first in my class from the very first day I entered school. In college I was Phi Beta Kappa. I graduated medical school at nineteen years old, Alpha Omega Alpha, but they wouldn't let me practice because of my age. My father wanted me to be a Rabbi. My mother wanted me to be a cantor. Yoselle Rosenblatt she said—better than Caruso. What did they know? My mind was bursting out of my cranium for knowledge. I wanted to know everything. They shipped me to freedom while they went to their Gotterdammerung in the ovens of Treblinka, and for what? So that anti-Semitic bastards can get to be first on line, *(Stressing the words.)* by accident. *(Gar doesn't respond but only looks at him.)* What do you want? Autographs? I have plenty. Babe Ruth, Ignaz Paderewski, Enrico Fermi. Are you a fagela? I've got Oscar Wilde, Dag Hammerskjold, J. Edgar Hoover. What shall I trade you for your seat?

GAR: I'm not interested

BERNIE: You want cash? I've got plenty. How much? *(No response.)* You don't like money? So why did you take? In uniforms they came, with guns, and took. No asking—not like a schnorrer—with force—just take. Your kind. Money, power, possessions—but not the mind. The artistry and brilliance of the mind was not yours to take. You could destroy it but not possess it. So what did you have but your own inferior genes—sheep—being led by a suicidal shepherd. You have strength but I have universal genius. *(Pause.)* You want Shakespeare? I've got Shakespeare. Now there was a genius and a goyim—but you never know. There was probably some Jewish blood—on his mother's side, of course. *(Pause.)* So, what'll it be? How much? *(He takes out a checkbook and a pen.)* Will you take a check? The money's good.

GAR: Look, I'm not really sure how to get through to you but I don't need anything and I don't want anything, except to sit here first in line, and listen to Beethoven.

BERNIE: Oh, sure, what do you know putzala? I'm surprised you're not listening to Wagner or Mendelson, you traitor. I bet you own a Mercedes, you bastard. I know you. 1936—I saw you in Munich, in the stadium. You can't go far. It's all on film. Riefenstahl—Olympiad—you were shocked by that schwartzer from America who refused to salute. I thought you would choke on your lachshincken and pinkelwurst *(Gar puts his headphones back on and continues to eat and drink.)* What kind of wine is that? Rhine wine? Sure, sure— fermented by the Rhine maidens who are guarding their precious gold. Where are the hops, you Kraut? Huh? No beer? Huh. Bier auf wein, dass lasse sein, wein auf bier, dass rat ich dir. Any good Kraut knows that.

GAR: I'm not German.

BERNIE: Right Sure You're not German and it never happened. What about Otto Frank and the diary, huh. You think he made it up so he could publish a book? What about the shoes? All those shoes! You think maybe it was a warehouse sale at Bergen-Belsen? Go ahead Judas, deny.

GAR: *(Removing headphones.)* Look, I'm not German. I've never been to Germany. I'm really sorry about the inhumanity of the holocaust but I had nothing to do with it. As a matter of fact, I'm a pacifist.

BERNIE: Well, let me tell you something, Mr. Butterfly lover who never squooshed a caterpillar in his life—I'm dying here. Do you understand? You're killing me and I know you don't want to do that. Where would you hide? Argentina? They only eat meat there. You wouldn't like it. They'll track you down. You'll be arrested. The trial won't be easy on you. Ladies and Gentlemen of the jury, the defendant is charged with the murder of six million and one Jews. We are only interested in the last case—that of one Bernie Gittelstein who took his own life by running in front of a bus because the defendant…What's your name?

GAR: Gar.

BERNIE: Gar? Gar what? Garfield? Gargoyle? Garbanzo? Edgar? Gargantua? Garbage? *(He hits himself on the head.)* That's it I knew it. The defendant—this piece of garbage—wouldn't let Herr Gittelstein get in front of him on line. We will be seeking the death penalty and because this garbage is a pacifist, when convicted we will execute him by drowning—in the pacific ocean.

GAR: It's just Gar It's not short for anything.

BERNIE: *(Extending his hand.)* Bernie, short for Bernard. Gittelstein. Not Steen. Stein. I'm a German Jew. Do you know what that means?

GAR: It means either you or your ancestors were from Germany.

BERNIE: Close but no cigar. There are two kinds of Jews in this world. German Jews and all the others.

GAR: Is that so?

BERNIE: My grandfather was an educated man—a doctor. He wouldn't sit at the same table with a Russian or a Polish Jew. And why not, you ask? Because they chewed with their mouths open and quite often they would wipe their mouths on the same schmutzicked part of the napkin they already used. And that's when they used a napkin at all.

GAR: I see.

BERNIE: You are a man of very few words. Is this not your native tongue. Would you be more comfortable in another. I'm fluent in many languages. All the usuals plus Latin, Swahili, Hebrew and Yiddish, Romansch, Papiamento *(I like vacationing in Aruba.)* and Greek.

GAR: I speak good English. I just don't feel like talking when I'm trying to listen to music. Besides, you're doing all the talking.

BERNIE: You look like a reasonable man, even though your mischugganah parents must have been from another planet to give you such a name. All I'm asking is something very simple. I'm appealing to your sense of honesty and fairness. To your Christian nature. I'm begging—please. I need to be first in line. It'll destroy my mind if I'm not. I'll do anything you ask, to take your place.

GAR: Look, if I let you take my spot will you leave me alone so I can listen to music?

BERNIE: *(Excited.)* Yes, yes, yes, yes, yes. Even though it's impossible for me to keep my mouth shut, I won't bother you. I promise.

GAR: I'll do it on one condition.

BERNIE: What, what! Anything.

GAR: When the number one is called you must go in.

BERNIE: Go in? I never go in. I don't really care to go in. I just want to be first on line. In, doesn't interest me. Only first.

GAR: That's the deal. Take it or leave it.

BERNIE: But I can't go in. I don't want to go in. *(Pause.)* I'm afraid. *(Pause.)* Have you ever been in?

GAR: I've never been first.

BERNIE: Never.

GAR: Never.

BERNIE: I'm glad there are people like you. If everybody wanted to be first my life would be such a mess.

GAR: What do you say?

BERNIE: I need to think about this. *(Soliloquy-like.)* I must be first but I don't want to enter. i like having the cake but to put it in my mouth. I don't know. It's never happened. I don't know what to expect. I'm happy with first. I'm afraid. What if I don't like what I see when I have crossed the line? There would be no going back. Life would be different. I might be very uncomfortable. Would I still like to play chess? Am I strong enough to handle change? Where would I hide when it's dark. Will there be place to hide. What would happen to my autograph collection? *(Back to him.)* I don't know. This is a big step. *(Pause.)*

GAR: Never mind.

BERNIE: No! I'll do it. I'll take it. I have to be first. I'll risk anything to be first. *(Pause.)* OK. Let's switch. *(Gar gathers his things and moves a few feet stage right and sits. Bernie observes*

this nervously, then takes his place at the head of the line.)
Dankaschoen!

GAR: Your welcome. *(Gar sits nonchalantly, eating and drinking and totally unruffled by the change. While the final strains of the ode to joy begin to get louder, the lights go slowly from white to red to purple during which time Bernie becomes quite disturbed and agitated. The volume increases as the stage goes to black.)*

GANGSTER APPAREL

Richard Vetere

serio-comedic, 2 Men

Louis (30s) a well-dressed hit-man, and Joey (20s–30s) his less-natty partner.

Scene: a dingy motel room in Queens

> *As they prepare for a job, Louis does his best to convince Joey that clothes make the man.*

LOUIE: Hey, where the hell you been? Another five minutes and I was going to call your mother!

JOEY: I'm sorry. I couldn't find the place so fast. It's in the middle of nowhere.

LOUIE: I know. The boss picked it. He wants us to be discreet. He says Frankie 'Snails' owns it. *(Nodding to his socks.)*

JOEY: What are you doin', Louie?

LOUIE: *(Ironing pants.)* What does it look like I am doing? *(Nodding to his socks.)* Huh?

JOEY: What?

LOUIE: Silk.

JOEY: Silk? Wow.

LOUIE: The boxer shorts…*New.*

JOEY: Nice. Louie? We gotta talk.

LOUIE: About what?

JOEY: I don't know…I want to go to the beach. I want to see girls in bathing suits.

LOUIE: It's winter. Go to the beach. You see a girl in a bikini, let me know.

JOEY: I'm not talkin' Rockaway, I'm talkin' Miami. Let's get on a plane. That's what I want to do.

LOUIE: The last time I was on a beach I was five years old and I was burying some snot-nosed punk in seaweed 'cause he broke my sunglasses. I hate sand, I hate rocks in my toes, and I hate that smell that comes up from Jersey. And no matter what beach you are on, I don't care where you are, you are going to get hit with that smell that comes up from Jersey! Plus, you walk on a beach and you step on dead things. You know how I don't like to step on dead things. You want to go to the beach? Go ahead. I like asphalt. You know what to expect when you walk on it. *(Louie steps to the bed where an expensive suit lies spread across it. Louie picks up the pants and hands them gently to Joey.)* Feel. *(Joey touches the pants roughly.)* Make nice! *(Joey touches the pants softly.)* Not any tailor. Guido on the corner near the deli. He makes the Boss's suits.

JOEY: Wow, Louie. So, what do you say? We go to the airport, buy a couple of tickets and we are outa here. We'll go where they don't have sand. Pick a place.

LOUIE: I like Queens. What's the matter with you? Things are happening for us here. Why do you want to go someplace all of a sudden? *(Louie slowly gets into his pants making that act somewhat of a dramatic artist moment.)*

JOEY: Things are going…too fast…

LOUIE: See? You have to learn to *enjoy* the *whole* thing. Go ahead…touch the shirt. *(Louie nods to a shirt which is hanging on a hanger from a hook on the wall. Joey walks to the shirt and touches it gently.)*

JOEY: Wow…

LOUIE: Georgio Armani.

JOEY: But the money it costs?

LOUIE: We are talking about clothes here. Who cares about the money? You think the Boss cares about the money?

JOEY: But he's *got* money.

LOUIE: You think he always had it? You know he didn't always have it. He was a guy just like you and me, Joey, workin' his ass off tryin' to make something of himself.

JOEY: Yea, sure, Louie. But I need…some time off.

LOUIE: You want a vacation? We'll take a vacation. But tonight, we have things to do. *(Joey carefully carries the shirt to Louie who puts it on with the same dramatic flair he did the pants as Joey watches every movement.)* The tie. On the bed. It took me a half an hour to pick the tie to match the shirt. *(Joey brings Louie the tie.)* You see, they compliment each other and at the same time—contrast. Silk. All I could afford was one but that doesn't matter. Watch what a tie does. Check it out... *(Louie slowly puts on the tie and when the knot is complete he stands in the middle of the room like a prima ballerina waiting for applause.)* Ba da bing! See?

JOEY: Wow…

LOUIE: The shoes.

JOEY: We got enough dough for the tickets, what do you say? *(Joey sees the shoes and runs to get them. He brings them to Louie.)*

LOUIE: Be careful! No creases! (*Louie takes the shoes and slowly puts them on after he reaches for a shoe horn. He puts on the shoes just as he did the other clothes, enjoying the act itself.)* Bally. I'd have twenty-two pair if I could buy what I like. I will someday. *(Pause.)* Go ahead…touch them. *(Joey gets on his hands and knees and touches the shoes.)* They cry out to be touched, don't they? I mean, Joey, they shine so nice they cry out to be *kissed!* Really kissed!

JOEY: They do?

LOUIE: Like you want to get down on your hands and knees and kiss them! I noticed that the other day with the Boss. He was walking out of the club, right? And I was sittin' out in the car like always and I watched him get into the limo and saw how his shoes were shinning from all the way over there! I mean, I was across the street and saw them shine!

JOEY: I was there! I was with you!

LOUIE: But you didn't see *it,* Joey! You didn't see what I saw! Those shoes cried out to be *kissed! (Pause.)* Comb… *(Joey takes the comb off the drawer and hands it to Louie. Louie's hair is so short that a comb can hardly go through it but he manages to push it through looking close to stream-lined perfection.)*

206 men's scenes

Fifty bucks for the haircut. Got it at Marco's. It's cut so close to my head it makes me look like I'm doin' eighty miles an hour! I am a man on the move!

JOEY: Nice. Real nice.

LOUIE: Now, get over here. Look in the mirror.

JOEY: Shit… *(Joey slowly walks to the mirror and looks.)*

LOUIE: That's what I mean, look at yourself, go ahead.

JOEY: I am.

LOUIE: And what are you thinking when you look? Huh?

JOEY: I don't look good.

LOUIE: You got it, pal. It's been what I have been trying to tell you…but you don't *see* it and you don't listen. *(Pause.)* Just two hours in this dump and I already got dirt on my cuffs! What time is it?

JOEY: Just about eight.

LOUIE: How do you feel? You feel loose inside?

JOEY: I feel loose, Louie, I feel loose.

LOUIE: I am glad you feel loose but you don't look *neat.* You know what I mean by *neat?*…I mean, sharp…I mean 'a man in control of his wardrobe." Get me my gun. *(Joey goes to a small bag on the chair in the corner and brings it to Louie.)* Go ahead…take it out.

(Joey takes out a brand new .38 pistol and places it on the drawer.)

JOEY: Wow…

LOUIE: It's new. Nickel plated. Did you hear me? New.

JOEY: It looks great.

LOUIE: Let's see your gun. Come on… *(Joey places Louie's brand new gun on the bed and slowly takes out a worn-out .38 pistol from his belt and humbly places it on the drawer in front of Louie. Looking at it.)* What is that? What is *that?*

JOEY: My gun.

LOUIE: Look at it! *Look!*

JOEY: Come on, Louie…*it works.*

LOUIE: It works? So what, it works! How can you be seen with that piece of shit? How?

JOEY: But nobody sees it.

LOUIE: Nobody sees it! I'm *seeing* it now! You *see* it. The cops who might bust you some day will see it! God forbid, Conchetta, your girlfriend sees it! What is she going to think? Huh? You think a piece like that will impress her? Come on, what's wrong with you?

JOEY: She did see it.

LOUIE: And what did she *think?*

JOEY: She didn't like it.

LOUIE: Can you blame her?

JOEY: You are right.

LOUIE: *(Holding his pistol.)* Now, If she saw you with this, what do you think she would think? Huh?

JOEY: She would be impressed.

LOUIE: *Yes!* So tell me, why don't you have a piece like this one?

JOEY: I don't know. I didn't think about it.

LOUIE: But these are the kinds of things you gotta think about!

JOEY: There are other things, maybe, like relaxin', you know? Gettin' away from it awhile.

LOUIE: And where is that going to get ya? Bus boy work at Abbrracciamento's?

JOEY: I don't know…

LOUIE: Come on, Joey…we started out in the same place you and I. Running numbers back and forth to Brooklyn…but now who gets the good jobs, huh? Who gets the big money? Who gets the important work? Huh?

JOEY: You.

LOUIE: And 'why'?

JOEY: You are smarter.

LOUIE: And what else?

JOEY: …You…*dress* better.

LOUIE: Yes!

JOEY: I *knew* that.

LOUIE: I always dressed better. Even when all I could afford was a Vidal Sasson jumpsuit…I wore it! Every nickel in my pocket went for a pinky ring! And not just any pinky ring—diamond! If I had five dollars in my pocket it went for a hair cut. Forget food! Maybe I was hungry but that's not important! *I looked great!* So sometimes I didn't sleep well…my clothes were pressed! The bottom of my shoes had holes in them but they were shinny on top! Do you understand me, Joey? You tell me who you want to be? You want to be a bum or do you want to be somebody?

JOEY: I want to be somebody, Louie.

LOUIE: You want to be somebody and tonight you're going out to work dressed like that? What is that on your feet?

JOEY: Sneakers.

LOUIE: Sneakers? Huh? Who wears sneakers? You ever see the Pope wearing sneakers? You ever see the Boss, god forbid, wearing anything but Bally's? Huh?

JOEY: No.

LOUIE: You know who wears sneakers?

JOEY: Who?

LOUIE: People who have no respect for themselves, that's who wears sneakers! And what kind of pants are those?

JOEY: These are jeans, Louie.

LOUIE: Jeans? Who wears jeans? You ever see Sinatra in dungarees? Okay, you want to go casual go *slacks.* A nice pair of black grey slacks but still with the Bally shoes. Pleated, pressed, neat. A nice button-down shirt…matching socks and a nice belt. The whole nine yards. The trick to casual is to *look* like you feel comfortable. So what you feel like your lying down on a bed of nails! Make people think you treat yourself good and they will treat you good. Huh? And that jacket? What are you a low life? A low life off the street wears sneakers, jeans, and a leather jacket with a hole in the elbow! Nobody important dresses like some kind of low life even in his own house! At home? Try a robe with a silk lining…good slippers! And PJ's? Silk. Always silk. And try black. Black is right. The cops bust in on you and see you dressed in a nice robe with silk lining, a silk pair of PJ's and good slippers and they will treat you like *somebody!* You understand me, Joey?

JOEY: I am not a low life.

LOUIE: I know you are *not.* That is why I am taking the time out to tell you all this. I am going up in the Club and I want you around me, Joey. We have done some *things* you and I. You know that. Some *things* together and I want you on top with me when it happens. Guys who do *things* together should stay together. To keep an 'eye' out for each other. We got a *history* together, pal, and you know that. Like they say—"if the walls could talk." *(Louie gives Joey a long, hard look and Joey returns it.)*

JOEY: I would never talk. Are you sayin' I would talk? Come on, Louie, I don't believe you—you insult me. I should walk home right now.

LOUIE: I didn't say a word to that effect. What are you talking about?

JOEY: I did one to five for you when I got busted on the bar job and I never said a word.

LOUIE: No, you are right, Joey. Of course you are. You did that one to five for us. You did. *(Louie walks over to a suit hanging on the closet door knob and tosses it on the bed.)* There. That is for you.

JOEY: Huh?

LOUIE: Go ahead, try it on. We ain't got time. *(Joey slowly approaches the suit in awe.)* Yo! Joey, you don't examine it— you wear it! It's a suit. Had it made for you. Special.

JOEY: You had it made for me?

LOUIE: Tailor made. You owe me $1,200.00…

JOEY: *What?*

LOUIE: What are you getting for tonight?

JOEY: I'm gettin'…five thou…

LOUIE: With that money you can afford to look your best. Joey, listen to me…tonight I change your life. You got that? One day you will look back on *this night* and say to yourself…"I recall the *night*…Louie changed my life for me." Now, put it on…hurry. *(Joey undresses taking off his jacket, pants and shirt. As he does, Louie looks at his gun, Joey's gun, and shakes his head 'no'. Standing in his boxer shorts Louie hands him the pants, the socks, the shirt and tie.)* Now go over *it* all with me.

JOEY: *(Dressing.)* I park the car on Bleecker.

LOUIE: Right. Bleecker faces east…You sit in the car…good.

JOEY: Then I wait and at nine fifteen you come walking down Bleecker toward my car.

LOUIE: Good. Then what?

JOEY: He comes out of the restaurant at nine fifteen…

LOUIE: Because we know he's got a meeting in Jersey at ten thirty and he is never late.

JOEY: And that's it.

LOUIE: No! That is not *it!* There is something else!

JOEY: Right! If he's got one bodyguard I blink the lights once…if he's got two bodyguards I blink the lights twice.

LOUIE: Twice for two. *(Joey is half dressed as Louie takes his brand new pistol and put it in his belt.)* I will then walk up behind him like *this*…Ba ba bing! *(Louie holds his pistol in one hand and aims it as if he is aiming to shoot at the back of someone's head. Acting it out.)* And pop him twice in the back of the head. I know his bald head like I know the palm of my hand. I am behind him so I go *bam!* Then when the first bodyguard turns around I go *bam* twice right through the heart! Now, if the other bodyguard is there ready to pounce on me, what happens?

JOEY: *(Acting it out.)* I am right there with you, Louie. I put two slugs into him. Bam! Bam!

LOUIE: *(Watching Joey.)* Good. Very good. Then what?

JOEY: Back to the car we go. Nonchalant-like. Then we drive right on Broadway and left on Delancy…Then over the bridge and back to Queens. Safe and sound.

LOUIE: *(Flings imaginary dice.)* Then a nice drive down to Atlantic City. I guarantee they open the gold gates of the Taj for us! The best food! The best broads! *(Joey is now dressed. Louie looks him over. Joey does not seem comfortable in the expensive clothes.)* You got to look comfortable in them. You just don't wear clothes, you become the clothes you got on. You understand me? It's a mental attitude. You are a *somebody* so walk like a somebody. You know? Look, tell me how you are gonna walk up to this bodyguard when you got to *pop* him tonight? Tell me.

JOEY: Like I always walk.

LOUIE: Show me. Go ahead. Hurry, we ain't got no time. *(Joey bops instead of walks across the room.) No!* No! You walk like that and the whole street will know you are a hood who's gonna pop some big shot!

JOEY: Then how should I walk? I want to know.

(Louie walks gracefully and slowly takes out his gun.)

LOUIE: Like this…see? I am a man who enjoys *walking*…see? Then, take out your piece like this…with finesse…style… then you aim at his head and pop the bastard. Like that. Look *good* doin' it. Come on, pal, you don't have to go to college to know how to look good when you are shootin' somebody! Don't you watch TV?

JOEY: I'll do it right, Louie.

LOUIE: And this gun, man, Joey. How the hell can you shoot such a big man…a man who is so famous…so important with a gun like that? Aren't you embarrassed?

JOEY: I didn't think of it, I really didn't.

LOUIE: You're only shooting his bodyguard true…but it's the principal of the thing! If the Boss saw what you carry he would be insulted.

JOEY: I'll get a better gun.

LOUIE: Don't let me down, pal.

JOEY: *(Looks in the mirror.)* We look good. Louie…we look good.

LOUIE: *(Joins Joey in the mirror.)* Movie stars, or what?

JOEY: We look up there. We definitely do. *(Louie takes out some cologne and puts it on. He puts it in Joey's face. Joey has a big smile as he does it.)* I got to thank you, Louie. This is the night which changed my life. Thank you for making me see myself as I was, so I can change myself to be better.

LOUIE: No problem. Just do me a favor. Burn those clothes. I don't want anybody I know to think I would know somebody who would dress like that...*ever again.*

JOEY: These clothes are gone forever. *(Joey places the clothes like rags in a bag.)*

LOUIE: The 'time'?

(Joey checks his watch.)

JOEY: We should make a move.

(Louie and Joey check each other in the mirror again.)

LOUIE: We look good...we smell good...anything missing?

JOEY: I was wondering...Is it important what you are thinking in your head, you know?

LOUIE: Go ahead...

JOEY: When you, Louie 'pop' a guy, what are you thinking?

LOUIE: When I 'pop' a guy on the street what am I thinking? You mean, when I am there and all those well-dressed people are around and the car's are driving by and people are going to eat dinner and talking and everybody is out for the night on the town to have a good time and I am there with my brand new piece and this suit and my new hair cut and I get behind the guy and I 'pop' him...*What am I thinking?*

JOEY: Yeah?

LOUIE: I am thinking how good I *look!* I am thinking how fabulous I look! What else would I be thinking? Why? When you are out there 'poppin' a guy, what are you thinking?

JOEY: I don't know. Lots of things. I sometimes think how hungry I am...what's on TV that night...sex...that kind of stuff.

LOUIE: So you see? You see what I am telling you all night?

JOEY: See what?

LOUIE: It's not what you think! It's not what is inside your head... It's how you *look* that matters! Who cares what you are thinking when you are doin' it! When you are eating dinner...when you are *doing* your girlfriend, who cares what you are thinking? It's how you *look* that matters!

JOEY: So when we do *it…we've got to look good!*

LOUIE: You got it, pal! And one day when we are famous the papers will say "Louie Falco and Joey Pugg are the two best dressed hoods in town."

JOEY: I can't wait.

LOUIE: Let me tell you something…that is all people really care about. How other people think of them. So, make sure your mental attitude is the right one for you. Think positive thoughts…*look good.* Dress to kill.

JOEY: I like that—'dress to kill.'

LOUIE: Ready, pal?

JOEY: Do I look ready, or what? *(Joey looks in the mirror again with Louie beside him.)*

LOUIE: Two pretty good-lookin' guys, huh?

JOEY: The clothes make the man.

LOUIE: This big shot should appreciate how much it matters to us how good we look when we 'pop' him.

JOEY: He should have no complaints. *(Pause.)*

LOUIE: Let's not fall in love…we'll be late. *(Louie and Joey quickly pack.)* You know, after Atlantic city there is a nice little shop on Austin Street we should check out…Excellent handker-chiefs… *(Louie slips a silk handkerchief in Joey's breast pock-et then puts one in his own.)*

JOEY: Nice. Very nice. Can't go wrong with the right handker*chief.*

LOUIE: They have a great assortment. Silk from the Far East. You'd love 'em, Joseph.

JOEY: Really? Well, I'll look forward to it, Louis. *(Looks into the mir-ror proudly.)* Man, you sure could pick a suit. *(Joey and Louie look sinisterly into the mirror.)*

LOUIE: Let's do it.

(Louie and Joey collect their bags, walk to the door and open it. A harsh white light from the parking lot suddenly fills the room. They stand in it a moment: it is the white light of real-ity, the starkness of existence, the destiny of the journey awaiting them. They step out and exit. Song: Sinatra's The Way You Look Tonight plays but in a distorted way. Lights out.)

HEMLOCK: A GREEK DINER TRAGEDY

Bob Jude Ferrante

serio-comedic, 3 Men

Socrates (55) well-known philosopher, Plato (24) his well-known student and Crito (32) his lesser-known friend.

Scene: ancient Greece

Here, Socrates and his greatest pupil bicker on the eve of the master's forced suicide via hemlock.

○ ○ ○

(Lights. A "Greek" vista—two ionic columns and a limestone bench—lit to create a hollow, empty effect. Plato sits on the bench, trying to write on papyrus. He stops, holds the scroll up to the light. Shakes his head. Puts the scroll on his knee and scratches something out furiously. Enter Socrates. Passes Plato from behind. Stops to regard him. Slips closer so he can read over Plato's shoulder.)

SOCRATES: One 's' in justice, boy.

PLATO: *(Looks up.)* Oh? Socrates! *(Sits up straighter.)* Good morning, sir.

SOCRATES: You should watch the spelling, son.

PLATO: Yes, sir. *(Looks down sullenly.)*

SOCRATES: Maybe it's time for us to talk. Have a minute?

PLATO: Yes, sir.

SOCRATES: *(Sits next to Plato.)* To tell you the truth, your performance in the Academy has left a bit to be desired. You're obviously bright. Why don't you try to make more of an attempt...er...

PLATO: Plato.

SOCRATES: Right. You're the young poet.

PLATO: No, sir. I'm not a poet, I'm...

SOCRATES: Speak up, boy!

PLATO: I don't know.

SOCRATES: *(Sighs.)* Neither do I.

PLATO: But…sir? Everyone respects you. A beacon of wisdom.

SOCRATES: A beacon that doesn't write anything down. When I'm gone, it'll all be…

PLATO: Someone should write it down for you.

SOCRATES: Someone? *You?* You can't spell.

PLATO: Only the hard words—'justice' and 'truth.'

SOCRATES: *(Mocking.)* Profound, boy. You should become a philosopher. Then you could sit around all day—on a bench like this—thinking deep thoughts. Your mind will grow broader. And so will your ass! Here. *(Grabs Plato's scroll.)* — Let's see this!

PLATO: No! It's not finished! *(Struggles to retrieve his scroll; Socrates is a lot taller.)*

SOCRATES: Hm. *(Reads.)* "Deeds accomplished for the good of the many would be deemed Just, even at the loss of the few, no matter their qualities." Hey. This is kind of funny.

PLATO: No!

SOCRATES: "But why sacrifice the few? Because of 'Justice?' Sounds I make? What if the sounds were 'pike-fish?' Or 'side-dish?'" Pike-fish! Side dish! *(Calls offstage.)* Hey, Crito! Get your ass in here! I think you want to hear this! First class material!

PLATO: *(Whimpers.)* Please…

SOCRATES: Pike as a side dish—sheer genius. I'm getting an appetite. *(Enter Crito.)* Crito! The kid's got the gift! Listen: "Philosophers postulate we have a higher purpose. But look at our design—it differs not from the beasts; as they live, so do we: feeding, defecating, breeding only to continue? Why? And where is the higher purpose?"

CRITO: Who wrote that?

SOCRATES: This kid here. Play-dough.

PLATO: *Plato! Plato!*

CRITO: It's magic. Let me. *(Takes scroll.)* "Yet who asks these all-

216 men's scenes

important questions? Who is this philosopher? Yet another beast; fed by the same food, subject to the same desires. An animal among animals." This kid wrote this?

SOCRATES: Yeah. Riot, huh?

PLATO: Please!

CRITO: Funnier than Homer. You say your name was Mayo? Okay, Mayo, I think you ought to go see about having this stuff read aloud in theater or something. More laughs per papyrus than Euripedes.

SOCRATES: You rip-a dese robes…

CRITO: You pay for dese robes! *(Socrates and Crito dance around Plato in glee.)*

PLATO: Please.

SOCRATES AND PLATO: *(Dance and wave the manuscript.)*
Oh oh wi-hi-hi-his-dom,
oh bay-bay, oh bay-bay,
cuh-huh-hum to me.

PLATO: *Hemlock!*

SOCRATES: Oh. Right. *(Stops; Crito keeps dancing. To Crito.)* Will you stop that nonsense!

PLATO: Then you understand? They'll kill you.

SOCRATES: I suppose.

PLATO: With poison.

SOCRATES: Hemlock. Right? Unambiguous.

PLATO: It will hurt.

SOCRATES: No. It's merciful.

PLATO: But slow?

SOCRATES: No, swift.

PLATO: Yes, then. But just?

SOCRATES: Yes. Just.

PLATO: But why?

SOCRATES: I don't understand.

PLATO: Why? Interrogative. As in 'what for.'

SOCRATES: Please. It's obvious. Didn't you pay attention? They proved it. My words and I. We corrupt.

PLATO: You?

men's scenes 217

SOCRATES: We decay society. My words and I. My mind's eye. All evil.

PLATO: You're wrong!

SOCRATES: You disagree, even after I ridicule your work?

PLATO: No! I mean…

SOCRATES: You're not being clear. Think it through. Use logic.

CRITO: Do I hear it right? You're guilty?

PLATO: Yes. He is.

CRITO: I thought it was a joke! The whole trial thing! I never thought they'd find you guilty!

SOCRATES: *(To Crito, fiercely.)* We're all learning so much today! *(Despairing.)* Nothing left now but to wait.

PLATO: No! You must live! And fight!

SOCRATES: Fight. That's easy for you to say. *(Sits on the ground.)* I'm old. And I've done enough damage. Better to spare Athens. Funny You spend your life building a body of work. You get really wrapped up in it. You never think it will hurt anyone. Because it's a blast—thinking things maybe nobody's thought. Then you get a bird's-eye view of the damage. And the voices whisper through the curtain, echo through the gallery, scream in the halls for justice. For blood. I will wait here for them.

PLATO: No! Don't be a fool! Don't be a hero!

SOCRATES: What was in that papyrus you just wrote?

PLATO: You've got it backwards. I was talking in general. Not specifically referring to you. You're my—

SOCRATES: Hypocrite!

PLATO: —teacher. *(A beat.)*

SOCRATES: You disgrace the Academy. Leave my sight.

(Plato walks to the edge of the stage, sits on the edge and watches. Enter two cardinals in Inquisition robes. Cardinals seize Socrates and lead him offstage.)

PLATO: The fool. He listened. I don't know anything. I'm just a boy. *(Bends over to write.)* His last words?

CRITO: Damage done! What damage now to Athens, deprived of

her light! Athena! You have abandoned us, you inconstant woman! *(Exits, shaking his head.)*

PLATO: Something to make them wonder. Something humble. What am I doing! More words! How can I keep doing this! They drag him off to death—all I can think about is what his last words were! I'm a monster! How many more will die because of me! I deserve to die! There's no other choice! *(Shouts offstage.)* You! In the robe! Come back, take me! Take me! *Take me!*

HOT AIR

Richard Willett

serio-comedic, 2 Men
Michael (30s) a man grieving over the death of his one-time lover,
and Danny (30s) a sympathetic stranger.

Scene: here and now

> *Michael has just discovered that his ex-lover, Benjy, has been*
> *killed in a car crash. Here, he dials Benjy's phone number and*
> *finds an understanding stranger on the other end of the line.*

○ ○ ○

DANNY: Hello?

MICHAEL: Oh…Hello. I'm calling for Ben Matell…Is he still at this
number?

DANNY: No. He was here before us. We get mail for him sometimes. Uh…I think he died.

MICHAEL: Yes, he did. He was in a car accident.

DANNY: Oh. Then how come you're calling him?

MICHAEL: Well, you never know. *(Pause.)* He drank. I imagine,
although I do not know, that he was drunk when this…acci-
dent occurred. He got me drinking. I swear to God. Never
touched the stuff before we met. He was a bad influence.
But he mixed a damn good martini. *(Pause.)*

DANNY: Really.

MICHAEL: I'm sorry. It's just that I…We hadn't spoken in a long
time, and I kept calling this number, thinking that I'd say
something…profound, and then when I finally had the nerve
to let it ring, he was gone.

DANNY: Were you…a couple?

MICHAEL: Yes. For almost two years. Well…I say that, but it was
really eighteen months.

DANNY: That's pretty good, I guess. These days.

MICHAEL: Is it?

DANNY: My girlfriend and I are about to celebrate our first anniversary. That's our first anniversary of living together anyway. Although we moved in pretty quickly; that was my doing.

MICHAEL: Benjy and I talked about that. In those first months of wild romantic flush. We talked about it a lot, in fact. I sometimes think I'll never talk about it again with anyone—no matter what. Why do we do that to ourselves? Why do we always make those plans that in the end seem so pathetic?

DANNY: You have to make plans.

MICHAEL: You sound like a very reasonable sort of person.

DANNY: Oh…well…

MICHAEL: Not long before we broke up, we took a trip together, to Hawaii. Have you ever been there?

DANNY: No. I hear it's great.

MICHAEL: It's very beautiful. And romantic. I mean, people say traveling together can ruin a relationship, but I don't know, with us it was more the coming back that seemed to ruin it. We bought almost exactly the same shirt without realizing it. And on the plane home we fell asleep together, in our matching Hawaiian outfits, holding hands. *(Pause.)*

DANNY: So what do you think went wrong?

MICHAEL: Huh? Oh, who knows? In the beginning, the way we contrasted with each other seemed magnetic. But there was a sad place in him somewhere, that I didn't get to often enough, because he wasn't given to self-examination, and grew irritated when I pursued it. The place where he would refuse to laugh at any of my jokes and *(Referring to the martini.)* down these in one shot, like water. (*He downs the martini in one shot, like water.*)

DANNY: It's a funny kind of gift, that sadness.

MICHAEL: We became oddly clumsy at the end, physically. We used to bathe together. I still have…in fact…one of those inflatable bathtub pillows which I always had difficulty filling but which Benjy managed to blow up for me, months ago. He had this…tremendous chest capacity. But then, I guess, you

men's scenes 221

wouldn't understand…what that might mean…to a person. I'm preoccupied with that pillow now. I realized suddenly one day that it was his breath trapped inside. *(Pause.)* We fell, in the bathtub, the last time we were together, for the first time in my life I had one of those household accidents they're always telling us about, a real pratfall, with Ben almost coming down on top of me, which might have finished me off. That night he walked in his sleep. I woke up and saw him opening the front door of my apartment and about to stride, buck naked, into the hallway. I started calling his name, but to no avail. He actually went through the door and shut it before I got there. Then he opened it again and came back, looking kind of sheepish. "What are you doing?" I asked. And he replied, very tightly, "I am trying to go to sleep." *(Pause.)* I should let you go.

DANNY: I've enjoyed talking with you.

MICHAEL: You seem like a good person.

DANNY: I have my moments.

MICHAEL: Well, good night then.

DANNY: Good night.

NO MEAN STREET

Paul Boakye

dramatic, 2 Men

Arlington (20s) an HIV-positive hustler and Marcus (11) his estranged son.

Scene: an inner city, anywhere

Arlington visits Marcus despite the objections of the boy's mother. When Marcus discovers his father's gun and plays with it, Arlington reprimands the boy, creating an emotional environment in with Marcus is finally able to give voice to his fears about Arlington's disease.

○ ○ ○

(Arlington and Marcus are seated on a bench. Music from an ice-cream van can be heard in the distance.)

ARLINGTON: Do you realize you had your mother worried to death? *(Pause.)* Marcus, I'm talking to you.

MARCUS: What?

ARLINGTON: Don't you know better than to play with guns?

MARCUS: I wasn't playing with it.

ARLINGTON: What were you doing then?

MARCUS: I wasn't playing with it…You shouldn't have it anyway.

ARLINGTON: Marcus, that's not the point, it's for your protection.

MARCUS: Why?

ARLINGTON: Look, there's a lot a people round here don't want work. Want everything but don't wanna do nothing. Some come like animals, break into your house, kill you, take what you have. What I have is mine. I work hard for it and no…

MARCUS: That ain't no way to live.

ARLINGTON: I know that ain't no way to live but that's life.

MARCUS: So if dog bit you, you gonna bite it back.

ARLINGTON: *(Chuckles.)* Marcus, Marcus, Marcus…

MARCUS: If you carried a condom for protection, Dad, instead of a gun, you wouldn't have AIDS.

ARLINGTON: Who told you I've got AIDS?

MARCUS: I ain't deaf, you know, I heard you and Mum arguing.

ARLINGTON: You're too smart, you know that?

MARCUS: Do you love my mum?

ARLINGTON: Yeah, I love her. I do love her.

MARCUS: But you both said you were gonna live together and be alright.

ARLINGTON: It's not that simple son. It's just not gonna work out between me and your mum.

MARCUS: Why? Because you've got AIDS?

ARLINGTON: I haven't got AIDS. I've got HIV. I've got the virus that causes AIDS.

MARCUS: Are you a battyman?

ARLINGTON: Don't be stupid, Marcus. 'Course I'm not gay. Anyone can get AIDS, y'know.

MARCUS: Are you gonna die then?

ARLINGTON: Everything dies, you know that. I could get run over by a bus tomorrow. Things get born get old and die.

MARCUS: Yeah, but you're gonna die young and skinny like them people with AIDS on telly.

ARLINGTON: I don't wanna die. I wanna live to see you grow up.

MARCUS: What if Mum dies of AIDS, what if you both die of AIDS, who's gonna look after me?

ARLINGTON: I'm here for now, y'know, en I? Your mum's here. We're both here.

MARCUS: Yeah, but you're gonna die. *(Marcus starts to cry. Arlington tries to comfort him. Marcus flinches, pushes him away.)*

ARLINGTON: Marcus, don't be stupid. It won't rub off, y'know. I'm here for now...I ain't going nowhere...and I need you to be strong for me to be strong. Marcus, look at me. Come on. I never really had the kind of father-son relationship people suppose to have, y'know, 'cos my old man was a bastard, he really was. I grew up with a lot of stress in the house. I never

224 men's scenes

got to know him. I missed out on a lot, and if I ever wanted to get to know him now, well, he's dead so…Look, Marcus, there's things I got to sort out in my own head…I dunno, Maybe I should go and see a counsellor…but I don't wanna treat you like a stranger no more, y'know, 'cos you're my son. And I love you. I never told you that before, but I do…you're all I've got. *(Marcus turns and hugs him.)* Come on. I brought you here for a reason. *(Gives him the keys.)* I've got a surprise for you in the boot.

(Marcus jumps up, goes to the car, opens the boot, finds a computer.)

MARCUS: Wow! Dad, is it mine? Is it really mine?

ARLINGTON: Yep.

MARCUS: Wikid! Wait 'til Mum sees this. Wow! Thanks Dad.

ARLINGTON: *(Smiling.)* Come here a minute.

MARCUS: What is it?

ARLINGTON: Close your eyes and hold out your hand. *(Marcus does so. Arlington places a condom in his outstretched hand.)* What's that?

MARCUS: *(Opening his eyes.)* Daad!

ARLINGTON: *(Laughing.)* You skinning up your face?

MARCUS: What d'you think I am?

ARLINGTON: A condom can save your life. You know how to use one?

MARCUS: 'Course I do.

ARLINGTON: Good! Keep it in your pocket for now.

MARCUS: You're out of order, Dad.

(Arlington laughs, ruffles his son's hair.)

ARLINGTON: Come on. *(Arlington puts his arm round Marcus. Marcus puts the condom in his pocket. They walk off.)*

PAINTING X'S ON THE MOON

Richard Vetere

dramatic, 2 Men

Lou Barbota (30s) a handsome Queens gangster, intelligent and dangerous, and Nick Dante (30s) an impoverished, yet sarcastic artist.

Scene: a taxi cab

When Lou's wife tells him that Nick's art is the real thing, the gangster decides to find out for himself.

○ ○ ○

(Night. Queens Boulevard. Lou steps over to Nick who pulls up the car.)

NICK DANTE: *(Into car phone.)* Yeah, I see him now.

LOU: Action Car Service?

NICK DANTE: Yeah, I got your call.

(Lou gets into the car by sitting in a chair behind Nick.)

LOU: I want to go to 66-56 Long Island Expressway Service Road.

NICK DANTE: It's a ten buck ride. *(He turns wheel.)*

LOU: Hey, you go left here…

NICK DANTE: No, left's tonight.

LOU: What?

NICK DANTE: Tonight's Tuesday. On Tuesday's I don't make left's. Wednesdays I don't make right turns. Thursday's I don't back up. And don't worry, I will get you there in the same amount of time.

LOU: So, you invented a little game for yourself, huh?

NICK DANTE: You spend eight hours in a car and let's see what you do.

LOU: I like that. I have had experience with monotony, myself. I've been stuck in one place all day and night. And you know, if you give into it, you will go nuts. So, you come up with little things to keep yourself busy.

NICK DANTE: You don't look like you drove a car service.

LOU: I've had a lot of brain numbing jobs. They were a kind of confinement, too. But some good came out of it—the time spent alone made me think about God.

NICK DANTE: With a world full of people, the only way human beings can feel less lonely is by hoping that there is a God! That is rich.

LOU: Hey, we all want to feel that somebody made us so that we ourselves are not responsible for the terrible things we do. We want to remain children forever believing in a benevolent parent waiting there to forgive us our every awful act.

NICK DANTE: My parents didn't forgive me anything.

LOU: Well, I figured that if there is a God there is one thing we could be sure of about Him—and you know what that is? He is *accurate.* He doesn't waste time. He gets to the facts.

NICK DANTE: To the truth.

LOU: Forget the truth. You know what Balzac says?

NICK DANTE: French novelist. Wrote "The Human Comedy."

LOU: Right. And he says, "Truth is perception." Everybody sees what they want to see and they call what they see the truth. Ha! You can twist the truth around for it to be anything you want it to be. People are real good at that. But to be accurate? To see what is really there—only God can do that.

NICK DANTE: You don't look like an intellectual.

LOU: Like I said before—I've learned to educate myself. I like books. They fit nice in your hand and they never change their story on ya.

NICK DANTE: *(Stops car.)* Here's 66-56…

LOU: Pull over there…

NICK DANTE: Sure. *(Lou takes his knife out of his pocket.)* You want money? It's in my glove compartment.

LOU: So, you're the artist?

NICK DANTE: What's it to you? You a critic?

LOU: I like that. Pretty tough when a guy has a knife on ya.

men's scenes 227

NICK DANTE: The worst you can do is kill me and that would be better off than I am now.

LOU: So, you think you have it hard?

NICK DANTE: *(Sarcastic.)* No, I like driving around Queens six nights a week.

LOU: A woman I know bought a painting from you.

NICK DANTE: If she wants her money back tell her I already spent it on the rent.

LOU: She's Diane Kelly. The movie star.

NICK DANTE: I don't watch TV.

LOU: She's my wife.

NICK DANTE: Good for you.

LOU: She said she went up to your place before and you two screwed your brains out all over the place. In the kitchen, on the floor, in the bathroom. She said you two were like a maniac screwing team.

NICK DANTE: That never happened.

LOU: You calling her a liar?

NICK DANTE: I'm telling you the truth.

LOU: From whose eyes, pal?

NICK DANTE: Mine. And that's all I give a shit about.

(Lou takes a closer look at Nick.)

LOU: You look like you got problems. What's the deal? You got a wife, three kids and a sick mother?

NICK DANTE: No, worse. I got a vocation to be an artist.

LOU: Come on, artists make money. Look at Peter Max.

NICK DANTE: You look at him.

LOU: Ha! I know what you mean. So, you feel sorry for yourself?

NICK DANTE: Big time.

LOU: Where did you get the idea to do that painting Diane bought?

NICK DANTE: I get all my ideas from one place.

LOU: And where's that?

NICK DANTE: My dreams. I paint what I dream.

LOU: And your dreams don't sell?

NICK DANTE: Your wife bought the first one I sold in two years.

228 men's scenes

LOU: I like your stuff.

NICK DANTE: Good. Write a review in the Times. *(Lou puts away the knife and hands Nick fifty bucks.)*

LOU: You want to sell paintings?

NICK DANTE: Who do I have to kill?

LOU: *(Writes address.)* Ha! Come to my house tomorrow and bring all the paintings you can carry. Here's the address.

NICK DANTE: You for real?

LOU: I collect art.

NICK DANTE: Like the wife.

LOU: Heideggar said that Nothingness exist in a state of Dread, not as something isolated and apart from the world. Looking at that painting of yours, I get the feeling that you swallow *nothingness* for breakfast. You put terror in the dark eyes of nothingness. I have one question for you—how do you do that?

(Nick perplexed, doesn't have an answer.)

PORTRAIT OF THE VIRGIN MARY FEEDING THE DINOSAURS

Jeff Goode

serio-comedic, 2 Men

Jesus and Mephistopheles.

Scene: a wasteland

Here, the Devil does his best to tempt Jesus in a somewhat updated version of this popular tale.

○ ○ ○

(Jesus sitting on a rock, playing his guitar.)

JESUS: Mary had a little lamb.

Little lamb. Little lamb.

Mary had a little lamb, his fleece was white as snow.

(He sits for a while He looks at his watch. Pause. Enter Mephistopheles, in a foul temper.) You're late

MEPHISTOPHELES: Blow me, Jew-boy

JESUS: That's it, I'm leaving. *(Jesus walks out.)*

MEPHISTOPHELES: Wait wait wait wait! *(Mephistopheles runs out after him. He reenters with Jesus.)* Come on, I had a bad morning. Do you want to do this or not?

JESUS: Okay.

MEPHISTOPHELES: Okay, are we calm now?

JESUS: Get on with it.

MEPHISTOPHELES: I'm not gonna start if you're gonna be testy.

JESUS: *(Pause.)* I'm sorry.

MEPHISTOPHELES: Okay…So what do you want to do?

JESUS: I dunno. What do you want to do?

MEPHISTOPHELES: Let's go grab some brewskis, watch some football.

JESUS: Sounds tempting, but no.

MEPHISTOPHELES: Come on…

JESUS: No.

MEPHISTOPHELES: What do you mean, "no"? Come on, I'll buy, whaddaya got to lose?

JESUS: Thank you, but I really don't think I should drink.

MEPHISTOPHELES: It's not like it's a sin.

JESUS: I know that.

MEPHISTOPHELES: Well, come on, one beer.

JESUS: No.

MEPHISTOPHELES: Come on, you pansy, what are you afraid of?

JESUS: I don't want a beer.

MEPHISTOPHELES: You fuckin' lightweight!!

JESUS: Is this going to be temptation, or just verbal harassment? 'Cause I can get that at home…

MEPHISTOPHELES: Well, what is this? How am I supposed to have a chance if you're going to take this Puritanical attitude about drinking? Next thing you know, you'll be telling me you don't like rap music.

JESUS: I'm not trying to be Puritanical about anything. *You* were an hour and a half late and I had a bottle of wine while I was waiting. And I don't want to mix.

MEPHISTOPHELES: Oh.

JESUS: Besides, your body is your temple

MEPHISTOPHELES: Well, okay, let's do something else.

JESUS: Fine, let's do something else.

MEPHISTOPHELES: …What do you wanna do?

JESUS: I dunno. What do you want to do?

MEPHISTOPHELES: Oh, I know!

JESUS: What?

MEPHISTOPHELES: Let's hot wire a car. Go for a ride.

JESUS: Nope.

MEPHISTOPHELES: It'll be fun.

JESUS: Thou shalt not steal.

MEPHISTOPHELES: Oh…right. Shit.

JESUS: That was too easy.

MEPHISTOPHELES: Gimme a break, I'm just getting warmed up. *(Thinks.)* I know, we could blow up a church.

JESUS: Are you kidding?

MEPHISTOPHELES: Did I say "church"? I meant an abortion clinic.

JESUS: You want to bomb an abortion clinic?

MEPHISTOPHELES: Sure, why not?

JESUS: Thou shalt not kill.

MEPHISTOPHELES: What if we didn't kill anyone?

JESUS: With a bomb?

MEPHISTOPHELES: We can wait till everyone goes home for the night.

JESUS: Hmm.

MEPHISTOPHELES: You can't pass this up.

JESUS: Let me ask you something.

MEPHISTOPHELES: What?

JESUS: Suppose *you* owned an abortion clinic.

MEPHISTOPHELES: Uh huh.

JESUS: What would you do with it?

MEPHISTOPHELES: Oh, I don't know…

JESUS: Just the first thing that comes to mind.

MEPHISTOPHELES: Um…

JESUS: Would you bomb it?

MEPHISTOPHELES: Bomb it?

JESUS: Would you blow it up?

MEPHISTOPHELES: Hell no!

JESUS: Y'see?

MEPHISTOPHELES: No. What's your point?

JESUS: You wouldn't want someone to blow up your clinic if you had one, so you shouldn't blow up someone else's. Do unto others as you would have them do unto you.

MEPHISTOPHELES: Oh. Waitaminute, I've never heard that before.

JESUS: I made it up.

MEPHISTOPHELES: You can't do that.

JESUS: I just did

MEPHISTOPHELES: That's not fair!

JESUS: Are you about done? I'm already an hour and a half behind schedule.

232 men's scenes

MEPHISTOPHELES: Okay, okay, I got it. I know what you wanna do. Let's go beat up some homos.

JESUS: Do unto others…

MEPHISTOPHELES: That's *not* in the Bible!

JESUS: It should be.

MEPHISTOPHELES: I can't believe you're gonna stand up for a bunch of dykes and faggots.

JESUS: Judge not lest ye be judged.

MEPHISTOPHELES: There you go again! You made that up.

JESUS: Love thine enemies.

MEPHISTOPHELES: Stop it!

JESUS: Let him who is without sin cast the first stone.

MEPHISTOPHELES: Alright, that's enough! I've got one thing to say to you: *Abomination.* Homosexuality is an abomination, that's…that's…

JESUS: Leviticus 20:13.

MEPHISTOPHELES: Leviticus! Right! Right there in black and white: homosexuality is abomination and must be…I don't know, killed or something.

JESUS: Thou shalt not kill.

MEPHISTOPHELES: I know, but…hurt or something, whatever it says in the Bible. I defy you to find one biblical defense of homosexuality. *(He goes offstage to get a Bible.)*

JESUS: And you think that makes it okay?

(Mephistopheles comes back with a Bible and a baseball bat.)

MEPHISTOPHELES: Hell, yes! Why not? There is nothing in here—*(I got a bat.)*—that says we can't bash some gays. Am I right?

JESUS: Hmm.

MEPHISTOPHELES: I mean, this is perfect. You sure you don't want a beer? I mean, we go downtown, hit a few bars, *(Hit a few gays.)* And God is on our side!

JESUS: I see.

MEPHISTOPHELES: And I mean, I'm not saying we should *kill* anyone, but a few broken bones, contusions. Permanent brain damage.

JESUS: This abomination thing really gives us some latitude.

MEPHISTOPHELES: Oh yeah.

JESUS: I mean, why stop there. Proverbs 6:19: False witnesses are an abomination. Something should be done about that too.

MEPHISTOPHELES: That's what I like to hear! Clean up the judicial system! Make the world a better place!

JESUS: And people who divorce and get remarried to the same people: Deuteronomy 24:4. That's an abomination.

MEPHISTOPHELES: Liz Taylor! I hate her!

JESUS: And what's Proverbs 3:32? Oppressors?

MEPHISTOPHELES: Oppressors and bullies! I wanna kick their asses!

JESUS: Oh, and Luke 16:15: Dishonest accountants. Now that is an abomination before God!

MEPHISTOPHELES: You're tellin' me?? When I see people cheating on their taxes, God, I just want to rip out their fuckin' hearts and piss on 'em. Faggots and cheaters, same damn thing, we oughta round up the whole lot of 'em, put 'em in camps and... *(Mephistopheles suddenly remembers the audience. To audience.)* I mean...I didn't mean that the way it sounds. No, it's okay if you want to cheat on your taxes. Really. I mean, what's an abomination anyway? It really doesn't say. I mean...

JESUS: Gotcha.

MEPHISTOPHELES: You son of a bitch. And I mean that the way it sounds.

JESUS: Well, I gotta go. I'm late for supper.

MEPHISTOPHELES: Waitwaitwaitwaitwait!

JESUS: It's been fun.

MEPHISTOPHELES: Wait, just five more minutes.

JESUS: Tempting, but no. *(Jesus exits.)*

MEPHISTOPHELES: You can't do this to me! I'm not through with you yet! What about right and wrong? Black and white? What about family values, you stupid hippie faggot?!?! *(Storms out, muttering.)* ...Somebody give me my gun.

S.O.S.

Richard Willett

serio-comedic, 2 Men
Brian (25) gay, attracted to his straight friend, Adam (25) an actor.

Scene: here and now

Here Brian and Adam engage in very light flirtation as they do acting warm-ups.

○ ○ ○

ADAM: She finally fell off the fuckin' silver dollar.

BRIAN: *(Picking up a beer for himself.)* Huh?

ADAM: *42nd Street.* I asked her how it was going, and she said "Well, I finally fell off the fuckin' silver dollar last night, so at least that's out of the way." *(Pause.)* So you're not…going out with…anybody?

BRIAN: No.

ADAM: For how long?

BRIAN: You don't want to know.

ADAM: Who was the last girl you dated?

(Pause as Brian takes in this misconception about him.)

BRIAN: It wasn't of any consequence. *(Pause.)*

ADAM: Some of the most influential people in my life have been… gay. A professor of mine in particular I'm thinking of. I sometimes think there's something in the gay experience that gives people a kind of…I don't know, substance, as artists, as people. It's enviable. *(Pause.)*

BRIAN: Why are you telling me this?

ADAM: I don't know. I just thought maybe…

BRIAN: *(Defensive.)* Is there something about me that makes you think I'm gay?

ADAM: No, I didn't—

BRIAN: *(Even more defensive.)* Do I look gay? Do I sound gay?

ADAM: Actually no, not particularly. It was more something I just sensed about you.

BRIAN: *(Sarcastically.)* Great!

ADAM: No, I just—I think maybe that's why I came over and talked to you in the first place, at the audition. I mean not the gay thing but…There you were, sitting on the floor with your Steinbeck.

BRIAN: Hemingway.

ADAM: Huh?

BRIAN: *The Sun Also Rises.* Remember? You *thought* it was Steinbeck.

ADAM: Whatever.

BRIAN: You told me you cried when you read *The Red Pony.*

ADAM: You see, I often feel as if I have no really deep convictions about anything. I can play any conviction you give me, but I've never felt that I really knew much of anything…profound, you know. I've never felt that my view of things was unique or important. And sometimes it seems that if you're gay, you're just sort of given that automatically. *(Pause.)* My girlfriend and I have a lot of gay friends. *(Pause.)*

BRIAN: *(Quietly.)* Well, you guessed right. Congratulations. Go all the way to Park Place. *(Pause.)* Does that change anything?

ADAM: No. Why would it change anything? *(Brian shrugs.)* I'm straight, you're gay: so what? *(Pause.)* I mean, you knew I was straight, so nothing's changed from your point of view.

BRIAN: Yes, I knew you were straight. It would have been hard to miss, since you've mentioned your girlfriend approximately ten thousand times since we met. *(Pause.)*

ADAM: Are you attracted to me or something?

BRIAN: What?

ADAM: You seem a little ticked off.

BRIAN: No, I'm not attracted to you. Why would I be attracted to you? Does the whole world have to be attracted to you? *(Pause.)*

ADAM: So are we going to go to this audition today or not?

BRIAN: Maybe.

236 men's scenes

ADAM: We have to get you psyched up. *(Pause.)* I've got an idea.

BRIAN: What?

ADAM: We should do a little repeat exercise here.

BRIAN: No.

ADAM: To limber up. I always go into these things so stiff.

BRIAN: I don't think so.

ADAM: Come on. It'll encourage emotional availability.

BRIAN: I don't like emotional availability.

ADAM: *(Studying him.)* You're resisting me.

BRIAN: I'm—No. I said I didn't want to do this.

ADAM: You're resisting me. *(Pause.)* You're nervous.

BRIAN: I'm not nervous.

ADAM: You're nervous.

BRIAN: Stop it. I'm getting nervous. *(He stands and prepares to leave.)*

ADAM: *(Standing also.)* You're moving away from me.

BRIAN: And you're following me.

ADAM: I'm following you.

BRIAN: You're following me.

ADAM: I'm following you. *(Pause.)* You don't want to look at me.

BRIAN: I don't want to look at you?

ADAM: You don't want to look at me.

BRIAN: I don't want to look at you.

ADAM: Why?

329 PACIFIC STREET

R. J. Marx

dramatic, 2 Men

Gustave Beekman (40s) German émigré, proprietor of a male
house of prostitution, and Elberfeld (30s) a Nazi spy.

Scene: Brooklyn, NY 1942

*Beekman runs a popular business that caters to American
Navy personnel and politicians. Here, the affable Beekman is
paid a visit by the sinister Elberfeld, who blackmails him into
becoming a spy for the Third Reich.*

○ ○ ○

*(Lights up in the kitchen. Elberfeld is with Beekman. Music
and voices blend together from the other room.)*

BEEKMAN: Who are you?

ELBERFELD: I think you know that. Undoubtedly you've been waiting for me all along. Or someone like me. It was inevitable,
wasn't it, Gus. You're simply too valuable. Too well-placed.

BEEKMAN: I don't want any part of it.

ELBERFELD: Oh, but you will.

BEEKMAN: How did you get into the country? They'll arrest you,
you know. They'll arrest you and hang you. They hang
German agents here.

ELBERFELD: You have no idea how easy it was. We pulled the U-boat
off the shore of East Hampton. It is part of Long Island.

BEEKMAN: I am aware of that.

ELBERFELD: Your humor is unappreciated. We were unhindered and
undetected as we moved close to the shore. I and three com-
panions disembarked—it was 3:55 a.m.; all was silent. We
rowed in a dinghy to the shore. Still, we were completely
undetected. The small town slept. When morning dawned,

we simply blended in with the population. That may show you the level of preparedness of your adopted homeland.

BEEKMAN: You speak English very well.

ELBERFELD: So do you.

BEEKMAN: I repeat: I am not an agent.

ELBERFELD: I know that. But you soon will be.

BEEKMAN: I will tell you now. I am violently, vehemently opposed to the government of the Third Reich—

ELBERFELD: I don't give a shit, Gustave. Is that the proper colloquialism?

BEEKMAN: I don't need to take this from you. *(As Beekman starts to leave the kitchen, Elberfeld forcibly stops him in the tracks. Elberfeld grabs a kitchen knife and sticks it close to Beekman's neck.)*

ELBERFELD: You cook, too? Such a fine host. You know, I will without conscience slice your throat right now. While those fairies are making love I will quietly and quickly move out into the night and disappear into a city with a million hideaways, and I will find another Gustave Beekman to do my work for me. I have killed, and I will kill again. Do you feel the blade? *(Beekman struggles to nod.)* Will you work with me?

BEEKMAN: You must have the wrong man—

ELBERFELD: *(Laying down the knife.)* First you tell me I have the wrong house. Now, it is the right house. Then you say I have the wrong man. Am I to believe that? Or will you soon change your story. We know a great deal about you. *(He pulls out documentation papers.)* You say you are Swiss? I am quite familiar with the region. I recognize your accent as distinctly German. *Frankfurt-am-Main,* am I correct? I am a language expert. Oh. Will you look at this? Here it reads— "Gustave Beekman—application for visa, 1934, for United States." Well, look. It does say, residence, Bruckenstrasse, in the Sachsenhausen District. Very lovely. Not far from the river, was it? I notice the application was denied.

BEEKMAN: Who are you? Why do you bother me?

ELBERFELD: How did I get hold of these papers? Could they possibly be forgeries? Unlikely. I have an article here in a newspaper. Pardon—it is yellowing now. About how you were in a raid in a bar. *Der Schlafsitz.*

BEEKMAN: No German! Not in here!

ELBERFELD: "The Roost." Not very subtle, was it. Your kind were the first that we cracked down on. Your little tavern had been quite popular. You advertised throughout the continent. You attracted *abweichen*—male deviates—from all over. As I see you are here. You have a head for business, Beekman. That is useful.

BEEKMAN: It is not true—

ELBERFELD: Spare me, Gustave. They called you "Madame Nazimova" in Germany. How sweet. She was a marvelous Garbo. You'll have to show me your impersonation of her someday. I hear it was a "scream." What do they call you now? Don't bother to deny it. You have left your trail. You lied to get into this country. We know who you are. The others may believe your story, Gus, but we know better. You ran from us, Gus, you were not a loyal German citizen. You fled the fatherland. You are a traitor to the Fatherland. But now— now is the chance for you to make good. You would like assistance, perhaps? You would like your loved ones out of Germany? Some precious person…a boy? Is there a young man, you have perhaps formed an attachment for?

BEEKMAN: No one!

ELBERFELD: You have sought a young man named Dieter.

BEEKMAN: How do you know that?

ELBERFELD: We have your letters to the government. Repeated queries. You've made many mistakes, Gustave. It's not wise to put such things in writing. Oh, yes, I have those letters as well. "To whom it may concern: I am writing regarding the whereabouts of Dieter Mannheim, a twenty-four-year-old male, fourteen Seehofstrasse. Any information would be appreciated." Then this. "To whom it may concern: I am deeply troubled by the disappearance of Dieter Mannheim, fourteen Seehofstrasse. Perhaps the proper authorities could investigate—" Then, you begin to get testy, impatient. You start asking questions. "I have heard of deportations. I am concerned about the whereabouts of Dieter Mannheim, fourteen Seehofstrasse."

BEEKMAN: I want those letters!

ELBERFELD: We have thousands of letters like that, Gustave, from thousands of others better than you, from every city in Germany, Austria and Poland!

BEEKMAN: *(After a pause.)* Do you—know?

ELBERFELD: Know?

BEEKMAN: Where he is.

ELBERFELD: Ah.

BEEKMAN: Do tell me about Dieter. You know about me, you know my Dieter Mannheim. What do you know about—and the others, Oskar, and Thomas?

ELBERFELD: You're a very bad liar, Gustave.

BEEKMAN: Yes, yes, of course, why do you torture me? I want to find my Dieter!

ELBERFELD: Ah, but now, you're asking something of us—

BEEKMAN: You must have word on some of the others, you know so much—don't you have anyone that you care about? Anyone that you love?

ELBERFELD: I love the Fatherland. I love the Commander-in-Chief.

BEEKMAN: No! Tell me, is there no one in your life, no one you have known, or loved, a relative, perhaps, who has not been taken away…deported? Who has not been lost, to hate, and anger, and the self-loathing of a nation?

ELBERFELD: Whoever has been taken, they deserved it. They are better off where they are now and they are serving the Fatherland in a more useful manner. As will you, here. You know, among the papers I have here is a legitimate Swiss birth certificate and papers.

BEEKMAN: So?

ELBERFELD: You entered America with a Swiss passport. A forged Swiss passport purchased on the black market. These papers will confirm your identity as a Swiss.

BEEKMAN: I am an American now. It is the American cause which I support.

ELBERFELD: That's irrelevant. One phone call to the authorities here and they will be at your doorstep. Such deception is not welcome in times such as these.

BEEKMAN: What would happen to me?

ELBERFELD: You would be deported, of course.

BEEKMAN: To Switzerland?

ELBERFELD: Don't be naive, Beekman. You could join your friends. Oskar, and Thomas. And…Dieter, was it?

BEEKMAN: You do know where he is then—

ELBERFELD: Of course I know!

BEEKMAN: You would never make that call. You would be turning yourself in at the same time.

ELBERFELD: Hardly likely. Anonymous tips are taken very seriously by the American government in this highly sensitive time. As well they should be.

BEEKMAN: Sir, Mr. White—

ELBERFELD: I am Elberfeld. Wilhelm Elberfeld.

BEEKMAN: *Herr Elberfeld*—if you would, if you would please understand. I now have a life here. I am free. I am among people whom I—whom I care for. You know as well as I, I cannot return to Germany!

ELBERFELD: That's the point, isn't it, Beekman?

BEEKMAN: You would do to me what you have done to the others. Why won't you tell me what has happened to my Dieter? To my friends? Where are they? What is being done to them! Tell me where Dieter Mannheim is! Tell me where I may find my lover!

ELBERFELD: So that is your price—so little. One germ.

BEEKMAN: I must know. You must tell me, I do beg you. Don't you have a shred of humanity?

ELBERFELD: You don't understand, Gus. This is the new humanity, our rebirth. Without the miserable little weaklings, the cowardly Jews, the simpering, mincing little faggots—la la la la la—we will exterminate them, do you understand, like *der*

242 men's scenes

schadling, das ungeziefer, vermin you know what we do to *der gleichgeshlechtlict*—your kind? *(Beekman shakes his head.)* We load them onto trains and take them to labor camps. All the camps are primitive. No comforts are allowed. No clothes are issued. We separate them, the men from the women, the fathers from the wives, and the children from their parents. Sometimes we rape the women. Would you want to rape the men? I'm sure one of your boys here might be interested. *(Beekman spits at Elberfeld.)*

BEEKMAN: You are not worthy of kissing the shoes of one of my boys. Not one of my boys would sink so low as you have sunk.

(Elberfeld calmly wipes his face.)

ELBERFELD: Our national spirit is unemotional, cool and calm. Look at you, Gus, you spit and claw like a woman. It is true. You are not a man. You are less than a man. *(Pause.)* But it is not too late for you. You can avoid this unpleasant deportation, and save your friend Dieter as well. I can assure you, he is quite safe…for now. You can stay in your new world here. Perhaps, with my assistance, I may even be able to find a way for Dieter to join you here. Your friends here will never know that you are feeding us little bits and pieces, little fragments, really, insignificant fragments. It is not too late for you, Gustave. You are a German. *Heil Hitler*—

BEEKMAN: No— *(Elberfeld then grabs Beekman at the crotch and begins to twist. For Beekman, the pain is excruciating. Elberfeld releases his grip.)*

ELBERFELD: I will contact you. *(He leans away from the kitchen to rejoin the others.)* Aren't you going to bring the drinks?

BEEKMAN: Drinks?

ELBERFELD: The reason you came back here. *Der Senator* asked you to bring him drinks. Good night, Gus. I shall return. *(Elberfeld exits the kitchen door, out into the night.)*

THE WORGELT STUDY

Kate Moira Ryan

dramatic, 3 Men

Henry (50) a developer, Hatter (60–70) founder of the Worgelt Foundation and Ari Dayan (30–50) an agent with the Mossad.

Scene: inside a display of the Worgelt Study, the Brooklyn Museum

As a young student of architecture in Germany, Hatter was tricked into designing the crematoriums used to dispose of those murdered at Birkenau. In 1985, his unhappy past finally catches up with him.

(Hatter, Henry and Ari Dayan a member of the Mossad, the Israeli secret police 1985. Outside Trey's hospital room.)

HENRY: Hatter, this is Ari Dayan. He is from the Mossad.

HATTER: The Mossad? I don't understand. Is that some sort of prayer group you belong to Hatter? Someone from the synagogue? To pray for Trey? Services for George?

HENRY: No, Hatter. Mr. Dayan is a detective from Israel.

HATTER: You are a long way from home Mr. Dayan.

ARI: Mr. Worgelt, forgive me for bothering you here, but we tried your house.

HATTER: There is nothing left to my house.

ARI: I'd like to ask you a couple of questions if you don't mind.

HATTER: As long as it is short.

ARI: Were you a student in Heidelberg during the thirties with the Worgelt foundation?

HATTER: Yes, I was.

ARI: Then you must know why I am here.

HENRY: If he does then I am the only one kept in the dark.

ARI: *(Unrolls plans.)* You designed a system for I.G. Farber, yes? This is your handiwork?

HATTER: *(Studies the plans.)* I left Heidelberg. This is why.

HENRY: I don't understand.

ARI: Mr. Rosenfeld, the plans are for an efficient way to dispose of the dead.

HENRY: The dead? What dead?

ARI: Dead Jews. This design is for the crematorium at Birkenau.

HENRY: Birkenau.

HATTER: Do you read German Mr. Dayan?

ARI: Yes.

HATTER: *(Puts his head in his hands.)* Mein Gott.

HENRY: What? Hatter? What?

HATTER: The fire. I had saved the letter from Farber. It was burned in the fire. It is my only proof. My only proof.

ARI: That you did not design the crematorium?

HATTER: I did. But, I did not know what it would be used for. In that letter…

HENRY: How could you not know? How could you?

HATTER: The Worgelt Institute was a think tank. One branch of it tried to solve social problems.

HENRY: Like the Jews.

HATTER: No, the problem was presented. If there was an epidemic like the Spanish Flu in 1918, how would one dispose of thousands of bodies in a hygienic and expedient manner.

HENRY: So you designed the crematorium.

HATTER: Yes, that is my design.

HENRY: What about the gas chambers? Did you design them also?

HATTER: After I designed this for Farber, I never designed again.

ARI: The letter to you from Farber what did it say?

HATTER: It outlined the problem they wanted me to solve.

ARI: How convenient to have a letter in a house that was burned to the ground.

HATTER: I lost my grandson in that fire. I have another one in a burn unit. Convenient isn't the word I would use.

HENRY: The past is the past. Mr. Worgelt made an unknowing mistake when he was young. He is sorry. Is there anything else to discuss?

ARI: Yes, there is.

HENRY: What is it then?

ARI: Whether or not Mr. Worgelt should stand trial for war crimes.

HATTER: War crimes? I left before the war. I was here during the war.

HENRY: You can't be serious.

HATTER: I killed my tutor in a cave in Greece. I knew I was being used. I knew it. He wanted me to go back to Heidelberg. I said, no. So I pushed him. He was one of them, a National Socialist.

HENRY: You killed Herr Schweig?

HATTER: I was raised separate from my peers here in the Hudson Valley. Then I was sent to Germany to complete my education. My world was hypothetical. Completely totally thought oriented.

HENRY: But, you knew something was the matter.

HATTER: Of course I knew. My fellow students were disappearing. I knew.

ARI: Back to the I.G. Farber plans.

HATTER: I didn't realize until the newsreels of the concentration camps that were shown right after the war ended. Then I knew. I knew what my design was used for.

ARI: And you made no effort for reparations.

HENRY: His design was taken for him.

HATTER: Let me speak Henry. My wife was unfaithful. My son began to show signs of mental illness, I had a young daughter. My wife died in a tragic shooting which my son witnessed. My son had a lobotomy and my daughter needed me. My son blew his brains out. I thought I had been punished enough. Until, the fire. Believe me Mr. Dayan, I am a man who has paid for his mistake. If you are going to charge me with designing the crematorium, then charge me in my family's deaths too, I have burned them alive. Everyone of them. My touch is like a match to plastic. *(He exits into Trey's room.)*

HENRY: You can't take him. I don't care who the hell you are. You can't.

ARI: And you, a Jew say that.

HENRY: My son will die if he leaves him. I know he will. You can't take him. You can't.

ARI: There is such a thing as justice.

HENRY: Mr. Worgelt didn't know and if Farber is saying he did, then they're just passing the goddamn buck. He wasn't even twenty years old when he designed the goddamn thing.

ARI: You can't even say it.

HENRY: I am living it. Look around me.

ARI: I can extradite him to Israel.

HENRY: Go find fucking Mengele. Go find that fucker.

ARI: You think we are playing around?

HENRY: Do you know who I am?

ARI: You're a real estate developer. Housing for the middle class, right? Suburban tract housing. Little boxes.

HENRY: Israel could use some little boxes. The refugees keep coming, don't they?

ARI: You can't buy justice.

HENRY: I see it as a reparation. I will make some calls. You really have no idea who I am, do you Dayan?

ARI: Who will you call?

TWINGES FROM THE FRINGE

Bob Jude Ferrante

serio-comedic, 2 Men

Donny (30–50) a sadistic theme park owner, and Nader (20–50) a consumer investigator.

Scene: here and now

> *Here, Donny is interviewed by a public servant regarding the rather deadly nature of the rides in his park.*

○　○　○

> *(Donny sits at his desk. Behind him on the wall is a poster that reads DonnyWorld. Nader enters, looking around at the office.)*

DONNY: *(Extends hand.)* Donny J. Ostman. *(Nader takes it.)*

NADER: Pleasure. Marty Nader, Public Safety.

DONNY: *(Sits; motions for Nader to sit.)* Nader? Any relation to—?

NADER: No!

DONNY: You must hear that a lot.

NADER: I can't *recall. (Brief pause; Donny gets the joke; laughs. Nader joins him.)*

DONNY: Good one! By the way…Coffee? Juice? Scotch?

NADER: No, thanks.

DONNY: Come on. A little nip. It's after lunch.

NADER: Mr. Ostman…

DONNY: Call me Donny!

NADER: Donny, I'm a public servant. Anyway, can we get down to this?

DONNY: *(Pours himself a scotch.)* I really don't understand this investigation. At DonnyWorld, we strive to provide an educational, entertaining and safe family experience.

NADER: Of course, uh, Donny. But we've had reports, and I just have a few—

DONNY: —Reports! *(Points to the poster.)* Just look at these happy families! We have a saying here at DonnyWorld: "We *love* families!"

NADER: Perhaps we could…discuss some of the rides?

DONNY: Very proud of our rides! We spent millions!

NADER: Okay, this first one, then: "Wonders of the Amazon."

DONNY: We sent a team of biologists to Brazil for *six months.*

NADER: "Children dive into a simulated river, stocked with piranhas and urethra beetles, while natives blow curare darts at them."

DONNY: A reproduction of the Tarahumara coming-of-age ritual.

NADER: But, real piranhas?

DONNY: We have *another* saying here at DonnyWorld: "There's no substitute for the real thing."

NADER: How about this one: "Ten-Story Drop?"

DONNY: Ah. My personal favorite.

NADER: "Children are lined up at the edge of a simulated office building and tossed off the edge."

DONNY: Helps them get over the fear of heights.

NADER: Do they tie bungee cords to these kids?

DONNY: No.

NADER: And they fall onto…some kind of padding?

DONNY: No. Concrete sidewalk.

NADER: Any kind of safety harness?

DONNY: Yes. There is a harness. We do strap them into a harness.

NADER: That's a relief. Title II safety harness?

DONNY: Well, no. But it's imported leather, real chrome studs. We're not *cheap!*

NADER: *(Pause.)* Let's move on.

DONNY: *(Pouring another.)* Mind if I have another?

NADER: "Acid Trip." Kids, sealed in Plexiglas™ bubbles, are dropped into an acid vat. Farm animals are dropped in; the kids watch as they dissolve.

DONNY: *(Slugs it down. Pours another.)* They can learn all about the wonders of animal biology:

NADER: Oh, like, "Dissolving now on your left, a cow's pancreas."

DONNY: You don't have to be *smug.*

NADER: "Space Walk." Kids are put into a steel tank, hung from an umbilical, and the air's sucked out.

DONNY: I can see you have no appreciation for science.

NADER: "Undersea world." Kids are strapped to the bottom of a tank, it's filled with water, and sharks are let in.

DONNY: *(Slugs it down. Pours another.)* You're a goddamned *philistine!*

NADER: And how about "Razor slide?"

DONNY: —Fuck 'em! I admit it! Kids! I hate 'em! The little midget bastards! I hope they all *die!* Die die die die! Yaaaaah!

NADER: *(Rises.)* Guess our meeting's come to an end.

DONNY: *(Rises.)* Perhaps…we could come to some kind of arrangement?

NADER: *(Turns.)* I don't think so.

DONNY: Come on. There must be…Idealist, right? I own a fleet of whaling ships. I'll spare a whale if you forget this silly lawsuit.

NADER: Thank you, Mr. Ostman. *(Walks out.)*

DONNY: *(Calling after Nader.)* Wait! World peace?! *(Falls back into his chair.)* Well. That went well.

(Lights.)

1996 SCENES – PERMISSIONS

AFTERLIFE by Jack Gilhooley. Copyright © 1997, by Jack Gilhooley, all rights reserved. Reprinted by permission of the author. All inquiries: Jack Gilhooley, 7342 Golf Pointe Circle, Sarasota, FL 34243, (941) 351-9688/351-9548 (fax), jackgilhoo@aol.com

ASK NOSTRADAMUS by R. J. Marx. Copyright © 1996, by R. J. Marx, all rights reserved. Reprinted by permission of the author. All inquiries: R. J. Marx, 31 Ridge Road, Katonah, NY 10536

BURNING DOWN THE HOUSE by Jocelyn Beard. Copyright © 1996, by Jocelyn Beard, all rights reserved. Reprinted by permission of the author. All inquiries: Jocelyn Beard. RR#2 Box 151, Patterson, NY 12563. kitowski@computer.net

THE COYOTE BLEEDS by Tony DiMurro. Copyright © 1994, by Anthony DiMurro, all rights reserved. Reprinted by permission of Rosenstone/Wender on behalf of the author. All inquiries: Ron Gwiazda Rosenstone/Wender, 3 East 48th Street, New York, NY 10017, (212) 832-8330/759-4524 (fax)

CUTE BOYS IN THEIR UNDERPANTS MAKE IT BIG (IN SHOW BUSINESS) by Robert Coles. Copyright © 1996, by Robert Coles, all rights reserved. Reprinted by permission of the author. All inquiries: Robert Coles, 80 Warren Street, # 16, New York, NY 10007

DANCE WITH ME by Stephen Temperly. ©1996 by Stephen Temperly. Reprinted by permission of the author. All inquiries: The Shukat Co. LTD., 340 W 55th Street, Suite 1A, New York, NY 10019. (212) 582-7614.

DETAIL OF A LARGER WORK by Lisa Dillman. Copyright © 1994, by Lisa Dillman, all rights reserved. Reprinted by permission of the author. All inquiries: Douglas Michael, Frieda Fishbein Associates, PO Box 723, Bedford, NY 10506, (914) 234-7232, fishbein@juno.com

DOUBLE OR NOTHING by Michael Ajakwe, Jr. Copyright © 1997, Michael Ajakwe, Jr. Reprinted by permission of the author. All inquiries: Dytman & Associates, 9200 Sunset Blvd. #809, Los Angeles, CA 90069

THE ENDS OF THE EARTH by David Lan. ©1996, by David Lan. Reprinted by permission of Faber & Faber. All inquiries: Judy Daish Assoc., London.

FAMILY OF HORRORS by William Gadea. Copyright © 1996, by William Gadea, all rights reserved. Reprinted by permission of the author. All inquiries: William Gadea, (212) 462-9135

FIRST ON LINE by Albert Verdesca. Copyright © 1997, by Albert Verdesca, all rights reserved. Reprinted by permission of the author. All inquiries: Albert Verdesca, 26 Fisher Road, Katonah, NY 10536

FRAGMENTS by John Jay Garrett. ©1996, by John Jay Garrett. Reprinted

Smith and Kraus *Books For Actors*
SCENE STUDY SERIES
Scenes From Classic Plays 468 B.C. to 1960 A.D.

The Best Stage Scenes of 1995

The Best Stage Scenes of 1994

The Best Stage Scenes of 1993

The Best Stage Scenes of 1992

The Best Stage Scenes for Men / Women from the 1980s

THE MONOLOGUE SERIES
The Best Men's / Women's Stage Monologues of 1995

The Best Men's / Women's Stage Monologues of 1994

The Best Men's / Women's Stage Monologues of 1993

The Best Men's / Women's Stage Monologues of 1992

The Best Men's / Women's Stage Monologues of 1991

The Best Men's / Women's Stage Monologues of 1990

One Hundred Men's / Women's Stage Monologues from the 1980s

2 Minutes and Under: Character Monologues for Actors

Street Talk: Character Monologues for Actors

Uptown: Character Monologues for Actors

Ice Babies in Oz: Character Monologues for Actors

Monologues from Contemporary Literature: Volume I

Monologues from Classic Plays

100 Great Monologues from the Renaissance Theatre

100 Great Monologues from the Neo-Classical Theatre

100 Great Monologues from the 19th C. Romantic and Realistic Theatres

A Brave and Violent Theatre: 20th C. Irish Monologues, Scenes & Historical Context

Kiss and Tell: Restoration Monologues, Scenes and Historical Context

The Great Monologues from the Humana Festival

The Great Monologues from the EST Marathon

The Great Monologues from the Women's Project

The Great Monologues from the Mark Taper Forum

YOUNG ACTOR SERIES
Great Scenes and Monologues for Children

Great Monologues for Young Actors

Great Scenes for Young Actors

Multicultural Monologues for Young Actors

Multicultural Scenes for Young Actors

If you require pre-publication information about upcoming Smith and Kraus books, you may receive our semi-annual catalogue, free of charge, by sending your name and address to *Smith and Kraus Catalogue, P.O. Box 127, Lyme, NH 03768. Or call us at (603) 922-5118, fax (603) 922-3348.*